NEPAL IN TRANSITION TO DEMOCRACY

About the Editor

Prof. Anjoo Sharan Upadhyaya, Ph.D. is India Chair at the Central Department of Political Science, Tribhuwan University and Professor, Department of Political Science at Banaras Hindu University, India. She holds a Ph.D. from Banaras Hindu University in Political Science and Master's from Allahabad University. She has done post-doctoral research at Woodrow Wilson International Center for Scholars, Washington DC (1993), London School of Economics and Politics, U.K (1986,1990). She has also obtained an International Diploma in Conflict Resolution from Uppsala University, Sweden (1990).

Professor Upadhyaya has been serving on the faculty of Department of Political Science, Faculty of Social Sciences, Banaras Hindu University for the past 35 years. Apart from teaching, she has served as Director, Institute of Conflict Resolution and Ethnicity (INCORE), UU/The United Nations University, NI, U.K. (2001-02), Dean, Faculty of Social Sciences, Director, Integrated Rural Development Programme, (1998-2000), Head, Department of Political Science (1998-2001 and 2004-07) and has been the Director Centre for the Study of Nepal, Banaras Hindu University since 2006.

Professor Upadhyaya has published extensively both nationally and internationally on themes related to issues of self-determination, ethnicity, conflict, federalism, gender and development. She has taught and lectured on these issues widely at various universities in India and abroad, some of them being Concordia University, University of Toronto (Canada), Wellesley College CT, University of Maryland, MD, Stanford University, CI (2010), International Peace Research Institute, Oslo (PRIO), University of Brisbane, Darwin University, (Australia), Karlstad University (2009 and 2008), Stockholm University, University of Lund (2009), (Sweden), Air Force Academy, Silver Spring (2004), Freie University, University of Magdeburg (Germany), and European University at Cracow, Poland (2007).

NEPAL IN TRANSITION TO DEMOCRACY

Edited by

Anjoo Sharan Upadhyaya

CONCEPT PUBLISHING COMPANY PVT. LTD.
NEW DELHI-110059

ISBN-13: 978-81-8069-918-4

First Published 2013

Published and Printed by

Concept Publishing Company Pvt. Ltd.
A/15-16, Commercial Block, Mohan Garden
New Delhi-110059 (India)
T: 25351460, 25351794, *F*: 091-11-25357109
E: publishing@conceptpub.com, W: www.conceptpub.com
Editorial Office: H-13, Bali Nagar, New Delhi-110 015, India

Cataloging in Publication Data--Courtesy: D.K. Agencies (P) Ltd. <docinfo@dkagencies.com>

Nepal in transition to democracy / edited by Anjoo Sharan Upadhyaya.
p. cm.
Contributed articles.
Includes bibliographical references and index.
ISBN 9788180699184

1. Democratization—Nepal. 2. Nepal—Politics and government—1990- 3. Economic development—Nepal. I. Upadhyaya, Anjoo S. (Anjoo Sharan)

DDC 320.95496 23

Preface

At present Nepal is in the process of framing its new Constitution. Great opportunities and challenges lie ahead of the nation that has a very rich and diverse culture, society and geography. Ever since the country was unified there existed deep rooted disparities between regions, ethnic groups and linguistic units of the country. Various methods of accommodating these diversities and strengthening them have somehow not worked well in the system in the past. There are powerful reasons to turn Nepal into a Federal democratic structure. Nepal has been transiting in a new era. Transformative ideas and trajectories are being conceived and there is an unprecedented urgency to bring in a real democracy, which not only accommodates the assertion of common masses but also satisfies their basic human needs. Stable progress in areas concerning civil-military relations, election reforms, multiparty system, gender justice, laws concerning *dalits* etc. are needed. It is indeed a long drawn endeavour and warrants among other imperatives constant scholarly review of the past and the present as well as the future projections.

The present book entitled 'Nepal in Transition to Democracy' is a collection of scholarly articles on contemporary Nepal with a view to initiate fresh discussion on the subject. We have tried to include an enormous range of issues written by renowned authors and scholars from both India and Nepal. This book drawing on various facets of Nepalese society and polity will offer fresh insights into our understanding of Nepal.

The first chapter 'Nepal's Turbulent Politics and Democratic Uncertainty' by Prof. Lok Raj Baral focuses on the turbulent phase of development and uncertain political situation in Nepal. Nepal's present transition is qualitatively different from the previous transitions; unitary structure would change into federal form with a view to correcting the ensuing social, political, economic and regional disparities. The author tries to put light on the principal identifiable sources of uncertainty, i.e. parties and identity politics, agenda of restructuring of state and its ramifications, crisis of governance, inter-party conflicts and atmosphere of mistrust, and external factors. He not only analyzes the present situation but also makes an effort to provide useful recommendations for the future.

The second chapter by Prof. Dev Raj Dahal is 'Nepal's Quest for Inner Party Democracy'. Popular demand for inclusive or participatory democracy in Nepal has opened debates about the democratization of political parties and an improvement in their political structures, procedures and political culture for attaining democratic responsiveness. Nepalese parties are formed largely on the heritage of political movement, rebellion and leadership split. Leaders of all the mainstream parties come from middle and upper classes of society. This paper recommends the enhancement of democratic character of Nepalese politics and transformation of small elite base at the top to become representative of the nation's social diversity. The inner party democracy is also a solution to the proliferation of armed groups caused by political closure and negation, lawlessness caused by factional fights and the corrosion of state power, alienation of youth and group-enclosed extra-party social movements in all types of democracy.

The third chapter of the book is 'Is There a Transition to Democracy in Nepal? Understanding its Nature and Implications' by Prof. Ganga Bahadur Thapa. This article's purpose is to address to what extent social organizations that do not share the rules of the state can successfully triumph and what specific kinds of mechanisms would facilitate political stability and also be able to remove corrupt and bad politicians in the face of increased expectations with potentially destabilizing demands to steer clear the challenging path to democracy. This article is not devoted to explaining democratization, but is limited to explaining the breakdown of insurgency as well as authoritarianism that may or may not be replaced by regimes that are more democratic.

The fourth chapter 'Federalism in Nepal: Issues and Challenges' by Prof. B.C. Upreti examines the reinstallation of democracy with the successful Jan Andolan 2006. There had been three major issues involved in the restructuring of the state: abolition of the institution of monarchy and declaring Nepal a secular republican state; inclusive democracy and the federal structure of state. On 26th May, 2008 Constituent Assembly decided to abolish the monarchy and declared Nepal a republican state. There has been an understanding that Nepal will have an inclusive democracy with a federal structure. The author deals with the problems and prospects of the issue.

The subsequent chapter of this book 'Restructuring State and Society in Nepal Post-Accord Challenges', deals on the promises and challenges of the post-peace accord in Nepal. Professor Upadhyaya discusses ramifications of a democratic transference of an evolutionary and homegrown fusion of Maoism that is yet to be reckoned in practical terms. Though there is a consensus on setting up of a democratic Nepal, the challenges ahead for the newly emergent Nepali polity are stupendous. The question that arises is how the changing political matrices will address issues of citizenship, ethnic harmony, equal sharing of development benefits, political inclusion, recognition of Terai languages and promotion of gender equity.

The next chapter is entitled 'Civil-Military Relations in Nepal' contributed by Dr. Bishnu Pathak. Civil Military Relations are the relationships between state-civil society, citizenry and military organization(s). It is a politico-legal concept initiated by western democratic nations/societies and developed alongside the progress of democracy, particularly after the end of the World War-II and the establishment of the United Nations. The principal aim of this chapter is to enhance the level of understanding and to commence a debate and discussion on CMR among the concerned actors such as civil, military, combatants of the Maoist Army (MA) and citizenry in Nepal.

The seventh Chapter is 'Media Contribution in Transfer of Power in Nepal' written by Mr. Binod C. Agrawal. The chapter is based on the first-hand interaction with Nepal media persons and available secondary data on the growth and development of media in Nepal and political events. In spite of several political upheavals and turmoil gradually private entrepreneurs took over media within Nepal youth within Nepal and emigrants to other parts of Asia provided continuous information that contributed to influence the struggle for democratic power to people.

The Eighth chapter 'Role of State for the Development of Micro Finance Sector in Nepal' by Ms. Yashmita Awasthi, discusses the role of state on developing micro finance sector to enhance access to financial services to a majority of un-served and under-served poor and low income households with emphasis on two aspects: sustainable financial services and enhancing access to financial services to un-reached. In this paper, a review of different schools of thoughts on this subject is done and state's role is discussed considering country context, realities and environment within which existing financial market operates. Further, this paper emphasizes sustainability and mass outreach at the outset in cognizance of significance of the debate for financial sector development and the fact that often policy makers' concerned on providing services to poor tend to ignore issues relating to permanency of services.

The ninth chapter 'Economic Development Imperatives and Impact of Globalization in Nepal' by Sujit Ranjan Prasad and Raman Ranjan examines the conditions, contributions, change, and challenges that Globalization had on economic development imperatives in Nepal.

The next chapter is 'Fiscal Federalism: The Indian Experience and Relevance for Nepal' by Dr. Anil Kumar Jain and Dr. Parul Gupta. The authors argue that the rich and diversified experience of India in respect of fiscal federalism is of extreme relevance for Nepal so as to transform Nepal into a democratic, divergent and progressive nation state, for which federalism is necessary. Towards this scheme of restructuring Nepal into a 'nation state', it should recognize the equality of all cultures and languages: devolve powers to enable all groups to exercise powers to rule and promoting individual freedom. This task is full of challenges arising from diversities, presence of numerous ethnic groups, loyalty of certain groups to their community, different languages and dialects, etc. Therefore, the scheme of federalism must be agreed by all population and its characters need to be set forth by consensus.

The eleventh chapter 'Bridging the Indo-Nepal Relations through Telemedicine Initiative' by Dr. Preeti Singh discusses Indo-Nepal relation in the field of telemedicine. In the health context of Nepal, telemedicine is rising and currently being implemented. Information Technology (IT) is poised to revolutionize health care trade through new thresholds in human connectivity. SAARC Telemedicine centre established in Nepal with the assistance of Rs. 4.88 crores from the Government of India is an initiative in this respect. Overall economic status of Nepal is far below India, there are vast areas of economic cooperation that must be identified particularly in the field of investment in joint ventures and transfer of technology ensuring benefits to both countries what is known as "Win-Win" effect. India's cooperation to Nepal is essential in a greater scale in future not only to sustain its development activities but also for poverty alleviation.

The next chapter is 'India's Economic Miracle and its Impact on Nepal' written by Prof. Hari Bansha Jha. He examines the economic relation between India and Nepal and the impact of growing Indian Economy on Nepal. He emphasises that more and more engagement is required at Business to Business (B&B) level to dig out potential opportunities, promote information dissemination, and organize trade fairs, exhibitions and different other business activities. However, for all this an enabling environment will have to be created in the country to restore the confidence of Indian investors.

The next chapter is 'Developing Women Entrepreneurship in Nepal through Small Scale Industries' by Dr. Usha Kiran Rai and Monica Srivastava discuss about the developing women entrepreneurship in Nepal. Women entrepreneurship, in a formalized sense, is a relatively new phenomenon in Nepal. Although certain ethnic communities in the country, especially the Newaris and Tibeto-Burman Highland Groups such as the Sherpas, Gurungs, Thakalis are known to have a long tradition of women being involved in small business enterprises. It is only within the last ten years that the concept of women entrepreneurship has progressively gained some acceptance in the overall dominant majority within the Nepalese society. Gender equality and economic development go hand in hand.

The last chapter of the book is dealing with the 'Millennium Development Goals' and the Changing Status of Nepalese Women' written by Prof. Anjoo Sharan Upadhyaya and Ms. Afreen Khan make an effort to explore the changing status of women in Nepal with the purpose of examining the achievement of the Millennium Development Goals as stipulated by the United Nations Organizations.

We hope that this book will provide a good understanding of state and society in Nepal and pave fresh ground for further analysis of the socio-political matrix of this significant country that is currently in a very critical stage of its development.

Varanasi
2nd November, 2011

Anjoo Sharan Upadhyaya

Acknowledgements

Special thanks to the authors of the articles; colleagues of the Centre for the Study of Nepal, and Malaviya Centre for Peace Research, Banaras Hindu University for their support in editing the volume; to B.P. Koirala India–Nepal Foundation for supporting many events and activities; to Afreen, Ajay, Prashant, Mani, Sanjay and Jitendra for being there for us always, to Manish and Pratima for composing to Banaras Hindu University for providing the intellectual synergy much needed for any such endeavour and to Professor Priyankar Upadhyaya for his constant encouragement.

Contents

Contributors

Lok Raj Baral, Executive Director, Nepalese Centre for Contemporary Studies, Kathmandu, Nepal.

Dev Raj Dahal, Head, Friedrich Ebert Stiftung Sanepa, Lalitpur, Kathmandu, Nepal.

Ganga Bahadur Thapa, Professor of Politics, Tribhuvan University, Kathmandu (Nepal) and President Centre for Democracy and Conflict Analysis.

B.C. Upreti, Professor, South Asian Study Centre, Rajasthan University, Jaipur, India.

Anjoo S. Upadhyaya, Professor of Politics and Coordinator, Centre for the Study of Nepal, Banaras Hindu University, Varanasi, India.

Bishnu Pathak, Director, Peace and Conflict Studies Centre, Convener of South Asia: TRANSCEND International and Board Member of TRANSCEND Peace University.

Binod C. Agrawal, Researcher, TALEEM Research Foundation, City Plaza, Sterling City, Bopal, Ahmedabad, India.

Yashmita Awasthi, Assistant Professor, Jeevan Deep Institute of Management and Technology, Varanasi, India.

Sujit Ranjan Prasad, Researcher, Faculty of Management Studies, Banaras Hindu University, Varanasi, India.

Raman Ranjan, Unit Manager, ICICI Prudential Life Insurance, Patna Hub Branch, Patna, India.

Anil Kumar Jain, Professor of Economics & Dean, Faculty of Social Sciences, Banaras Hindu University, Varanasi, India.

Parul Gupta, Assistant Professor, DAV Institute of Management, Faridabad, India.

Preeti Singh, Assistant Professor, Jeevan Deep Institute of Management and Technology, Varanasi, India.

Hari Bansha Jha, Executive Director, Centre for Economic and Technical Studies, Nepal.

Usha Kiran Rai, Professor, Faculty of Management Studies, Banaras Hindu University,Varanasi, India.

Monica Srivastava, Researcher, Faculty of Management Studies, Banaras Hindu University,Varanasi, India.

Afreen Khan, Senior Research Fellow. Centre for the Study of Nepal, Banaras Hindu University, Varanasi, India.

1
Nepal's Turbulent Politics and Democratic Uncertainty

Lok Raj Baral

Nepal's present transition is qualitatively different from the previous transitions. But the fate of the ongoing transition is also fraught with the grave dangers of being unsuccessful as in the past, despite the fundamental issues raised by it for correcting the distortions of the Nepali state. Moreover, changes underway are for peace, progress, stability and democracy. The Unified Communist Party of Nepal (Maoist) (UCPN-Maoist) is in the process of transformation from being an underground and insurrectionary party into being a systemic party; the moderate Nepali Congress, the Communist Party of Nepal (United Marxist-Leninist) (CPN-UML) and others have embraced a common political ideology of pluralist democracy along with the Maoist, despite its ambivalence; the traditional state structures such as army, police and bureaucracy are on the agendas of restructuring of state. Nepal's unitary structure would change into federal form with a view to correcting the ensuing social, political, economic and regional disparities. Thus, such political metamorphosis is so overwhelming that cannot be dismissed easily by turning the clock back.

However, such inclusive and encompassing changes are no less daunting in view of the interplay of internal and external forces. Internally, the political elites of Nepal now need to be imaginative and courageous for taking ahead the agenda of democratic consolidation. Since there have been explosions of issues and problems all around, it is quite natural to prevail uncertainties during the turbulent phase of development.

Nevertheless, Nepal's uncertain political climate prevailing today is not an uncommon phenomenon. The post-Rana politics (1951) was perennially fraught with uncertainties. The political stability provided by the absolute monarchy was no less uncertain as the political regimes created by the monarchs were always vulnerable to the crisis of legitimacy. Political parties that were hard hit by the imposition of absolute monarchical rule following the coup staged by King Mahendra in 1960 opposed it. In 1990, the royal regime collapsed due to the mass movement launched by the same oppositionists who had all along been demanding the demise of partyless regime. It was hoped that the crisis of legitimacy would no longer hover over the new multiparty system introduced under the 1990 Constitution. Acclaimed as the best democratic constitution Nepal had ever produced, the political actors–parties and the Kings–failed to own the Constitution due to clash of interests. If the parties failed to abide by the spirit of constitutional monarchy as argued by them while enforcing it, the Kings tried to carve out a space for active monarchy. Moreover, political uncertainties continued despite three elections held under the Constitution. On the contrary, high degree of political instability prevailed when the parties' leaders picked up quarrels for petty interests. Thus, instead of conducting the affairs of the state efficiently and democratically, political parties encouraged the King to be ambitious as in the 1950s.

Although the *Jan Andolan II* (2006) was a turning point in the modern history of Nepal, political uncertainties continue to rule the roost as if Nepal is yet to pass through the turbulent phase. Both the prospects of integration and disintegration have simultaneously arisen with the plethora of ethnic, dalit, Tarai and other regional groupings demanding their proportionate shares in power, resources and other benefits to be catered by the state. Since the Nepali state was discriminatory in nature and functions, only some privileged caste/class groups monopolized the state power and resources depriving other ordinary people of such advantages. Moreover, the basis of the foundation of the modern Nepali state was faulty due to caste/religious prejudices that the rulers of Nepal had invariably displayed in politics, economics and administration. So today's demand of restructuring of Nepali state is an endeavour to correct such discrimination perpetrated by the state. And demands put up by various deprived and marginalized groups or regions cannot be construed as the seeds of disintegration.

To be more specific, the post-*Jan Andolan II* (2006) developments show some sources of uncertainty for building a new Nepal which is the goal of the movement itself. The principal identifiable sources of uncertainty are: parties and identity politics, agenda of restructuring of state and its ramifications, crisis of governance, inter-party conflicts and atmosphere of mistrust, and external factor.

Parties and Identity Politics

The three Parliamentary elections held in 1991, 1994 and 1999 under the 1990 Constitution indicated that all sections of communities, regional groups and other minorities were within the fold of national parties. Whoever tried to whip up the ethnic and regional feelings could not get a single seat in the three Parliaments as ethnic, regional, and other minority groups' members came to parliament on political parties' quota.[1] So despite the lackadaisical approaches adopted by the parties towards the agenda of balanced representation, parties were mainly successful in enlisting the support of these groups. Such pattern has now been significantly changed by the new political landscape in which identity politics is likely to play a dominant role. And the Maoist's ten-year long insurgency, particularly the Maoist party's effort to sensitize the marginalized sections of society to be conscious of lingering social, economic, political and regional disparities perpetrated by the Nepali state, is responsible for giving rise to such feelings. Democratic deficit experienced in the post-1990 politics also led us to rediscover democracy in relation to the rise of identity politics.

Is ideology replaced by a new identity politics Nepal is now undergoing? Are ideological parties declining in the melee of ethnic and regional trends that are perceived by some people as also the trends of national disintegration? Can Nepal survive the challenges posed by such developments? Is it the right time to assert ethnic and regional demands when all such agendas could be addressed by the Constituent Assembly? Can Nepal transit to a new democratic order as per the spirit of *Jan Andolan II*? Many more questions can be raised in light of the emerging trends in Nepal. How do principal parties survive in the wake of new ethnic, regional and other kinds of upsurge depends on their understanding of the emergent realities in the country.

It has been argued that most major parties have lost their support bases in Tarai, in *jan jatis*, and in other regions where ethnicity and other group identities are now working independently of parties. Creating Tarai as a single federal unit, full proportional representation system, inclusion of Tarai people in the army and other state agencies, right to self-determination etc. have posed challenges to the builders of new Nepal. Similarly, various ethnic and tribal groups have been demanding full proportional representation, autonomous regions on the basis of ethnic composition of regions or Pradesh. And the parties are under pressure whether or not they should concede the demands of these groups and the Tarai people. So far the issue of making Tarai as a single autonomous region is concerned, it has become contentious issue as the Tharus have rejected the idea of converting the entire Tarai as a province. The Tharus and also the Muslim and the Dalits want their own separate identity and do not like to be identified with one Madhesh Pradesh.

The Tarai demographic landscape has changed significantly due to migration from the hills to the Tarai. In about six Tarai districts stretching from Jhapa to the East and Kanchanpur to the West, more than 50 per cent population is of hill origins. "Geographically, the Tarai proper, or Madhesh, is not one continuous strip of territory but comprises of three distinct units: Eastern Tarai–from Jhapa to Parsa; Central Tarai–Nawal Parasi, Rupandehi and Kapilbastu; and Western Tarai, from Banke to Kanchanpur."[2] Between these units are the inner Tarai districts of Chitwan and Dang. Chitwan has 83.7 per cent hill population followed by Jhapa with 69 per cent, Morang with 51 per cent, Nawalparasi with 57.2 per cent, Dang with 62 per cent and the Far Western district of Kanchanpur with 61.5 per cent.[3] Moreover, identity politics based on ethnicity is increasingly becoming fractionalized with several districts trying to be different from the Madhesh movement. The agenda of making Nepal a federal state therefore seems to be encountering difficulty because of the much hyped sentiment of Tarai regionalism.[4] However, the deal struck between the agitating Madheshi groups and the SPA Government clinched the issue of one Madhesh, One Pradesh and of "right to self-determination". The eight-point agreement reached on February 29, 2008 has rephrased this agenda in these words: "The structure of the Madhesh and other autonomous regions, power devolution between the centre and the provinces and the allocation of resources will be done through the Constituent Assembly by keeping intact the sovereignty, unity and integrity of the country". Regarding the group recruitment of the Madheshi into the Nepal Army, the agreement lays down: "Madhesi, including other marginalized groups, will be recruited group-wise in Nepal Army so as to ensure the principle of inclusiveness."[5]

Interestingly, the hill ethnic communities also want full proportional system of representation, autonomous regions with the right to self-determination. Although these issues need to be discussed in Constituent Assembly (CA), all these communities and regional groupings want them fulfilled now. Continuing agitations, often igniting violence across the country, have not only put the CA election in peril but Nepal is also emerging as an uncertain, if not failed, state. Government is losing its credibility day-by-day as it can neither ensure security nor deliver goods and services to the people. Since the CA election is taken as the single most important agenda for a smooth transition to democratic stability, peace and progress, people want to give a chance to the SPA leadership until the CA elections. If the parties fail to hold elections by settling some outstanding regional and ethnic issues, the prospect of conflict will be high.

It should be understood that the very concept and dynamics of present state system is undergoing a sea-change along with the powerful impacts of globalization. The old Westphalian state-system is changed owing to the rise of multiplicity of ethnic, regional, religious and economic factors. The impact of globalization on 'creating hybrid identities' has produced radical effects on the structure of power. And Nepal is no exception to it with the people showing unprecedented awareness of their role in the spheres of the state and society. Inclusive democracy, sharing of power and resources, distributive justice and state as a cooperative enterprise has not only challenged paradigmatic rationale of the past but also have made people assertive and articulate to make the state system more rationale.

Restructuring of State and Imperative of Federalism

Coming close on the issue of ethnic and regional politics, change from unitary to federal system has dominated today's political discourse. It is one of the vital components of the restructuring of state. Some people do not subscribe to the agenda of turning Nepal into a federal state. They argue that Nepal's ethnicity, geographical division, unitary tradition etc. go against the spirit of federalism. On the negative side, some serious objections raised are: federalism as a disintegrating factor for Nepal; federalism can be created only on the basis of willingness of independent states who want to join the new federation voluntarily; federal units to be created on the basis of ethnicity would neither be feasible nor sustainable; Nepal's population, geographical position, ethnic heterogeneity etc. are not favourable for federal structure; resources cannot be mobilized if Nepal is divided into various federal units; nor can a country handicapped by limited capacity to produce more due to difficult terrain and mountains produce enough to sustain such divisions. Moreover, as the arguments against federalism go, security cannot be provided to the people under the federal structure.

Such negative arguments apart, Nepali political forces have committed themselves to turning Nepal into a federal state. But what type of federalism it would adopt would be decided in the CA. Only theoretical commitments are made with a view to pacifying the aspirations of the people. So federalism is likely to be one of the difficult agendas of new Nepal, despite its acceptance by all the principal parties and ethnic and regional groupings in the country. What are the compulsions for it and why cannot the unitary structure function in the new Nepal need more serious discourse.

Federalism is a new subject for Nepal because of its long centralized, unitary tradition and elite orientation. Integration of small principalities or little kingdoms was understood only in physical sense as the conqueror or unifier embarked on the expansion of territories under the sword of the Gorkha ruler, whose understanding of ethnic and cultural mosaic had nothing to do with broad meaning of pluralism. Although Nepali society has always been plural due to diverse social groups, cultural and religious diversities, the Gorkhali political culture articulated by Hinduized rulers and the caste-oriented elites (Brahmin and Chhetri) prevailed in the country. With the passage of time, the ethos of the Nepali state became parochial subjugating other groups to the state-owned social, political and religious ethos. Assimilation rather than accommodation became the guiding spirit of the Nepali state.

Given the emergent realities in today's Nepal, some reasons for turning Nepal into a federal state can thus be identified. First, deep-rooted disparity gaps existing since the unification of the country cannot be improved without removing such disparities. Second, sharing of power and resources need to be balanced so as to redress the grievances of Tarai people, ethnic groups, dalit, gender and other deprived sections of society and regions. Third, the centrality of Kathmandu should be changed by creating regional units as the traditional approach of decentralization or devolution of power would not be adequate to address the aspirations of people. Finally, since a nationwide psychology is already created for federalism, other options such as full decentralization or devolution of power etc. are not adequate. Nor can such measures convince the people in general. The Nepali rulers who invariably were not tired of talking of "decentralized democracy" in the past turned out to be deceptive when the *de facto* power and resources continued to be the monopoly of power wielders and their lackeys. Later, even under the so-called democratic regime in the post-1990 period, politics and administration failed to make a departure with the past.

What course then Nepal would adopt if federalism is taken as the seed of destruction of the state itself. Will Nepali state break into pieces if it goes federal? Can the unitary state structure now retain the integrating trends as were made out in the past? What do we mean by integration of the country in the present context? Are old myths and symbols capable of keeping the country intact? Some of these questions are loaded with the baggage of history and seem to be quite influential to make some pundits hypersensitive to the new demands and ideas that come from the protagonists of change. The remedies provided by these critics are also charged with emotion. It is true that the much touted ethnic basis of federalism is fraught with dangers for creating animosity and mistrust between and among communities. Nor can ethnicity work as the cementing factor in highly heterogeneous socio-political context of Nepal. The linguistic division of the country is not also a plausible basis for carving out regional entities because of complex mixture of all languages. An acceptable formula therefore needs to be explored by all those who want to use federalism as a strategy for forging national consensus. Federalism based on animosity and emotion or revengeful attitudes cannot last long as the very concept and practice of federalism is based on cooperation and trust.

Federalism is not also a panacea that cures all diseases or ills afflicting the ongoing developments. Some of the concerns raised by critics are based on examples cited from other countries that were/are in the processes of disintegration. Yet, some events can be influenced by the men in the helm of affairs but sometimes such events would prove disastrous despite efforts to be made by leaders. South Asia has undergone such traumatic experiences in the past and is now struggling for survival regardless of the forms of government—unitary or federal.

The spurt of violence in Tarai and the demand for converting the entire belt as a single regional unit are singled out as the seeds of disintegration of the country. Other demands related to end regional disparities are legitimate and should be considered sympathetically by the ruling parties. Nevertheless, Tarai as one federal entity is not a plausible solution to maintaining Nepal's territorial integrity and national unity because of nature of physical location of the country and of complex human settlement pattern. The north-south cooperation for sharing natural resources would also be difficult if regional units are created without taking into consideration the long tradition of hill-Tarai cohabitation.

Nepal's ground realities and popular aspirations might not be comparable to other situations; nor can arguments raised against federalism in Nepal be universal. India didn't accept the idea of right to self-determination while making the present constitution but the Soviet Union under Lenin accepted it theoretically believing that the federal units would not secede. On the contrary, the Indian Union accepted 'centralized federalism' vesting key powers with the Centre. It does not mean that India is a unitary state making the state governments subservient to the Centre. States mostly carved out on linguistic basis have now become more crucial than ever before for running both Central and Regional Governments. This is how cooperative federalism is working showing "unity in diversity".

Some principles and rationale should be accepted while designing the state along federal line. They are: no breach of unity and integrity of Nepal; harmony to be maintained among communities and regions; search for economic viability and administrative rationale; and judicial distribution of resources and power between the centre and federating units. Demands for 'right to self-determination' and Tarai as a federal unit are negotiable in view of their irrelevance in actual practice. The Tarai groups, individual leaders and the people in general are for Nepal's unity and territorial integrity. Moreover, the right to self-determination can be exercised only in extreme conditions that continue the pattern of exploitation of people. Similarly, a serious study is essential for creating regional units on the basis of the spirit of cooperative federalism. Any step to be taken by the movement leaders and groups should be both plausible and sustainable.

Thus, parties are under pressure to make democracy inclusive by opening the accesses to less privileged groups but the atmosphere is now charged due to the explosion of group mobilization and pressure tactics mounted by various sections of communities and regional groups. Autonomous regions, federalism, proportional election system are advanced as the principal demands accepting the diversities of the country. If the political parties would have foreseen these demands and had opened negotiations with some of the leaders, things would have been made easier. Moreover, some demands need to be seriously studied for making them sustainable. What the agitating groups need is only to keep a vigil on the implementation of policies accepted by eight parties.

It must be clear to us that creating autonomous regions independently of hills or Madhesh would neither be feasible nor sustainable. There must be a harmonious and integral relationship between the hills and Madhesh as the complementary relationship is an essential ingredient of federalism. "Cooperative federalism" is positive because each unit of federal structure, even if they are autonomous to a certain extent, needs the help of the other.[6]

Creation of autonomous units within the existing structure of population in different parts of the country is problematic. Nevertheless, a suitable model can be designed by examining the Nepali reality and also with a view to mitigating the grievances of each region and communities. In India, linguistic basis was followed to carve out states within the Indian Union, but after the linguistic states were created, the dominant groups within each state "often discriminated against their own linguistic minorities". Stories of disparity gaps between the Hindus and the Muslim, between regions have frequently fuelled the conflict in India. Such problems only urge the ruling elites to be more judicious and vigilant in order to reduce the disparities, if not completely eliminate them.

The bungling created by the agenda of the Interim Constitution and the failure of political parties to set some principal agendas by way of making the new Nepal have also made each community restive. All political parties, both ruling and outside, should think that the present developments have given them a unique opportunity for making a New Nepal. For democracy demands vigilance and assertiveness with which people can ventilate their feelings and grievances. This process makes a series of profound transformations in economic, social and political structures and relations. So the occasional rise of the masses and demands being made by the people are positive for the future of democracy. However, political parties are likely to face a multitude of challenges as they can no longer take people for granted. Nor would they be able to understand the new identity politics that creates its own space within democracy and makes the former [democracy] stronger and broad.

Crisis of Governance

The most unfortunate part of the whole exercise in the post-2006 period is both the crisis of leadership and crisis of governance. It was expected that the political parties would set a new precedent while conducting the affairs of the state. But all such hopes were dashed when the same old style of politics, distribution of patronages, partisan interest and favouritism and nepotism as in the "patrimonial system" are replicated in the new Nepal. The new political party–the Unified Maoist–which did get a chance to head the government by virtue of being the largest party in the Legislature-Parliament or in CA–is not entirely different from other parties insofar as its lust for power is concerned. On the one hand, the Maoist leaders boast that they would not be bogged down in the "dirty parliamentary game", power-capture, not the making of a new Constitution, seems to be their ultimate aim. Prachanda, the supremo, failed to garner majority support even after fourth round of election due to their trust deficit between the Maoist party and the other parties. It seemed that all major players of Nepali politics have failed to take the peace process to a logical conclusion and to make a new Constitution for which they had been elected to the CA.

It is not a question of getting frustrated by sudden setbacks suffered by the direction of Nepali politics. Yet, degree of irresponsibility and lack of vision and direction has become worrisome to those who had aspired for a New Nepal in accord with the spirit of the *Jan Andolan II*. When non-issues dominate the daily headlines creating distrust and confusions in the minds of people, credibility of political actors start eroding too. Recent developments have shown that all the core leaders of the so-called mainstream parties are on the slippery slope. And for developing democracy like ours, the role of political leaders is always crucial. Their commitment to the principles and processes would only lay the foundation of system espoused by the spirit of the people's struggle.

Rashtravad (nationalism), the issue much often raised by politicians, smacks of the same old strategy of mobilization for wrong cause. In the given context, politicians in general are on the fast track of being discredited due to irresponsible statements and speeches they make from time-to-time. If one goes by their speeches and interviews etc., they turn out to be empty alienating the people further from them. '*Rashtravad* in peril' is thus taken as a strategic ploy to hide failures, either in government or outside. Since the date for completing the writing of the Constitution by CA has been postponed till May 2001 due to shifting strategic positions taken by some of its constituents, parties' leaders who are indulged in power game may again fail to complete the process. The view expressed by the Maoist party chairman, Prachanda that the "*rashtravadi* elements close to the former King" should also find space in the new alignment of forces, have distracted the attention of all from the main agenda of CA election. *Rashtravad*, which is generally understood in Nepal as anti-Indianism, is likely to add more complication if responsible parties and leaders start repeating the same old game.

The ambivalent roles of Maoist leaders have also given rise to distrust between the Maoist and other parties and external powers, especially India. Those who believed in the transformation of the Maoists into mainstream multiparty system, lack confidence due to Maoist penchant for its dogmatic ideological commitment. Although they have been able to win maximum seats in the CA and also headed the government for about nine months, their activities and orientations are believed to have gone against democratic spirit.

Changed Political Picture

The new political dynamics in fact began with the results of the CA election of 2008. It not only changed the inter-party relationship but also sowed the seeds of distrust and the trends of unhealthy competition between the UCPN (Maoist) and the two principal parties–the NC and the CPN (UML). The result also brought the Madheshi parties into political limelight making them as effective power brokers. Of the total electoral seats of 575 allocated for both majority (first-past-the post) and proportional systems, the Maoists wrested 220 seats, while its major competitors, NC and CPN (UML) respectively getting 110 and 103 seats. The 26 members would be nominated by the government on the basis of understanding among the major political parties.

Table 1.1 and 1.2 that show parties' position and social representation pattern in the CA make substantive change in making democracy inclusive.

The CA election based on parallel systems put a brake on the major parties like the Maoist, the NC and the CPN (UML) for wresting comfortable majority (301). The Maoist party that had bargained heavily for accepting the whole PR system suffered a great deal in the PR system but could gain 50 per cent gain from the majority

Table 1.1: Parties' positions in CA election Results, 2008

Sl. No.	*Political Parties*	*FPTP Result*	*PR Result*	*Total*
1.	CPN-Maoist	120	100	220
2.	Nepali Congress	37	73	110
3.	CPN-UML	33	70	103
4.	Madheshi People's Rights Forum	30	22	52
5.	Tarai-Madhesh Democratic Party	9	11	20
6.	Sadbhawana Party (Mahato)	4	5	9
7.	Janamorcha Nepal	2	5	7
8.	Nepal Workers and Peasants' Party	2	2	4
9.	Janamorcha Nepal	1	3	4
10.	Independent	2	0	2
11.	Rarstirya Prajatantra Party	0	8	8
12.	CPN-ML	0	8	8
13.	CPN-United	0	5	5
14.	Rastriya Parjatantra Party-Nepal	0	4	4
15.	Rastriya Janashakti Party	0	3	3
16.	Rastriya Janamukti Party	0	2	2
17.	CPN-Unified	0	2	2
18.	Nepal Sadbhawana (Anandi Devi)	0	2	2
19.	Nepali Janta Dal	0	2	2
20.	Federal Democratic National Fourm	0	2	2
21.	Samajbadi Prajantantrik Janata Party Nepal	0	1	1
22.	Dalit Janajati Party	0	1	1
23.	Nepal Pariwar Dal	0	1	1
24.	Nepal Rastriya Party	0	1	1
25.	Nepal Loktantrik Samajbadi Dal	0	1	1
26.	Chure Bhawar Rastriya Ekata Party Nepal	0	1	1
	Total	240	335	575*

* 26 members would be nominated from various sections of society to make a 601-member CA.

Table 1.2: Social Representation in CA

Population Groups	*FPTP Result*	*PR Result*
Janajati (Hill)	59	88
Janajati (Madheshi)	18	27
Madheshi	48	76
Muslim, Churaute (Bangle dealer)	7	9
Dalit (Madheshi)	2	11
Dalit (Hill)	5	29
Others (Hill) Brahmin, Chhetri	101	95
Total	240	335
Women	30	160*

* The total strength of women in the CA adds up to 197.

Source: www.election.gov.np

system. So the UCPN (Maoist) is stuck with 220 seats in a House of 601. The smaller parties have made gains in CA election, thus forcing the major parties to work together or for *sahakarya* (cooperative action) without which the functioning of government would not be possible. It is "consociational" or power sharing democracy that defies the "winners take all" approach. The emergence of Madheshi People's Rights Forum (MPRF) and the Tarai Madhesh Loktantrik Party (TMLP) has also added a new dimension to Nepali politics. The Forum and the TMLP have won 52 and 20 seats respectively and have considerably been able to break the traditional hold of the major parties including the Maoists.

The post-CA election politics has become somewhat complex with the major parties reverting to confrontational politics. Nepali Congress and the Maoist seem to have entered into the politics of zero-sum game thus giving rise to serious doubt to the constitution making process. The major alliance partners have turned into foes or sworn rivals CPN (UML) and the Maoist.

The new political dynamics created by the 2006 movement and during and after the CA elections would be a great challenge to the political parties. Since no single party will have the dominant role, all need to embrace the culture of cooperation and understanding. But the manner in which the political parties seem to be conducting the politics of the new Nepal does not inspire the general people. From conventional point of view, Nepali politics is heavily dominated by the "left" forces as well as by the ethnic, regional and many other parochial trends. But, pluralistic democracy alone has triumphed as all left parties and others cannot find other escape routes, despite their numerous internal compulsions. Although the left trends have tried to inject some doses of radicalism into liberal politics, it is imperative that no political party can survive without having to embrace the agendas of common people. So democracy today cannot confine to statecraft in the Machiavellian or Chanakya's sense, nor can it remain abstract slogan of empty liberty. It can only survive with a human face.

The emerging trend of Nepali politics is a jigsaw puzzle that fails all assumptions and studies. Electoral gains of the Maoists have come out as a big surprise. All predictions that the Maoists would get third or fourth position in the post-election political hierarchy proved wrong with the Maoists replacing the two major parties, the NC and the CPN (UML). Now the CPN (Maoist) has occupied the first position after the verdict. The emergence of the CPN (Maoist) as a reckonable political force in the country has brought about a qualitative transformation in politics and society. Its 10-year long insurgency with a clear mission of abolishing monarchy, holding constituent assembly election for drafting a new democratic constitution, its emphasis on changing the election system for insuring inclusive democracy, its commitment to change Kathmandu-centric politics and administration by creating autonomous regions for distribution of power and resources, and to effective socio-economic programmes could prompt other parties to embrace them. But King Gyanendra's impatience for grabbing power by sidelining Parliamentary parties drove other parties to be closed to the Maoists. It also changed the mindset of general Nepalis that monarchy and democracy were incompatible in the context of Nepal.

It has also been demonstrated that the Nepali politics is heavily dominated by the 'left' trends. Even the oldest and largest moderate NC is relegated to second position, though its credibility didn't erode after it decided to transform its conventional role as a monarchist party. Its role during the movement and later has not diminished its status as a democratic party, despite much pressure put on it for continuing the *status quo*. The two parties–the NC and CPN (UML) have however failed to capitalize on their progressive image that they had gained during and after the second mass movement. The electoral setbacks suffered by them show that the Maoists have become the sole beneficiary of the new changes underway in Nepal. Yet, electoral gains sometimes prove to be momentary if the benefactor fails to perform up to the expectation of the people. If one goes by this assumption, the Maoist erosion has also set in with the leaders, particularly its chairman, Prachanda, becoming contradictory, often paranoid. His failure to continue in office and subsequent developments made him angry with other parties and India for their alleged role to oust him from power.

Critique of Post-2006 Political Developments

Movements, often launched for achieving the set goals, remain generally incomplete if politics continues to be in a state of flux after the change. The second *Jan Andolan* (2006), as others in the past, has "provisory achievements" which too are subject to 'interruption' and 'retrogression'. Some of the reasons for being abortive are: (a) interlocking relations between the revolutionaries and old regime; (b) elites ideological obfuscation; (c) lack of leaders' confidence, (d) impacts of retrogressive elements within organizations, and (e) international pulls and pressures.

The interlocking relationship between the forces of movement and the old regime, despite the latter being discredited and rejected by the people, seems to influence the political development after the movement. In the morrow of the so-called successful movement, political leaders cannot keep aloof from it not because of the lack of public support but because of their failure to give a definite mould to the spirit of the movement. Since they are preoccupied with the organized state and its force (army, police, bureaucracy and intelligence) whose help would also be crucial for them if there would be regime change in the real sense of the term, these leaders have to compromise even at the cost of the spirit of the movement.

Regime change alone is not the criterion of successful transformation of existing order. In 1951, there was only a replacement of rulers–from Rana to Shah, and from a core democratic point of view, it turned out to be a chimera. The retrogression was not partial confined to backlash to democracy; it was total as the Nepali state based on disparities and parochialism remained unchanged even during the era of party politics. The seeds of alienation had been sown through the imposition of monoculturalism, i.e., one language, one religion and one culture etc. The people of Madhesh took it as an imposition of the hill social and political culture patronized by the state, only to be resisted later. The post-2006 movement politics has however challenged the very notions of state and citizenship but not to the extent the French revolution had done for putting these two terms at the centre of politics. So the Nepali people need to develop a fresh attitude towards a democratic cohesive state with a clear perspective of state and citizenship. As of today, the state is projected as an enemy because of its parochial ethos and historical background, while the idea of citizenship is also not matured because of the long tradition of being *praja* or subject whose orientation was not compatible to the spirit of the movement. So the two fundamental aspects of modern democratic state are the harmonious relationship between the citizen and state.

Second, political leaders of Nepal have not yet internalized the core values of democracy despite being projected as the thoroughbred democrats committed to ending all forms of indiscrimination. Ideology should work as glue to highly fragmented society by forging cooperative and harmonious relations among the contending forces. If ideology is used as a strategy, then politics degenerates into an 'unprincipled struggle for power'. Nepal's political reality demands that all political forces including the Maoists should work together until providing stability to a new democratic constitution drafted by the CA.

Third, the decline of state is pervasive in all domains–economic, social, political, regional and psychological but political leaders fail to resurrect the sagging image of the state. Political parties themselves are on the decline giving rise to political spaces to regional, ethnic and other formations that are bent on promoting their own community and regional interests. Major parties yield to their pressures as they were, till yesterday, considered to be the support bases. Defiance of whip in Parliament by the members of major parties demonstrated that political leaders are increasingly playing subordinate role to individual members, a strange phenomenon observed in party system. Although parties in the conventional sense cannot work in the changed political landscape of Nepal, there seems to be a general decline of parties. Both the country and democracy suffer if the state and parties fail to be effective. At a time when Nepal needs "integral nationalism" in which all sub-national loyalties and identities converge, state based on people's will and parties need to be strengthened. Since both are exclusive to each other in democracy, force of the state alone cannot change the direction to catastrophe.

Four, one of the principal reasons for the decline of parties is the penetration of regressive elements who invariably point to the risks to be faced by the proponents of radical change. Most Parliamentary declarations and commitments remain on papers showing that the new government leaders are not separate from the landed aristocracy or the vested interest groups whose tentacles are spread everywhere. Linked to it is the absence of effective governance without which no substantive changes in people's living conditions could be introduced. As a result, people's confidence in the new regime also gets attenuated putting the regime itself in peril.

Finally, movements generally fail when people start losing faith in the capacity of political elites who in turn feel that they are subject to pressure politics intensified by native conspirators and external players thus injecting in parties' leaders a sense of fear and helplessness. Such lack of confidence is also created by the psychology of politicians that the state cannot survive without the support of external donors; more so at a time when resources for running the government and other institutions are depleted. Nevertheless, such pressures exerted by the foreigners are still positive inasmuch as most major powers have only warned the parties of possible risk factors in case they fail to comply with the established democratic practices and norms. So Nepal's agenda of democratic transformation continues to attract the external actors at least for the time being.

Summing up

One of the greatest contributions made by the *Jan Andolan II* is the changed mindset of the Nepali people. The Maoist people's war had sensitized the two agendas–end of monarchy and election to Constituent Assembly (CA)–to which other political parties also adopted in order to translate the wish of the *Jan Andolan II*. The declaration by the Interim Parliament stripping all powers vested in the King was a follow-up measure establishing the fact that the new Parliament, a combination of both the dissolved Parliament and of the new nominated members of the movement parties including the Maoists, was able to take such crucial decisions for changing the future course of Nepali politics. Some old myths were also exploded in the wake of new developments. These myths were: monarchy as a symbol of unity and integrity and continued loyalty of the Royal Nepal Army (now Nepal Army) to the monarchy.

Yet another significant aspect of the transition politics is that Nepali politicians seem to be too much preoccupied with external factors, particularly with the role of India, China and the US. Other donors such as the European Union have also created an impact on shaping the psychology of the new rulers of Nepal. India and the US have played important role in creating conducive atmosphere for peace and democratization. Their strong anti-Maoist positions have undergone significant changes during the movement and after. Indian facilitation and encouragement to conclude agreements with the Maoists has proved to be positive despite occasional difficulties suffered by the peace process. Nevertheless, it has been generally realized that these foreign powers are too visible to dictate terms for Nepali elites and are often misunderstood as interventionist powers.

Nepal today is in the throes of revolutionary change. Putting flurry of demands and resorting to *bundhs* and other forms of coercive actions have become a routine affair in the country. Fatigued with such agonizing trends, people feel that Nepal has the syndrome of both a 'failed' and an uncertain state. Deteriorating law and order situation, failure to deliver minimum goods and services to the people, unchanged mindset of leaders and lack of effective decisions to steer the course of new politics and lack of direction etc. are singled out as dismal failures of the SPA Government.

Yet, sometimes, such failures appear to be by-products of deliberate actions that try to keep cool the atmosphere in the country. Such cool and calculated approach needed when the scope of escalation of conflict was high. Weighing the gravity of the situation, the government thus preferred to use more carrot than stick during its two-year rule. So it might be painful for the time being, but its long-term positive impacts cannot be undermined.

But, a big question has arisen on the prospect of making a new Nepal. Will the parties rise above the partisan interest and work in tandem for some more years, despite their differences, or fall apart as some non-Maoist parties did in the past when the question of power arose? If the three major parties–the NC, the CPN (UML) and the UCPN (Maoist) can manage to make a constitution and hold election under it, then scope of consolidating democracy may be bright. Yet, for that to happen also, needs ideological commitment of all the forces. If the greed of power and privileges weigh against the principal agenda of peace, stability, development and democracy, as is being witnessed today (2010), Nepal's future itself is in peril.

Notes

1. Baral, Lok Raj. 1995. "The Emerging Trends of ..." *Asian Survey.*
2. For a more detailed picture of the ethnic composition of Nepal, see Pitamber Sharma. 2008. *Unravelling the Mosaic: Spatial Aspects of Ethnicity in Nepal.* Kathmandu: Himal Books.
3. *Ibid.*, p.13.
4. Bhim Prasad Bhurtel has given two reasons that give rise to suspicion and fear of the Tarai people. First, the Kathmandu rulers want to follow the division of the country into Zones and Development Regions as was done during the Panchayat (royal) regime. Such division was made in order not to allow the Tarai to dominate the hills/mountain regions. Second, The leaders of the Madhesh movement belong to the less developed areas of the Tarai as except the eight Tarai districts–Jhapa, Morang, Sunsari, Chitwan, Rupandehi, Banke, Bardiya, Kailali–other Tarai districts cannot produce sufficient food as needed by them. Since 90 per cent of the present Tarai leaders belong to the low producing districts stretching from Kosi to Kandaki, the demand for one Madhesh, one Pradesh would turn out to be unrealistic. See Bhim Prasad Bhurtel, "Madheshko Artha Rajniti" (Political Economy of Madhesh), *Kantipur Daily*, February 28, 2008.
5. See in detail, *The Himalayan Times* (Kathmandu), February 29, 2008.
6. See Baral, Lok Raj, "Imperative of Federalism", *The Kathmandu Post,* February 19, 2008.

2
Nepal's Quest for Inner Party Democracy

Dev Raj Dahal

Introduction

Modern political parties are the lynchpin of pluralistic democracy. As breeding ground of democratic aspirations they are also an engine of social transformation. They bring diverse sections of citizens into their structures and offer adequate electoral choice thus enabling them to exercise rights to choose leaders in governance. Political parties are also vital "instruments of winning and administering power and determining policy outcomes" (Criddle, 2003:140). Effective functioning of democracy presupposes political parties to adopt democratic principles and activities in their internal life. Popular demand for inclusive or participatory democracy in Nepal has opened debates about the democratization of political parties and an improvement in their political structures, procedures and political culture for attaining "democratic responsiveness."[1] Nepalese parties are formed largely on the heritage of political movement, rebellion and leadership split. The common ground, in relation to an inter-party collaborative platform, therefore, can be found in "*a political-economic regime of social democracy*" (Mishra, 2008: 14-16). Leaders of all the mainstream parties come from middle and upper classes of society. They require enhancing democratic character and transformation of small elite base at the top to become representative of the nation's social diversity, majority of them fall into the economic bracket of lower classes.

The 12-point agreement signed by Seven-Party Alliance and rebel Communist Party of Nepal (Maoist) in 2005 assumes political parties a "guardian" of people. The Interim Constitution of January 2007 entails the parties to adopt "*transparency and accountability*" in their functioning. Sound internal bookkeeping, reporting to electorates and information disclosure to citizens are vital civic functions. Modernization of an in-egalitarian stratification of Nepalese society can increase poor citizens' access to power and resources and enhance their confidence in the polity. These are also the solutions to the problem of growing extra-party civic engagement of subsidiary identities–women, Madheshis, Janajatis, Dalits, Adivasis, backward classes, business, etc. and balance common interests of parties, public interests of citizens and national interests of the state.

The inner party democracy is also a solution to the proliferation of armed groups caused by political closure and negation, lawlessness caused by factional fights and the corrosion of state power, alienation of youth and group-enclosed extra-party social movements in all types of democracy. Internal party democracy, dignified space for the opposition and resiliency of participatory democracy requires generations' efforts in fostering inclusive transformation of the nation's political culture. Left parties have sought to offer an alternative to elite oligarchy. But, Milovan Djilas, while analyzing a single Communist party-dominated regimes found the formation of new ruling class within the parties just as selfish as previous oligarchy (Djilas, 1961). The paternalistic tendency of leaders often considering themselves most competent and cadres incompetent (Bhusal, 2009: 32) is universal in many societies lacking civic culture. Karl Marx and Friedrich Engels, therefore, considered party democracy a crucial means to combat "group conspiracy". V. I. Lenin allowed freedom of criticism within the limits of the principles of party so that reform and unity of party are achieved. All political parties of Nepal prefer high necessity of party reforms as they provide learning opportunities for the next generation of leaders and followers. The only question is when, how, how far and how fast?

Where is Nepal's party politics heading in terms of laws, political structure and political culture? How is stability possible in the relations of political parties in Nepal so that they can collectively achieve national goals? Where are Nepal's reforms for inner party democracy heading? How long does it take to reform Nepal's political culture when highly personalized and fractious party leaders coexist uneasily with impersonal laws and institutions of the state? Can a strong sense of party identification of citizens so essential to their behaviour endure when party leaders and party intellectuals themselves develop flexible tendencies in their loyalties? How to build the capacity of parties to reform and think beyond partisan interest for national vision and goals? This paper revolves around some of these questions.

Changing Party Functions

The changing stratification of Nepalese society has produced highly mobile classes outside the institutional framework of party politics but well connected to national and international networks of values, struggles and collective action. The social mobility of underclasses of society from rural to urban areas and abroad continues to erode the traditional authority of feudal interests while entrepreneurial lower-middle classes have become an *elan vital* of democratic spirit, energy and expansion. The rational-choice behaviour of political cadres and voters has weakened the voluntary spirit in political participation. While 12-point agreement sought to institutionalize parliamentary polity, Comprehensive Peace Agreement (CPA) and the Interim Constitution have sought to bring "incoherence of political principles", among the mainstream parties and made the boundaries between "plural left", parties existing in Nepalese political landscape fluid and fluctuating. The outcome of CA election has changed power equation in favour of UCPN (Maoist) as it emerged the single dominant party but short of simple majority to form its own government. The demand of non-Maoist parties to shift political game from consensus to competition has added new element in this fluidity as power struggle assumed primacy over drafting a new constitution. In the absence of a modicum of party discipline along the line of common values and common attitude and accountability to inter-party accords there is no guarantee that Nepal's party system will restore law-governed regime, cohesive peace, progress and stability. The outcome is: "democracy has been transformed into a semi-anarchic regime" which has generated a fear of "the disintegration of the state" (Bobbio, 2002:298; Mainali, 2009:24-31).

The UCPN (Maoist) projects itself "anti-system" revolutionary party having belief in People's Republic while other parties do not have courage to defend the existing system as they are torn between fear of "state restructuring" and challenges posed by "political *status quo*". Nepali Congress (NC) and Communist Party of Nepal Unified Marxist-Leninist (CPN-UML) are locked in an uneasy tension between "politics as usual" at the centre and widening of socio-economic revolution at the grass roots level. The swelling of NGOs, civil society, professional bodies, media and small parties signals a budding political pluralism, each checking the other's power and authority and articulating the human rights of minorities.

Turmoil in inner party democracy has resulted in clashes in CPN-UML, NC, Madheshi Jana Adhikar Forum (MJAF), Rastriya Prajatantra Party (RPP) and Nepal Sadbhavana Party between the parliamentary parties and the mass section of the parties causing vertical split though NC has uneasily shelved its discord and allowed cadres of both Koirala and Deuba factions to compete for general assembly members. A large chunk of CPN-ML drifted back to mother party latter on. The Madheshi parties too formed a Madheshi Democratic United Front to fight for a single Madhesh federal state and proportional representation in governance. The UCPN (Maoist) is seeking "unity, struggle and transformation" which is closer to the line of CPN-UML Chairman J. N. Khanal's "reorganization, unity, struggle and transformation", and even a possibility for either national consensus or the left unity government. The self-image of CPN-UML is moderate left in the middle between what it calls "conservative NC" and "left extremist UNPN (Maoist)". In contrast, M. K. Nepal and K.P. Oli of the same party, like leaders of *ancient regime*, feel comfortable for a collaborative action with the NC so long as UCPN (Maoist) is not transformed into a civilian party by returning the lands it seized during conflict to rightful owners, dismantling of para-military wing of Young Communist League and rehabilitation and integration of Maoist combatants. The two lines of struggle maintained by UCPN (Maoist) makes it difficult to compromise "revolutionary path" it had given to the people as a surest way to emancipation.

The UCPN (Maoist) and Madheshi parties exhibit "movement tendencies" and maintain a very unstable relationship with society as their self-perceived image is a catalyst of radical change. Both parties also face conflict between soft and hard lines. But the class polarization sought by UCPN (Maoist) and territorial polarization by Madheshi parties frighten each other. The NC and CPN-UML, however, fear both for their lack of interest in governability and converging interest on sectoral demands though they sharply differ on land reforms, political pluralism and identity politics. Politics of

Nepal has thus become "overshadowed by both the desire for and the fear of expropriation" (Offe and Schmitter, 1995: 514). Changing functions of parties entail a search for the redefinition of identity based on current policies and bridge the disjuncture between their ideological brand and anti-ideological policies.

In a strong inner party democracy, political parties collect a variety of demands, opinions and interests of people, articulate to party committees, present competing policy packages and submit them to respective parliamentary committees for deliberation and consideration. Conversion of demands into public policy and feedback of citizens brings the system nearer to the life-world of citizens. Petty and personal demands of voters for small projects, job and problem handling are done through the links of party leaders to different agencies. Aggregation of citizens' demand is managed by political parties while articulation is done through pressure groups, interest groups, civil society, media etc. Factions within political parties also aggregate and articulate those opposing interests into alternative policies. Sometimes competing and sometimes common interests are formed across the party lines for articulation. In order to perform input functions, political parties should sufficiently maintain inner party democracy and cohere diverse public into enlightened understanding and democratic culture of cooperation based on popular sovereignty.

Nepal's rural life is changing very fast with changing structure in gender roles, social stratification and migration pattern as new social mobility from rural to urban areas provided by remittance economy, decline in agricultural production, proliferation of NGOs and civil society and sharpening of social ferment are exerting pressure for restructuring of the state, political parties and property. The implementation of federalism, regional autonomy and devolution of power in Nepal is sure to incubate many regional parties in the future if the leadership of national parties will continue to remain within the historically existing pre-capitalist traits (of paternalism where people look to the state for everything), feudal peculiarities rooted in patronage system and caste-bound prerogatives while vociferously posturing the language of Marxism, nationalism and liberalism to the public. The politics of caste and gender homogeneity maintained at the top echelon of mainstream parties is incongruous for a democratic rule because it reflects the non-representative character of politics and de-institutionalization of party system. The weakness of political leaders to stabilize democratic initiatives is mainly attributed to eroding distributive capacity of the state at a time when leaders have themselves unleashed unrealistic expectations and trapped democracy in a partisan politics.

Party Convergence into a Catch-All Type

The shift of Nepalese political parties from ideological formation to "catch-all" type, aiming to maximize supporters and members regardless of their commitment to party ideologies and programmes, indicates their perception of changing electoral base as well as the *Zeitgeist*. But, they appear weak in exercising the will of people in governance and attain a new constitution by an elected 601-member Constituent Assembly, stable peace and structural reforms. All the parties articulate two kinds of interests–*functionally specific interests* of organized groups of society such as businessmen, trade unions, media and NGOs and the *interests governed by primordial loyalties* of families, caste, religion, ethnic and indigenous groups and Dalits. The interests of peasants and workers, who constitute major segment of Nepal's population, are largely ignored as they are the most inarticulate, passive and unorganized group. As a consequence their voting behaviour represents high volatility and gradually veering towards the left. The catch-all tendency also marks the decline in ideological orthodoxy and fundamental policy differences among the parties. This has affected their organizational dynamics and weakened the social base of partisan attachment of electorates.

Otto Kirchheimer, while studying the political tendencies of parties in the Western Europe, argues that social change, bureaucratization, secularization, growing influence of media and the decline of political ideology have weakened the links between political parties and society and transformed ideological political parties into catch-all type. Its effects are: erosion of influence of individual party members; de-emphasis by parties of special class or religious appeals in favour of attracting diverse voters across population; autonomy of the leadership from internal checks and balances; and decline of ideology (Kavanagh, 2003:1). Due to the nation's social and cultural diversity, Nepal's political parties of all hues ingrain a tendency to mix class, gender, ethnicity, caste, region, age and other empirical components into their party programmes to fit with the catch-all criteria defined above. In contrast to Western tradition, there is an unwillingness of leaders to accept political defeat in elections and accept "rules of the game". This has generated a crisis of democratic authority and legitimacy of governance.

The catch-all parties have a more unstable political constituency, no definite policy focus and present a message that though carefully crafted, aims to combine as many disparate propositions as possible so long as they do not come into direct conflict or contradiction (Williams, 2006:2). The psychological wounds of fission and fusion of the Nepalese parties have not disappeared. Proliferation of factions in each party continues to affect vertically at the local level of party committees causing the erosion of trust between the factions. As a result, an individualized relationship of leaders with voters is becoming stronger than the general outreach of parties in society. This is causing the de-politicization electorates and increasing frustration of voters. The catch-all tendency and political interest in building grand coalition government in Nepal with all kinds of political combination has shifted contradiction from horizontal to vertical level–between the leaders and the masses and allowed the birth of identity politics–the politics of difference–and claim for the allocation of power and position accordingly. The centre-periphery and hill-Tarai cleavages have also deepened due to the tendency of party leaders and many civil society groups to use cultural differences of the nation for the expansion of political base. Electoral campaigns have already become multi-channel media-mediated rather than door-to-door canvassing and the leaders have developed a strong interest in executive power than production of good legislation. As a result, political parties have less power to mediate conflicting claims about common good.

The legitimacy of democratic parties comes from their representative character and the support they command from diverse citizens. Those who don't listen to the voices of citizens wither away. The politics of "difference" maintained by social groups, recently institutionalized group rights for women, Madhesi, ethnic and indigenous groups and people of remote areas by Nepal's political system and their assertion for "social representation" has taken precedence over political representation. Similarly, the demand for "participatory democracy" is contesting the boundaries of "representative democracy" sustained through party politics as channels of political participation have also become too diverse–extra-constitutional (militant wings of parties and ethnic groups), extra-parliamentary (distributional movement of social classes), extra-party (across the party caucus group) and anomic (109 armed groups). Twenty social minorities who do not have representation in the CA and ignored by parties are demanding a constitutional and political system that includes them in the future.

Political Modernization and Inner Party Democracy

Political modernization is a process of transmutation of pre-modern, caste-based and patriarchal authority and legitimacy of parties to post-traditional, rationalistic and electoral authority capable of broadening the political structures for mass participation and resolving conflicts to attain societal goals. Obviously, constitutionlization of political parties and policy coherence among them can achieve rule-governed behaviour and a semblance of political stability but it requires abolishing the culture of impunity for powerful political classes in the country. Institutionalization of party system equally demands the existence of robust party organizations independent of individual leaders (Hartlyn, 1996: 174) but supportive of state impersonality in the implantation of laws.

A defective democracy which lacks unitary legal order of modern state does not guarantee inner party democracy with adequate checks and balances in its internal life as it does not have sufficient political will to abolish the state of nature and enforce rule of law. So long as Nepalese leaders stick to multiple worldviews, the crisis of rule of law in the country will continue and political socialization of citizens will be steered in multiple directions, some even in militant way. Militarization and radicalization of politics in Nepal have already hobbled the system of constitutionalism and strained efforts for recovery from conflicts. Various political parties of Nepal hold dissimilar views about the transformation of party democracy as the representation of particular interest to general interest of public and remove the disharmony between ideological brands espoused by parties and actual programme contents.

The main cleavages among them are the class, caste, ethnicity, religion and region, not ideology. As a result, costs of cooperation between citizens and leaders have increased. The inner life of Nepal's left parties are generally governed by "democratic centralism", a concept which provides the freedom to members of political parties to discuss and debate matters of policy and direction, but once the decision of the party is made by majority, all members have to follow that decision. The latter represents centralism. By contrast, in inner party democracy party members are allowed to engage in the shaping of ideological, institutional and leadership competition as well as their continuous engagement in programme formulation and implementation. Non-left parties are less cohesive in terms of ideology, discipline and organizational affiliation. The socialization, mobilization and decision-making functions of parties tend to resolve both adaptive and integrative problems in society and transform intra-party sub-national loyalties into national identity.

Democratizing Ties with Ancillary Organizations

Horizontal expansion of political parties with ancillary organizations and vertical decentralization of authority to local units increase popular participation, deepen the tentacles of party in society, tie the bottom with the top leadership and broaden the cycles of reforms. In Nepal, the historical relationship between political parties and their ancillary organizations is marked by unequal patron-client ties. The leadership recruitment of party cadres for intra-party functions also indicates patronage politics. Ancillary organizations are now demanding their own representation in the party's various committees. As a result, political parties are now facing a tension between the accommodation of ancillary organizations' demands without visible representation and ancillary organizations' assertion in representation.

Trade Unions have formed Joint Trade Union Coordinating Committee (JTUCC) and seeking autonomy from party politics as they have discovered that their continuous "infantilization" and "subordinated role", for long has compromised their legitimate interests in social security, codetermination of public policy, free collective bargaining and domination-free relationship in society so that they can also cooperate with other trade unions. Women, Dalits, indigenous people, ethnic *Janajatis* and Muslims have also formed cross-party caucus groups, common curricula and struggling for group interests than general political interests. So long as political leaders mobilize the poor during elections and demobilize and desert them after the elections to shift to business interest, it would be difficult to inject more democracy in the parties as leadership opportunism thwarts the conversion of social power into political power. The important side-effect of this process is that when money talks the voice of civil society is subdued and the interest of cadres is compromised. This shows that party reforms driven by factional competition do not make them responsive to electorates unless civil society, media and public-interest groups apply external pressure for strong constituency service and renew democratic discourse. Transparent selection of candidates, regular organization of committee meetings and decentralization of power to them can strengthen democratic practice (Saud, 2009: 54-60).

Active Listening and Debate

Nepalese people and party cadres at the local level want their leaders to listen to their legitimate concerns and help resolve their problems. A culture of active listening by leaders opens the possibility for reducing the cycles of violent protests and brings dissident forces into constitutional bounds of dialogue, negotiation and compromise. Conversation on contending ideas, principles and practices by members helps evolve new concepts which are important to handle concrete contextual problems. Nepalese political parties cannot really grow without the creation of a trusting and communicative action between the leaders and cadres and peacefully resolve the conflict of divided societies. The leaders must come out in front of people, be honest about the situation and invite a few questions that require immediate response. The leaders' style of response defines the nature of relationship between cadres and the rulers. Open-ended dialogues and participation of cadres in various party committees give them ownership in the programme, build confidence for future leadership and help solve the problems through deliberative means. Ironically, most of the national conventions of parties in Nepal are hurriedly organized where delegates and cadres have little time to discuss about ideology, organization, policy, programmes and leadership questions. Authoritarian leaders do not encourage the habits of political debate because party schools' orthodoxy deprives them to learn multiple perspectives and adopt a culture of social learning. Regular meeting of party officials and leaders for intermeshing of perspectives based on communication about party policies and activities provide for a new system of rules to emerge (Habermas, 1997: 347).

Party Ideology and Policy Making

In Nepal, a small group of Kathmandu-based closed circle of elites steer politics from top without consulting the affected at the grass roots level. Only democratization process can enforce the party leaders to go to electorates, ideologize the cadres and balance the interest of interest groups within the party vying for influence on public policy and the interest of ordinary citizens (Prasai, 2009:5). Erosion of ideology has made strong party affiliation and policy debate difficult. Nepal is largely a "consumer" of public policy, political system and development paradigms. Planners, party leaders and parliamentarians lack intellectual capacity to "indigenize" policy and feed the social and contextual learning into its process. As a result, parliament is not a place where national policies are made by national reflection, guided by public opinion and public interest of sovereign citizens. The self-consciously organized civil society, NGOs and cause groups are, however, better engaged with the policy community of the state, Finance Ministry and donors for projects and increasingly compete with the state, political society and societal institutions though they themselves are fragmented, weak and largely group-enclosed. Little impact of agricultural and informal sectors on public policy demonstrates skewed development of Nepal while patronage-based ethnic and territorial bargaining remains strong within the parties. Previous model of modernization integrated urban areas to global modernity, now huge migration of rural workers to global capital market, 3,00,000 out of 4,00,000 youth entering into global labour market every year is shifting both voting behaviour and social transformation of agrarian, rural areas from feudalism to capitalism. This electoral change bears consequences for party reforms and party building.

Resolution of Factional Fight

The struggle of Nepal's political parties of all hues is the history of struggle of political factions' fight and split in leadership which are too numerous to document here. This affirms the thesis about the "iron law of oligarchy", according to which society is governed by a "small self-perpetuating elites at the centre (Michels, 1968:15). To him, masses are intrinsically weak to govern their organizations and democratically control their leaders owing to their educational, cultural and technological conditions. In Nepal, local leaders argue, "people have to follow leadership", except in the case of elections and agitations. The solution of the problems of parliamentary politics is not possible by extra-parliamentary means. Nor violent extra-constitutional change can stabilize civic culture. In Nepal, the tendency of top party leaders to bypass the party, parliament and government is evident from their "non-participation" in the parliamentary committees while generating interest in the creation of a High Level Political Mechanism outside the parliament for conflict resolution. Creation of flexible avenues of negotiation outside parliamentary framework to settle sectoral demands has eroded the authority of parliament and capacity of parliamentary leaders of parties to embed them in the daily life of general public.

The negotiation of semi-militant Madhesi, ethnic and Tharu movements and labour-capital often takes place outside the parliament. The demand of various social groups for functional representation has replaced the role of parties and parliaments (Held, 1987: 218) and marks a shift from representative to direct democracy. Despite a number of coalition governments political parties have yet to learn a culture of coalition, negotiation and compromise for collective public and national interests. "The willingness and habit of the political elite to reach good compromises with anyone willing to participate in the interest of the country is an essential contribution to promoting a democratic political culture" (Mayer, 2007: 36). A culture of compromise and trust and non-violent resolution of conflict are expected to enable leaders to participate constructively in the political process. The cost of party factionalism in Nepal is too high as it has often produced a series of deadlock and restricted political parties to achieve collective goals. Regular inter-party dialogues with independent intellectuals is expected to innovate ideas for common grounds appropriate for the resolution of factional fights.

Leadership Style

Joseph Schumpeter has reduced democracy into a process of competition for leadership selection and recruitment of personnel (1947: 269). Inner party democracy is an alternative to the totalitarian and authoritarian "leader party because it guarantees the control of leadership, its selection and the participation of its members in decision making" (Mayer, 2007:11). Political parties' democratic character is judged by the degree to which they allow party members to select their candidates for leadership of various layers of committees in election. Nepal's leadership is governed by sub-cultures and, therefore, critically lacks national vision and ability to communicate that vision beyond kinship, family and party politics though the mobility of cadres is stratifying Nepalese society and gradually shifting its political culture from introvert, closed society to extrovert one and traditional to modern attractive enough to generate hopes of democratic renewal. This will surely exert pressure on the central and district committees of parties to democratize and augment influence over party elites. The Nepali diasporas is also mounting pressure for the democratization of party leadership and a political culture of frank discussion in which party cadres, voters and even potential voters are encouraged to speak their mind and shape the agenda. The leaders' tendency to substitute oneself with the party has bureaucratized most of Nepalese leaders, generated a contradiction between their actual democratic aims and undemocratic functions and opened the possibility of coalition government of any sort under the imperative of the doctrine of necessity. These leaders are mainly responsible for the erosion of the founding ideology, identity and organizational discipline of parties without sufficiently adapting to changing context, actors, issues and aspirations.

A move away from careerist to transformational leadership is central to foster responsive civic political culture. "Leadership has the threefold task of diagnosing the situation authoritatively, devising a course of action designed to resolve or alleviate the problem, and mobilizing the political community's support for the leaders' definition of the situation and their prescribed policy response" (Tucker, 1981: 31). Growing group-bound social movements in Nepal are eroding leadership's traditional, charismatic and movement oriented legitimacy and the increasing autonomy and assertiveness of civic groups who demand leadership's rule-bound accountability in performance. The leadership of a mass membership party requires the loyalties of rank-and-file members coming from various strata of population, sound inner communication and occupancy of achievement-oriented role in the party.

Party Politics and Democratization of Public Sphere

In a culturally plural society like Nepal having 103 ethnic and caste groups, 7 religions and over 90 languages, deepening of political parties in society requires the participation and representation of these diversities and their contestation between formal constitutional equality and condition of inequality. Nepal's politics is less public and more partisan and personal. As a result, it leaves little space for the autonomy of public sphere where critical debates about public issues allow the formation of public opinion, articulation of alternatives, democratic will formation, agenda formulation and enable citizens to make informed choice. Party leaders' authority is often contested in media, institutional practices and everyday life by diverse social classes because kinship and family considerations are very strong in party politics than ideology and public institutions. The liberalization of society is considerably eroding the social base of feudal politics and the patrimonial leadership as well as its capacity to use the state to regulate economy, culture and disciplinary institutions. But it has also generated radical expectation of people beyond the ability of leaders to fulfil. The globalization process has injected cosmological consciousness and enlarging the level of participation. In contrast, an atrophy of civic institutions has veered Nepalese politics into an uncertain direction. The use of democratic means of struggle by women and under-classes of society have challenged the institutional closure practised by both traditional and radical leadership while the existence of militant groups in the bigger parties has legitimized violence in politics. De-linking violence from politics requires continuous socialization of party cadres in human rights code and civic education. Civic education encouraging critical thinking and values of democracy, development and peace are essential to the transformation of Nepal's predominantly rural societies.

Democracy Aid: Funding of Political Parties

Financial contributions to political parties are important incentives to make them effective organizationally and functionally, enable them to mobilize supporters and voters, run successful campaign and conduct political activities. The tissues that link the citizens to state and respond to popular accountability requires inner party democracy. But, if the money that influences party politics is "strings attached" they increasingly become responsive to the narrow webs of power and isolate the parties from democratic values and delivery of collective goods to common citizens. Ironically, party system in Nepal does not conform to an institutionalized system of agreed-upon rules as many of them are organized and run according to their party interest, leadership, institutions and programmes than *constitutional vision and principles*. This has made political sphere jarring, increased money's influence in politics, created unreasonable competition, soiled the wheels of corruption and impunity and reduced level playing field for weak actors–thereby making democracy a zero-sum game where opposition and powerless do not have any stake in it.

There is a strong interest shown by members of international community to work on party reforms in Nepal. At the empirical projects level donors are supporting their NGOs to promote the rights of women, Dalits, youth, Madheshis, trade unions, journalists, etc. which have exerted bottom-up pressure for party reforms but they are more connected to rights-based identity politics and less to citizenship building to deepen democracy in society and contribute to post-conflict reconciliation and peace building. Three areas are opened for international cooperation: first, many parties are affiliated with like-minded parties abroad and are governed by common values of solidarity. They together participate in regional and international forums and share each other's experience. Second, exposure visits and short-term trainings have also been provided to Nepalese leaders abroad. Third, there is an exchange of ideas and literature to brief each other, and finally, donors also support selective leaders of parties to foster clients in parties. Massive aid packages diverted to pre-political solidarity group, NGOs, civil society networks and consultants as a reconstruction strategy are creating parallel structures, weakening the representative value of parties and obstructing their authority and legitimacy. The need is to support the institutionalization of dialogue and increase leaders' willingness to cooperate across political divides and formulate necessary public policies to meet public needs.

Democratization of Inter-Party Relations

Democratic political culture requires avoiding "fundamentalist fallacy", a term which describes an attitude of parties which fails to understand that democratic process requires both competition between parties and certain amount of consensus about some rules of the democratic frame, basic rights and some macro objectives for the entire polity (Meyer, 2001: 5). Fragmentation of Nepalese politics and introduction of proportional election system have made the future of Nepal's Government coalition-based. This means without the democratization of relations among them for shared interest there is neither possibility for the formation of coalition government nor stability of regime. Trust building also requires sharing of common democratic values and ideological orientations. In Nepal, however, there is a disharmony between leaders' commitment to common values of human rights and democracy and expression of utilitarian instinct. This has created a tension between party ideology and identity and the reality of national politics. "Inter party dialogue can aim at identifying and overcoming common challenges in improving the functioning of the political system" (Angeby, 2005:8), seeking reasonable settlement of conflicting interests, ideology and identity and coordinating goals and actions in response to challenges. Nepal's political parties can perform better in competition with other parties if internal democracy contributes to cohesiveness and helps to maintain working relationship with other parties either towards the formation of government, undertaking public interest initiatives, achieving collective goods and resolving conflicts. Inner party democracy becomes stable when winners do not dictate the rules of game despite a decisive power advantage it enjoys.

Election Commission

Political parties in Nepal are required to register with the Election Commission (EC) for the legitimacy of their activities. Nepali laws prohibit undue financial influence on party politics and allow the EC to monitor financial transactions and flows including power to penalize the parties with the cancellation of election result or imprisonment for two years but this oversight function of the EC is largely ineffective. The autonomy of EC is questioned because election commissioners are selected on the basis of party loyalty. The institutional and legal frameworks can make political parties effective players in the polity. The EC has to frame strict rules to monitor political parties' commitment to democracy. This is especially important because decision-making is concentrated in a few elites, party discipline is weak and culture of impunity is strong. It is the responsibility of treasurer to do the accounting of party finance through external certified accountant, signed by him and submitted to the EC.

If political parties do not follow this practice, approved by themselves and the Constitution, then one must find the rationale for it–either arbitrary character of leadership, weakness of EC or lack of technical and financial efficiency of the parties themselves. The treasurer normally does reporting of the financial activities during national conventions. Since national convention occupies the leaders and cadres about elections of new leadership the delegates and voters are more engaged in lobbying than discussing about the detail of finance. It is possible to increase the technical, financial and management efficiency of the parties from outside support and the standardization of bookkeeping procedures. But, the control of arbitrary style must be done away with the internal democratization of parties. Corruption flourishes in the deinstitutionalization of the political system and an atrophy of civic life.

The denial by political parties to submit their annual income and expenditure statement to EC reflects the resiliency of old political culture of *Nepalese leadership to exercise power without accountability*. It has become easy to maintain because the symbolic fine of Rs. 100 is low as compared to the cost in the preparation of all details. It also reflects weak law-enforcement will of the EC. Ensuring transparency is not without cost. There are too many party laws. The problem lies in the attitude of leaders as they do not find any incentive for their sincere implementation or face costs in non-implementation of laws. Big parties should set examples in insuring transparency for small ones to follow. If money dominates election campaign it will be less representative. Too much emphasis on corporate citizenship in Nepal has skewed power relationship in society thus enervating the self-correcting mechanism of democracy–circulation of new elites through elections thereby making every citizen stakeholder of the polity.

That none of 74 EC-registered political parties of Nepal have publicized their annual financial report to public has made electorates and civil society difficult to understand the legal and illegal patterns of donations. The fragile nature of the state has inhibited the state authorities to demand the parties to follow "rule of law". The articulation of the need to transform "autocratic hierarchy" of party leadership (Bhattarai, 2009) into transparent and democratic one with effective public oversight on its conduct is one remedy. The EC must set a mechanism along with watchdog agencies to enable citizens to obtain information and judge the merit of financial income and expenditure in a transparent manner. There is a need to strengthen

Nepal's public sphere enabling it to organize informed debate and major public hearings including party's democratic and transparent operation.

Conclusion

Changing Party Functions

Despite pivotal roles played by Nepalese political parties in the modernization of state and society, the main challenges they encounter in the democratization process are: gaps between the ideology and policy, incoherence between constitution and constitutional behaviour, weak-enforcement of party laws, unstructured political participation of citizens moving beyond party, parliament and constitutional system, exclusionary political culture sustained by politics of negation, lack of balance between individual, groups and human rights, absence of mechanism of inter and intra-party conflict resolution and a tradition of centralized leadership facing tension with the social groups demanding regional, social, gender and inter-generational representation.

Inner party democracy bolsters general political democracy with democratization of parties as one of the political platforms to attract most supporters. Any attempt towards constitutional democracy helps to overcome democratic-centralism in the left as well as authoritarianism in the centre and the right and address democratic challenge from social movement groups and non-democratic challenge from 109 armed groups. Among all the available solutions to problems of politics in Nepal, inner party democracy is the most urgent and thus most promising way for Nepal's democratic future. First, it increases the social base of political parties. Second, it restricts anti-institutional social movements by means of inclusion and organized political participation in the life of society. Third, it fosters a culture of listening to the cadres and incorporates their demands. Fourth, it nurtures democratic ways of deciding public issues including the issue of leadership in the party. Fifth, it increases social responsiveness of leadership and abolishes hereditary privileges in public policy and public action by way of decentralization.

Note

1. "Democratic responsiveness is a complex process, somewhat like a chain whose links are causally connected. It begins with the policy preferences held by citizens, and moves link by causal link through such stages as voting, election outcomes, the formation of policy making coalitions, the process of policy making between elections, and public policies themselves" (Powell, 2004: 91).

References

Angeby, Martin. 2005. "Democracy and Social Integration", paper presented at a *Dialogue in the Social Integration Process: Building Peaceful Social Relations–by, for and with People*, organized by the Division for the Social Policy and Development of the UNDESA, New York, May 21-12 November.

Bhattarai, Binod, *et al.* 2009. *Transparency of Political Finance in Nepal*, Kathmandu: Transparency International.

Bhusal, Ghanashayam. 2009. "Inner Party Democracy in the Context of CPN-UML". In *Inter Party Democracy,* edited by B. R. Adhikary and K. Prasai (in Nepali). Kathmandu: CELCAR and FES.

Bobbio, Norberto. 2002. "The Future of Democracy", *The Polity Reader in Social Theory*, Cambridge: Polity Press.

Criddle, Byron. 2003. "Parties and Party Systems". In *Understanding Democratic Politics: An Introduction.* edited by Roland Axtmann. London: Sage Publications.

Djilas, Milovan. 1957. *The New Class.* Karvest: HBJ Books.

Habermas, Jurgen. 1997. *Between Facts and Norms: Contributions to a Discourse Theory of Law and Democracy.* Cambridge: Polity Press.

Hartlyn, Jonathan. 1996. "Latin America's Parties", *Journal of Democracy* 7(4). October.

Held, David. 1987. *Models of Democracy.* Cambridge: Polity Press.

Johnson, Chalmers. 1982. *Revolutionary Change.* London: Longman.

Kavanagh, Dennis. 2003. "Party Democracy and Political Marketing: No Place for Amateurs?" Paper presented to a conference on Political Communication in the Global World at Mainz, October 30-31.

Krichheimer, Otto. 1996. "The Transformation of the Western European Party Systems". In *Political Parties and Political Development*, edited by Myron Weiner and J. LaPalombara. Princeton: Princeton University Press.

Mainali, C. P. 2009. *National Identity and Federal System in Nepal* (in Nepali). Kathmandu: CPN-ML.

Meyer, Thomas. 2007. *From Authoritarian Leader Party to Mass-Membership Party*. Kathmandu: FES.

Meyer, Thomas. 2007. *Compromise: The Ideal Path to Democracy.* Kathmandu: FES.

Meyer, Thomas. 2001. "Political Parties, Citizen Initiatives and Political Communication in Democratic Politics". Unpublished paper.

Michels, Robert. 1968. *Political Parties*. New York: Free Press.

Mishra, Chaitanya, 2008. "Common Ground: Social Democracy", *Himal News Magazine*, May 1-28.

Offe, Claus and Philippe C. Schmitter. 1995. "Future of Democracy". In *The Encyclopedia of Democracy*, edited by S. M. Lipset, New York: Washington DC.

Powell, Jr., G. Bingham. 2004. "The Chain of Responsiveness". *Journal of Democracy* 15(4), October.

Prasai, Khagendra. 2009. "Inner Party Democracy". In *Inter Party Democracy*, edited by B. R. Adhikary and K. Prasai (in Nepali). Kathmandu: CELCAR and FES.

Saud, N. P. 2009. "Internal Democracy in Nepali Congress", In *Inter Party Democracy*, edited by B. R. Adhikary and K. Prasai (in Nepali). Kathmandu: CELCAR and FES.

Schumpeter, J. A. 1947. *Capitalism, Socialism and Democracy*. New York: Harper.

Tucker, Robert C. 1981. *Politics as Leadership*. Columbia: University of Missouri Press.

Williams, Michelle Hale. 2006. "Kirchheimer Revisited: Party Polarization, Party Convergence, or Party Decline in the 2005 German Elections?" Paper prepared for delivery at the 2006 Conference of Europeanists, Chicago, Illinois, March 30-April 1.

3

Is there a Transition to Democracy in Nepal? Understanding its Nature and Implications

Ganga Bahadur Thapa

Introduction

The prospects for peace and democracy-building in Nepal looked very promising in April 2006 after the *Jana Andolan II* (popular movement) brought down the royal regime through mass protest and political action. The most significant break with the past, symbolically and politically, was the resolution adopted by the interim parliament to abolish the 240-year old Hindu feudal monarchy and create a federal democratic republic. Although the newly elected Constituent Assembly (CA) whether will be able to draft a constitution acceptable to all political stakeholders and deliberative democracy in all dimensions: rule of law, accountability, responsiveness, freedom, and equality remains to be seen. Many believe that the post-CA Nepal faces demanding challenges, some as legacy of its long history of unequal economic and political development and others as offshoots of the Maoist insurgency. While Nepal appears to be stabilizing after several years of conflict and witness the final collapse of monarchy with Maoists becoming the principal beneficiaries, most critics assume that the Maoists are communists with an aim to ultimately create a truly monolithic regime, which is something way off in future, but for now they would encourage foreign-assisted capitalist development as the necessary precursor of socialism. The Nepali society had perhaps never witnessed the kind of activism emerging now to weed out roots of authoritarianism since the collapse of monarchical commissarial regime, although no plan for effective democracy is in place yet. Indubitably, radical changes have taken place since disgrace the monarchical-authoritarian rule suffered in April 2006, but Nepal has limitations–some real structural weaknesses, other inadequacies are the results of the failure to respond quickly to changing circumstances, particularly for radical changes to enable the marginalized and muzzled people to participate in governance. This article's purpose is to address to what extent social organizations that do not share the rules of the state can successfully triumph and what specific kinds of mechanisms would facilitate political stability and also be able to remove corrupt and bad politicians in the face of increased expectations with potentially destabilizing demands to steer clear the challenging path to democracy. This article is not devoted to explaining democratization, but is limited to explaining the breakdown of insurgency as well as authoritarianism that may or may not be replaced by regimes that are more democratic.

Conceptual Overview of Democracy

Until recently no one had anticipated that the world would change as radically as it did. The most profound political transformation of the late twentieth century was the self-destruction of the state communism in Eastern and Central Europe and the former Soviet Union. Drawing on the experiences on the nature of political governance, representation and economic system among the newly established democracies, there has been an increasing acceptance of a western model of democracy, following the 'third wave' perhaps with different methods and techniques, yet prospects for democracy in many of them are still somewhat new and uncertain, in particular, getting the proper institutions and making them work. With the end of the Cold War while the concept of democracy has increasingly come under to public debate, yet a distinctive feature of the globalizing world is a kind of diffusion of power, a pluralism of centres of decision-making and authority. Although the growing amount of research suggests that people may put up with considerably disappointing social and economic performance in the short run, the case becomes even more interesting when we observe still struggling what democracy is understood in procedural terms or what Dahl (1971) make the reference 'polyarchy'–denotes meaningful and extensive *competition* among individuals and organized groups, especially political parties; a highly inclusive level of political *participation* in the selection of leaders and policies, which includes, for example, regular and fair elections and a level of civil and political liberties and rule of law, electoral accountability and alternative sources of information–to ensure consolidation of political regime that democracy delivers on the promise freedom, equality/solidarity, transparency, and accessibility to power. The important question is *why* particular institutions and rights are considered democratic.

Democracy is a loaded term. In the literature of democratization, certain prerequisites are invariably stressed over, however. Despite variations in procedural arrangements of democratic systems, regular, free, and fair elections remain the determining factor to distinguish them from the rest. Moreover, the problems of democratization may vary significantly from one country to another, reflecting differences in size, location, history, culture, and level of development, yet theorists of 'third wave' transition consider election as a defining attribute of democracy. Participation, they contend, offers a means to identify and measure the magnitude of political democracy without having to deal with the problem of functioning democracy. However, it is debatable whether elections help achieve acceptable levels of governance, especially because even genuinely free elections by themselves do not necessarily sustain democracy. This is not to say that elections are not an important element in the process of democracy. But they constitute a small, albeit necessary aspect of democracy. Furthermore, nobody claims that election is a quick indicator of the stability of democracy[1] (Gutmann and Thompson, 2004; Sorenson, 1998; Dahl, 1989 and 1998). Similarly, scholars examine the processes by which transitions from non-democratic to democratic regimes took place and tell us that culture matters to laying the foundations for democratic institutions indicating that the drive to democracy derived primarily from indigenous rather than outside influences. This is also to say that reversals of democratic transitions, consolidations, and collapses can all result from a variety of dynamics. (Huntington, 1997; Huntington and Harrison, 2000).

There is no doubt democracy will leave its impact on the economic, political and social institutions. Yet the truth is that Cold War euphoria, "democracy versus communism", that divided the East and the West is now over. In other words, with the disappearance of communism as a credible threat, anti-communism substance of democracy has become obsolete. For the governments in Washington, Paris, Bonn, and London, besides the European Union and the World Bank, democratization is a priority in their policies. Again, if one defines democracy institutionally, except in a few isolate cases, western democracies did not actively push against authoritarian regimes for the sake of democracy until they were embroiled in severe domestic crisis due to deep economic and political problems. In many cases, the traditional elites have been monopolizing political power with substantial benefits to their people. But it is necessary to be clear that democratic society does not merely have representation in which political parties play a leading role, but it also exhibits what they intend to do when they come to power through fair elections. And citizenship involves civil, social, and cultural dimensions in addition to the political dimension brought about by the regime. Although a better democracy is one that enacts a wide gamut of all such rights, liberal democracy is much more complex as it involves a number of real situations, including cultural, socio-economic, and political dimensions. It has been argued that while modern democracy does not require uniform consensus, a well functioning democratic system is primarily dependent on citizens and creative consensus, not voters (Diamond, 1999). Thus, even one can expect most political problems to be settled by means of a competitive elections, it appears that election is not an adequate explanation, but a combination of various factors is desirable if indeed necessary to survive political crises for longer periods of time (Huntington, 1991; Tornquist, 1991; Dahl, 1971; Powell, 2000; Diamond, 1999).

Democratization typically creates a wide spectrum of politically significant groups with diverse and incompatible interests. A number of pluralist writers however maintained that democracy can be defined in a narrow manner which considers what is the best form of government or in a broader sense by asking what is the best form of society. It is reasonable to assume that while political reforms may liberalize military, police and electoral practices to a significant extent and "power fairly evenly dispersed in society with no single grouping having ultimate control over all issues" (Mitchell, 1996:15), but it is not enough, especially if the country has long history of authoritarian brutal past. To be effective, democracy promotion requires sufficient space to conduct its work. Some scholars claim that sustaining democracy as a type of political system, the resources and problems inherent in the economic and social environment, the attitudes and values of the citizens, and the strategies of the leaders are probably more important than variations in the institutional arrangements (Dahl, 1971). Indeed, citizen participation based on a proper functioning balance of power must bring about citizen satisfaction in relation to their basic needs such as education, health, employment, and economic well-being in order to attain social and distributive justice (Gunther, Diamandouros, and Puhle, 1995). Obviously, if one believes in government by consent, one must believe that the people may, as a matter of fact, change their political system. Without this, it would be impossible to have democracy, we aspire for.

It is important to note that there are always problems of grave nature in an alliance between an armed guerrilla and a political party that is committed to act within the institutional framework. There is also a view that violence is structurally rooted in many factors—economic, social, political imbalance, unequal distribution of resources, poverty, unemployment, ignorance, etc. There are also other socio-political factors facilitating violence, such as deeply rooted corruption and the abuse of instruments of oppression, whether they come from government institutions characterized by 'institutionalization of conflict' (Newman, 2004:150), or from other factions who view themselves as oppressed (Drury, Krieckhaus and Lusztig, 2006). It is precisely on this point, moreover, while the deliberations may sometimes be construed as differences between interest-based and value-based policies, we must be aware that democracy always remains in some sort of crisis. But, we must bear in mind that the transition to democracy generally takes one of four aspects: One, such routes arises from a defeat in war followed by the imposition of democracy from an outside power, as in Germany and Japan in the aftermath of World War II. Second, a faction, of moderate elements may encourage democratization from within an authoritarian regime and initiate a period of liberalization, as was the case in Latin America, Southern Europe, and Russia. Third, political mobilization by a cross-class alliance of those excluded from power, if successful in forcing regime elites from office, may bring about a democratic regime, as in the case of Philippines, Nicaragua, Czechoslovakia and many African countries. Finally, a sustained political mobilization from below by working class actors can force a regime to negotiate a transition to democracy, as is the case in South Africa and El Salvador (Wood, 2000:10; Tulchi and Bland, 1992). Yet, we are not sure that democracy can revive direct from anarchy as in the case of El Salvador, Mozambique and elsewhere because political theorists for Machiavelli to Huntington have warned against the possibility of a popular government arising right from militarization of political conflict. Certain elements are common to all systems, but each may be pervaded by its distinctive characteristics (Held, 1996).

Although democratization is defined as the transition of non-democratic regime to democratic polity, mere regime change is not tantamount to political transition. At the same time, even if, as many authors have argued, democracy is the best available means to propose political reforms, it does not present a sufficient condition that would help bring down brutal state repression, or for that matter resolve disputes, or set up political liberalization (Dowd, 2001). Consolidation, on the other hand, has been defined by the scholars as a process by which democracy becomes so profoundly legitimate among the citizens that it is very unlikely to breakdown (Mainwaring, O'Donnell; Valenzuela, 1992; Linz and Stepan, 1996). Many observers would argue that democratic political culture (Almond and Verba, 1965) is the basis for proper functioning of democracy. But, arguments based on political culture as an independent variable all too often lead to dead end.

The core meaning of democracy may be vague, but a well functioning democratic system must rest on fundamental normative agreements about proper political procedure and legitimate form of government.[2] The basic logic to the argument is that democracies may have high conflict carrying capacity, but there is no fix model of democracy as soon as one starts to examine it more closely, although it generally perceived political liberty, given that democracy requires individual choice with both individual and collective consequence to be essential to it. Similarly, democracy is not a consequence of the imposition of human rights and a state of law, it is precondition for the establishment of both. Even if some studies contend that liberal institutions are not required for democracy if all citizens have equal access to power and resources (Jalal, 1995), the fact that there are several routes to democracy and that these routes may not be the same methods of solution. The terms 'constitutional' and 'democracy', on the other hand, are linked in the definitions of a just liberal society, democracy as a system through which the majority, either directly, or through representative bodies, exercises decision-making political power, and the term constitutionalism only to refer to the creation of a basic law that restricts the capacity of the majority to exercise its political will. (Elster, 1988:1; Sanin, 2005)

In fact, from Aristotle to Hobbes to the present, analysts have debated various features of regimes, political institutions and cultures, specific institutional roles and practices, such as respect for human rights, civic freedoms, and independent judiciary, yet one of the challenges to democratic consolidation is the successful management of the military under democratic control. It would be useful to remind oneself that the consolidation of democracy is unthinkable without political parties. Yet again, during transition, there can be fragmented party system, moving beyond narrow institutional conceptions of political rule, and several of the newly formed parties may be transient in character, therefore, it is doubtful that they could manage the social, economic and political problems of the country. (Mainwaring and Scully, 1995). Whereas the chances to develop 'viable democracy' (Margolis, 1979) or 'strong' (Barber, 2003) can be significantly improved if consensus on goals does not evaporate with short-living and *ad hoc* actions. The thesis is that, a forward-looking nation requires reasoned political discourse which includes listening to the opinions and demands of the other interested parties and then seeking for a compromise. More appropriately, if state weakness is a factor in organized violence, the test of leadership cannot be based on its ability to deliver success with the support of those who habitually align themselves to meet selfish ends, but upon bestowing a vision such as paving the way for full-blown democracy. By any measure, the subject matter of social sciences cannot be treated by the sets of pre-established facts. But politics is not about lofty pursuit of public interest; it is about power–who gets what, when and how.

The Framework of Analysis: Nepal's Struggle for Democracy

Early Political History

Nepal had been a kingdom for at least fifteen hundred years under the authoritarian rule of a small section of elite and governing class. In its recent history it has always been composed of a familial core. Nepal has gone through several stages of political and social changes beginning from the early twelfth century, yet Nepal became a political state created through military conquest in 1768 by the Gorkha ruler

Prithvi Nrarayan Shah (1743-1775). The political system established by him was essentially militarist and despotic in character. As most of the people at the time had no say whatsoever in the political restructuring, the successive Shah Kings governed the nation in fact as well as in theory and established monarchy as the unparalleled political institution. Besides, the main goal of power struggles centred on the control over the king himself; and there was little progress in sorting out procedures for sharing power or expanding representative institutions. The political system after the making of Nepal was an absolute monarchy in which the king wielded supreme authority in both civil and military affairs of the state and prevalence of a powerful nobility side by side that brought new complications, tensions and turmoil in Nepali political life. As a result, regents, nobles, and feudal took away all effective complete control over the administration and politics.

However, Nepal took a fateful turn in 1846 when Ranas, a native feudal ruling clan made the monarchy captive by a bloody coup known as *kotparva* (massacre) and usurped complete control of the government by reducing the king as a puppet. After the *kotparva*, the Ranas became the only true beneficiary, who by the 1850s, established a dynasty of prime ministers and imposed their family dictatorship until they were overthrown by a people-powered movement in 1950. In fact, there was no difference between the state treasury and the personal fortune of the Rana ruler. They exercised almost unlimited powers over internal affairs and took for their own use whatever funds were available in the treasury. Jung Bahadur Kunwar, the main architect of the 1846 massacre who later held the surname 'Rana'[3] was blamed for setting up a family dictatorship but also eliminated the useless factional fighting at the royal court. The two basic objectives with which Jung Bahadur began his office were, first, 'to entrench himself in power as permanently as possible and, second, to pass on the prime ministership as well as other important offices of the state to his brothers and descendants in perpetuity'. They were not even answerable to the king from whom they had acquired power and authority. The ordinary people, some describe, were likened to *pauko dhulo*, the dust off their feet. At the top of the repressive political structure was the Rana Prime Minister from whom all authority followed. (Gupta, 1993)

By that time, it seemed that the continuation of Rana oligarchy without major political reforms was difficult, especially after the departure of the British Empire from the Indian sub-continent in 1947. The Rana furthermore found themselves in a very unfavourable situation after the installation of a democratic government dominated by the Indian Congress led by Nehru in India. Also significant was the event in the North in 1949 when communist power emerged victorious in China, threatening India's so-called security 'south of the Himalayas.' As part of their political reform, the Rana Prime Minister, Padma Shumshere on 26th January, 1948 announced a constitution that provided some freedoms to the people. However, it did not prevent the movement politics or party politics since the provisions underlying in the constitution were inadequate to establish democratic rule. Whatever the reasons, things became unbearable for the Ranas when King Tribhuvan flew to New Delhi in November 1950 via Indian Embassy in Nepal leaving the throne empty. It was altogether an extraordinary event in Nepal's political history, which also drew considerable attention of the world. At the same time, it provided moral support to the revolt as started by political forces and gave it the shape of national liberation movement. Anyway, several uprisings rapidly exploded in different parts of the kingdom, culminating in the victory of the pro-democratic forces in 1951.

The political system that prevailed after 1950 was a multiparty politics headed by the monarch, in which for the first time, ordinary Nepali got an opportunity to involve themselves in the process of nation-building. After the revolt against the Ranas, Nepal also struggled to overcome its long legacy of underdevelopment and to incorporate its varied population. Although political parties were crucial in the revolt that overthrew Rana rule, their constant wrangling conflicted with the monarchy's view of its own dignity and with the interests of the army. Under the new political dispensation, monarchy was still the supreme authority. On the one side, stood the king who controlled the most powerful force in the nation, the army, and found it an increasingly useful tool with which to wield his prestige and authority. On the other side, stood the newly formed political parties and a multitude of breakaway factions or small parties. However, as new political forces were less united to put a combined fight against the traditional power wielders, such as the Ranas and the king, this Tripoli struggle kept the country far from modernity. In a sense, however, the political changes of 1950, for the first time, granted the general public, through party agencies, a new situation where their voices had some meaning with basic democratic political elements.

The political parties were open, people were exercising some democratic rights despite patronage networks and political intrigue. In other words, the most impressive feature of this period was the freewheeling political activities.

But the struggle to restore democracy was a painful process as the environment was elitist, feudal, and anti-democratic. A number of internal and external factors are responsible for this. Among the internal factors, the political parties intensely competed and quarrelled over smaller issues, leading to quick cabinet reshuffles. Another factor is that due to limited experience, the new leaders could not properly handle the political power they had gained. Between November 1951 and February 1959, there was a succession of short-lived governments which ruled either according to the Interim Constitution or under the king's direction. It is also remarkable that on 18th February, 1959, for the first time the general elections for the Parliament commenced in Nepal in which the NC turned up with highest number of seats, 74 out of total 109 seats in the Pratinidhi Sabha, the House of Representatives; its victory was a milestone in the uncertain politics. In spite of this, Nepal once more moved towards monarchy and political uncertainty. Finding this weakness of the government, the king with the support of army and opposition forces dissolved the Constitution that barely functioned eighteen months. The following three decades under the non-party Panchayat System was a period of close politics headed by an absolute monarchy. Neither the opposition views were allowed to be aired, nor any checks and balances were exercised. All power was the monopoly of the king since all political authority remained in his hands. The king dominated the legislative process and retained broad powers, including the power to initiate constitutional amendments, assent laws, and declare emergency during which they could rule through decree. This period was another Dark Age for the people after the century-old Rana rule in Nepal. Within a short span of time, the new political system crushed all types of democratic activities successfully and silenced the opposition. There were many cases of repression, detention, imprisonment and brutality. (Singh, 2007 and Mathema, 1998)

The period of forced silence however was short-lived. Concerned by the massive student movement, political demonstration and considerable general unrest, King Birendra as a palliative tactic called for a nationwide referendum to determine the future form of government in May 1979. The referendum offered two choices: either continuation of the non-party Panchayat system with prospects for further reform or multiparty system. The referendum returned the Panchayat however with a slim majority; it secured 54.7 per cent of the votes cast on May 2, 1980 when 67 per cent of the eligible voters had participated. It did not improve the status of the common people from *praja* (subjects) to *nagarik* (citizens). Rather, the referendum legalized the political system that was forcefully and even dramatically imposed on the people some twenty-years ago. This, however, did not matter so long as the parties were not there and there were still restrictive regulations on broad political participation, but the amendment allowed more open elections. The amendment did not curtail the absolute power of the king, and there was enough room to rule without a formal check. Hence, it was a substantial gain for the king who was authorized by the people to occupy the central stage in politics.

Constitutional and Legal Basis

A description of the political framework within which development takes place must begin with the system created by the Constitution. While India, Bangladesh, and Maldives had been continuing with the same constitution without major breakdowns, Sri Lanka and Pakistan have had three constitutions each, Nepal experienced six different constitutions since 1948. Although a thorough assessment of constitutional exercise is necessary, we attempt a cursory inspection of Nepali constitutions. A brief perusal of the Nepalese constitutionalism shows that it first joined the ranks of those countries which prefer to have written, or specially codified, constitutions on January 26, 1948 when Prime Minister, Padma Shumshere promulgated the Government Act while reserving the final power in the hands of the Rana Prime Minister that provided for a Council of Ministers, a bicameral legislature, an independent judiciary, fundamental rights and principles of representational rule as a political institution for governing the nation, but it could not become a charter of freedom because it never came into force.

The 1948 Constitution was replaced by the Interim Government Act of 1951 which was announced by King Tribhuvan, but it also demonstrated that the king was not willing to share power with the commoners, this led to the worst political quagmire. The 1959 Constitution provided a bicameral legislature, multiparty polity and universal franchise. Most important, the constitution announced well-known rights to the people, namely, freedom of speech and expression; freedom of assembly; freedom of association and property rights. Independent judiciary was its another important feature. But sadly, this new democratic exercise could not be geared further when the king dissolved the Parliament and suspended the constitution after barely eighteen months in operation on December 15, 1960 on charges of mismanagement and incompetence.

After two years of emergency rule, King Mahendra appeared with a new political system known as 'partyless Panchayat' when in 1962 he promulgated a new constitution, but had to bear absolute monarchy with no freedom to dissent. A successful pro-democracy movement in spring 1990, and subsequent formulation of the Constitution of the Kingdom of Nepal, 1990 (2047 B.S.), that a real democratic exercise began in Nepal with Nepal became a Parliamentary democracy, consisting of legislative, executive and judicial branches. Its institutions consisted of the monarchy, the Parliament, the cabinet, the judiciary and other constitutional organs. More to the point, sovereignty of the people, constitutional monarchy, multiparty system and freedoms were guaranteed by the Constitution. The political system was based on the principle of separation of powers, with checks and balances, in which the executive was subject to the confidence of the Parliament and the law guaranteed the independence of judiciary. It should also to be remembered however that the 1990 Constitution had come to an end following successful movement in 2006 when CA was formed to draft the new Constitution.

Second Democratic Opening and Movement for Democracy

The collapse of communist regimes in Eastern Europe was an event of profound significance. Discussion about the virtues of democracy are increasingly diversified and modified all-around the world following the conclusion of the Cold War, particularly after the breakdown of socialism between 1989 and 1991 and subsequent rise of new states. Since then, democracy has become the most widely accepted system of governance, as it protects the people's fundamental freedoms of association, speech, belief, etc., and upholds the rule of law. There was a sort of renaissance in world politics with the emergence of new democracies that endeavoured to find a conducive role in the international arena. In many parts of the world, the 'third wave' of democracy is largely attributed to the failure of the political systems that were either despotic or proletarian. However, it is worthnoting that democratic consolidation is one of the most important tasks that newly-democratized countries face. Most countries that undergo democratic transition commonly encounter many of the same difficulties that other fledgling democracies face, while other obstacles arise primarily out of their specific political and social contexts. Many of these fledgling democracies are still transitioning out of their authoritarian brutal past, and where instability and disorder arise especially in countries with numerous political, religious, ethnic, regional, and class divisions. (Linz and Stepan, 1996; Huntington, 1991).

Nepal is no Exception

In this process, Nepal was not an exception as it has had a long history of authoritarian rule under absolute monarchs and other forms of autocracy. In early 1990, for the first time in Nepali history, a coalition of two opposition political forces, the NC and the communists was built-up under the command of Ganesh Man Singh, the supreme leader of NC. In subsequent political developments, a joint front was also formed under the joint leadership of K.P. Bhattarai, President of NC and Ms Sahana Pradhan (widow of founder of Nepal Communist Party: Pushpalal), the leader of United Left Front, a combination of seven left parties.[4] The basic task of this front was to accelerate the movement for the restoration of multiparty democracy and to uproot the thirty-year old Panchayat system. Professional groups such as lawyers, medicos, engineers, teachers, professors, students, peasants, and workers supported the movement. There were several incidents of street violence between February and April 1990 and some of them were very much intensified. Initially, the government responded with police action, but the popular resistance was so powerful that the police failed to control the masses. However, the military was not used to suppress the movement. By this time, unlike in the past, the movement received enough support from both inside and outside. As the pressure for greater political openness increased, on 49th day of the movement, i.e. April 8, 1990, King Birendra saw a threat to his throne and lifted the ban on political parties. This was the second democratic opening in Nepal.

The results indicate that, at the very least, the transition to democracy in Nepal after the breakdown of personalist ('personal' in Huntington terminology or 'sultanistic' in Linz's) monarchy in 1990 that have ruled for a very long time provided a ground evolve steadily towards a democracy with new methods of participation in decision-making process but thwarted by a wave of political violence, disorder, re-emergence of despotic traditional authorities with concomitant social and economic dislocation which led the monarchy to seize power. That is to say, Nepal's experiment with democracy since 1990 indicates that democratic transition and consolidation constitute two quite distinct processes of political change and that success in the first does not necessarily imply a similar success in the second. Of course, throughout its 240 years history, power has alternated between monarchy or other ruling clans with the former dominating. Such situation gave rise to a series of client regimes built around a dynamic boss who bestowed selective patronage to those who remained loyal towards him. In fact, Nepal has gone through several stages of political and social changes, and with the changes of times, the authorities did shift here and there at the top, but no powers were devolved to the people.[5]

The transformation of non-party politics to a multiparty system was indeed the most striking phenomenon of 1990 that fundamentally changed the Nepalese political system in three important ways. First, the power of the king was reduced to symbolism. Second, political parties were duly recognized to assume a political role in mobilizing the electorate towards their party programmes and policies and the competitive elections based on adult franchise. Third, the democratic rights of the people were guaranteed by the Constitution. These are important features that characterized the political transformation, ushering in a new era of political pluralism and democratic culture. But still, the big issue hanging at the forefront is whether democracy can be retained or not; because it faces challenges of enormous proportions. There is a pervasiveness of poverty, high-levels of political polarization, unaccountability and injustice. As a result, Nepalese are increasingly becoming weary of the inefficiency of government, incessant political feuds and rampant corruption that pervade the political life at almost every level. People are tired of years of botched reforms and economic decline that have left many millions of people living in inhuman conditions. Things won't change overnight, of course. But the current political dynamics do not ensure us that the ordinary Nepalese will receive greater political output for their safety and a comfortable future.

Judging from the above, Nepal's first democratic opening in February 1951 ended with a coup d'état engineered by King Mahendra, who revived absolute monarchy under the "partyless" panchayat system (1960-1990), a sultan-type monarchy where the ruler exercises power without restraint, at his/her own discretion and above all unencumbered by rules or by any commitment to an ideology or value system. It has again been substantiated that the king, his army and their guns were no match against the people's power. In fact, King Gyanendra's February 1, 2005 coup that revived active monarchy, by putting blame squarely on the parties, we are certain that bought to an end one of the most open political systems in South Asia is a reversion of competitive politics. The most remarkable feature of the post-February 1 regime was the gerontocratic character of the administration in which not only the boundaries of political conflict intensified with ideological polarization, death and suffering but also pursued survivalist strategies leading to robust authoritarianism. In taking power, the king took advantage of undeveloped political organizations in order to enhance his personal power, even while maintaining the regime's resilience in the face of pressures for democratizations. Yet the end of Gyanendra's regime was an inevitable outcome because its function resembled closely that of a French, Italian and German fascism. It became more repressive, intolerant of opposition, and denied freedom to people to support democracy as a political system. It must not be overlooked that if it were not for the crucial role of Maoists[6] (Thapa, 2006; Thapa and Sharma, 2009; ECHO, 2002; Singh, 2007:267-326) and active participation by the civil society, King Gyanendra's commissarial regime would not have been checkmated for another several years, irrespective of what it would have meant for the country.

Constituent Assembly Election: Reform from Below?

Many persuasively argue that until 2063 B.S. Nepal had no successful popular movement comparable to those in modern times. But it would be a mistake to believe that all transitional events are initiated and controlled solely by the reformers. In fact, until democracy is thoroughly institutionalized, the legitimacy of the regime would swing rapidly, driving the voters into performing desperate acts, some of which are extremely detrimental to the cause of democracy. Obviously, while a clear break with the past may be necessary, the continuation of power remains in force, which inhibits renewal. We understand that this invariably leads to crises in the state, not to speak of democratic consolidation. It does not appear any better at present either. However, the revolution that began in 1990 actually brought forth Maoist insurgency and the subsequent uprising of April 2006 and CA election on April 10, 2008, which even this can be termed as a distinct chapter in the lengthy process of the emergence of the new Nepali nation has opened a new window of opportunity to restore legitimate authority in the history of modern Nepal. By itself, this may not be particularly remarkable. Yet the important point is that one is inclined to believe that Nepalese can frame political issues in terms of various rights and freedom. Moreover, the synergy created by the Maoists indicates that their ideology and democracy may be compatible. It is abundantly clear that the stagnant equilibrium of three major forces–the palace, the political parties and the Maoist rebels–has now been swept away.

Since no political system can possibly achieve stability, legitimacy and peace without doing something for its people, Nepal's nascent democracy came under attack from the Communist Party of Nepal–Maoist (CPN-M), the most radical offshoot of the left-wing spectrum in Nepali politics which launched the *janayauddha* (People's War) or armed conflict in 1996 to overthrow both monarchy and parliamentary democracy characterized by the unspeakable brutality including torture, massacres of defenseless civilians of all ages, and constant fear of ambush, search and seizure and encounter killings both from state and Maoists side. Modern democracies depend a lot on the types and level of fairness of political institutions and uprooting of old mores, values and structures, yet a small armed rebellion that started in poor remote districts spread like a tornado taking 15,000 lives because politicians failed to address the causes behind the distress and had no clue about how to combat a guerrilla movement. And these former rebels are now ready to contribute to the society through manipulations within the system, albeit with a touch of enthusiasm for democratization. Again, the rise of Maoists' influence and its implications are multidimensional. But the paramount proposition about Nepali culture is that the values, beliefs and attitudes of Nepalese, albeit in a limited form, have changed them significantly from what they were a couple of decades ago.

None too surprisingly, while internal conflicts were part and parcel of Nepali political history, the Maoist insurgency (1996-2006) was different in that it was a grass roots rather than elite-dominated revolution. The Maoist "people's war" was a multidimensional phenomenon encompassing economic, political, cultural, and psychological aspects. It sought an end to social and political inequalities, ethnic/caste disparities, and discrimination against minorities and disadvantaged groups. Economically, insurgent demands included a nationalization of private property and a redistribution of land through revolutionary land reforms. In foreign relations, it wanted to redefine Nepal's relations with India by abrogating all "unequal treaties" with India and calling a halt to the recruitment of Nepali hill people to the Indian and British armies.

While there are varied interpretations to the word democracy, Nepal under King Gyanendra (October 2002—April 2006), who reversed the democratic opening was not the first king to have gained power intensified militarization, brutal repressions and horrible violence is a case 'authoritarian democracy', a beautiful oxymoron invented by Chilean dictator Pinochet to characterize his regime. (O'Donnell). Yet perhaps no one had anticipated that King Gyanendra's commissarial regime would fizzle out so soon and Nepal's monarchy would get dumped within Narayanhiti[7] although *Jana Andolan II*[8], was not a downright revolutionary transformation of political and social structure like the 'velvet revolution' of 1989 in Eastern Europe (Barker and Mooers, 1994) or any of the historic revolutionary changes: France in 1789, Mexico in 1910, Russia in 1918 or China in 1949. In fact, despite draconian security measures, the royal regime was unable to stop 'social unrest', 'labour strikes', 'student demonstration'.

Nepal still has a long way to be recognized as democratic. A look at the *post-Jana Andolan II* however showed that it has made great advances in encouraging freedom of speech and democratic rights. Yet again, while the mainstream theories of democracy assume that high levels of wealth and education enhance a country's chances for democratic rule, the demise of royal autocracy has had immense impact on public perceptions—it has created new space for public discussions and it has all but terminated the dialogue for partnership with the monarchy. This political change, no doubt, is a great shift, thanks to King Gyanendra who was incompetent to solve the economic and political crises and indifferent to react to the public aspirations.[9]

Obviously, since 2006 Nepal has experienced a shift from monarchical to republican rule, and this democratic transition has been accompanied by the idea of politics as a non-violent resolution of conflict and a means to ensure the equitable distribution of resources. Yet hybrid forms of wielding power exist; indicators of political rights and civil liberties remain modest. Nepal is not a case of democratization driven by the middle class, in which arguments are clarified, interests and values are elucidated, and agreements are built on a consensual reflection of majority public opinion. Whether Nepal will become truly democratic has yet to be seen; Nepalese are not overly optimistic about their political future. Liberal parties, including the Maoists seem to be thinking tactically rather than strategically, and their sole motive is to gain control of state power and resources. Nepal's experiment with democracy in the aftermath of a popular revolt indicates that political transition and consolidation are two distinct, and not necessarily interdependent, process. This is the nub of the problem.

While Nepal's 240 years old monarchy has made little contribution to democracy-building to promote political stability and economic prosperity of the Nepali people, yet together with a demoralized administrative system, ineffective security agencies and corrupt civil society, speak volumes on severe democratic deficit and an inherent lack of legitimacy, extra-constitutional actors often attempt to influence the reconfiguration of the political order, further weakening state structures. Nonetheless, the CA election was a sort of political earthquake which provided a unique opportunity to jump-start a new post-conflict political order, yet characteristically heading downhill towards fewer political rights and diminished civil liberties in terms of legitimacy of the institutions (normative) and their functioning and effectiveness (positive). Specifically, the Maoist guerrilla fighters now in CA have established themselves as a dominant political phenomenon in terms of "Mao-streaming" liberal parties instead of the liberal parties mainstreaming the Maoists with relative majority (238 in 601 member CA) in post-monarchy Nepal, many question marks are raised whether Maoists, the so-called proletarian democratic faithful to federal democratic republic in a variety of political shades, are sensitive to the wider public in terms of a 'democratic them' against an 'autocratic them'—a prerequisite to adhere to Nepal's fledgling democratic game to inadvertently escalating a process of effective representative democracy.

Equally important, even if democratic transitions at a critical moment in political time-frame sets off, as Rustow (1999) suggests 'prolonged and inconclusive political struggle', there is another more disturbing concern here. It would be premature to assume that the structural features of liberal democracy—individual rights, competitive political parties and regular elections—would not materialize. But, due to the inability of the ruling elites that determine the targets and timing for political actions, the legitimacy of the system may, over time, fall into question even if it promises stability in the long run. The problem is that despite the consensus reached among the divergent political groups, it still calls for agreeing to goals and methods that would enable other institutions to reform the polity and take the lead when situation demands. The apparent rise of ethnic and regional discontent in the past few months, it is impossible to predict which course of action would ultimately preserve the integrity of a multiethnic Nepal. When we look into the character of ruling cliques, instead of facilitating the concerned people to come together as trusting equals and for mutual benefit with respect, we find it at best as anxious to shift blame each other for whatever political setbacks the country might be experiencing.

Another factor is the inability or unwillingness, often profoundly so, of the political actors who struggle towards personal ends rather than to ascertain the implications of institutions and opportunities. As if to prove the point, an argument often advanced is that the post-transition governments ignore to address longstanding patterns of poverty and social exclusion. In fact, Nepal's history depicts the structures that have persistently segregated the elite minority from the impoverished majority. The politics has always been a game between the centre and periphery. The centre, whether elected or appointed, assumes a core position while the people are pushed to the periphery. The inner sphere, or the nucleus of the nation, is composed of decision-making elite. This elite centre controls the power and wealth of the country. The subsequent rings of society emanate towards the periphery, with the extreme periphery representing the group which is most distant from the centre of power. Such scenario is responsible to undermine support for democracy. (Blaikie, Cameron and Seddon,1983; Regmi, 1976; Shrestha, 1997). As a result, people's discontent has started to stroke fire for a series of social movement, including Maoist insurgency that erupted in February 1996. In fact, Huntington did note many years ago that in an "unstable social, economic, and political environment coming out of a civil war, a shift to democracy that is too rapid may prove counter-productive, if pressures for political participation cannot be accommodated by the newly created political institutions." (Huntington, 1991)

While institutional approach to democracy implies that it is a system of conflict regulation that allows open competition over the values and goals that citizens want to advance (Barber, 1998). It has been argued that transitions, the interval between one political regime to another, are formative, the development of democracy cannot be fully explained by any single factor; ultimately, a combination of internal and external variables. Upon close inspection, one would find that the transfer of power from king to the people following the successful people's movement in 1990 gave a chance to bring about a definite end to the traditional political forces devoted to serving vested interests and to build-up institutions associated with democracy in the newly opened political space, Nepal could not achieve a breakthrough in the evolvement of political process, rule of law, and economy in sharp contrast to many transitions that had occurred in the preceding decade. Whatever the initial expectations, Nepal's transition was delayed because its legacy deflected the efforts to create the institutions necessary for democratic consolidation. While the failure was ascribed to narrow vision sluggish pace towards political reforms, the underlying reason was that those who struggled for democracy wanted to cash in their sacrifices by acquiring power and position in the government rather than safeguarding people's interests. Extremely abhorring was the fact that the political parties themselves maintained fascist structure in the organizations. They were incapable to set-up a mechanism strong enough to address the social and economic agenda of the country (Thapa, 2006).

In Nepali context what we specifically need to keep in mind that the break-up of multiparty democracy in the past was not entirely the monarchy's fault, but a series of factors, chief among those being the politicians who pretend to represent citizens but serve only their narrow interests. We have seen that in spite of considerable changes at political level, the current political conglomeration is brimming with the strong presence of lumpen democrats and Leninists/Maoists in the interim legislature (awkwardly-named 'Legislature Parliament') who have no understanding of democratization. While their struggle might have been justifiable, democratic context requires different behaviour. We have noted above that many things have changed since the demise of royal autocracy. But in addition, the crucial problem facing the Nepal is that those excluded from power have little faith that they will have a just share of national resources. There is, then, an apparent tension not only in pursuit of its mission to work for the good of community but also a manifest debilitating contradiction in the style of governance and the goals it professes to attain. It makes little sense to argue in current circumstances that if Nepal's new polity acts in ways that Nepali people see as hostile to their interests, Nepali politics would produce does rise in armed rebellion against the state.

Another circumstance that made the Nepali case so particularly distinctive and complex consists is the corrupt and dishonest political leadership, and more significantly, the perpetuation of clientele rule. Again, Nepalese in CA elections voted for change by giving the Maoists an opportunity to address social and economic issues which presented itself as a party with clarity, yet Nepal is anticipated to drag with unconsolidated porous democracy, as noted above, largely because of limping proletariat driven by the expired versions of Marxism and Leninism and pompous democrats. We must not forget that transition implies a paradigm shift from state-centred myopia to a broad vision of constitutionalism. It is all the more important for Nepal where large segments of the population remain marginalized and not seldom confront, albeit with little advantage, that tends to make it more dangerous. The main fault line for instability in the Nepalese system are the fissures caused by those who wish to acquire or preserve their stake in the state's power structures. This is perhaps one of the main reasons why the political change to democracy did not work speedily and the country had to go through a turbulent period towards near disintegration. It need not be disputed here that by granting more powers to the army, police and intelligence agencies and at the same time curtailing political freedoms, the king effectively monopolized political space, resources and governance. Such conditions of political oppression have created a wide-ranging landscape of dissatisfied young people eveready to engage in militant activity that ended King Gyanendra's regime after 15 months in power.

Transition to democracy is a complex process, in Nepal, if history is any guide, the monarchy never acted as an accelerator in the process of socio-economic and political reform that would contribute to the well-being of the Nepali people, rather it acted as a brake and even reverse gear. Moreover, democratization is closely linked with the 'egalitarian transformative' order and a modern citizen is open to global cultures and can participate at various levels of society with relative ease. But, if only the few politicians run everything in spite of a successful revolution, the opportunity leading to revolutionary changes will just vanish either with a crisis coupled with yet another authoritarian hammer and compulsive decay or generate negative spillovers to disintegrate the fibres of the nation; for good intent does not always bring forth positive results. For example, after the collapse of Rana Regime[10] in 1951, King Tribhuvan did not convene a constituent assembly but gave a new constitution. King Mahendra killed Nepal's first version of democracy. Even though King Birendra had studied at Eton and Harvard, he maintained absolute monarchy through the panchayat system after he succeeded to the throne in 1972 (Thapa, 1996/1999; Rose and Joshi, 2004). In this connection, the transition to democracy in Nepal has been severely hindered by the country's oligarchical past.

No doubt, one factor in the failure of the parties to assert their power was their inability to maintain a consistent policy and a unified vision aimed at tackling simmering economic and political conflicts. This is evident in Nepal where the claims of democracy allowed the political leadership to impose misguided policies that kept too many of its citizens under their absolute control and got their whims fulfilled. In other words, all seek to be rulers over the people rather than to be the servants of the people (Lingle, 2005). While Maoists' insurgency is a contributing factor to Nepal's halting the process of democratization, the problem with Nepal's democracy is that it had become a toll for appropriating power rather than guaranteeing individual liberty whereby the interests of citizens come last–whether royalist or Maoist or democratic. The paradox in Nepal is that the period between 1996 to 2006 can be seen, on the one hand, a revolutionary doctrine based on Maoist ideology, and on the other, a military strategy of King Gyanendra, not least because militarization solves none of the underlying problems to which the democratic movement was reacting in 1990.

From Authoritarianism to Democracy: Discussion

Can we speak of a brewing crisis in democracy here? Surely this is an intriguing question. The normative view of defenders of constitutionalism is that democracy requires both majority rule and protection of fundamental rights, and so they find themselves having to defend judicial activism as well. Stability is based on a proper functioning balance of power. If the state elites can assess the national interests and respond soberly to shifting influences, the character of regime—whether democratic or authoritarian—is not an important consideration. Certain types of political strategies are more likely to succeed than others; yet the more intriguing question is: How political actors who struggle for personal ends rather than consolidate institutional processes and opportunities that always thwarted people's sovereignty set-up a sound edifice and the Maoists who missed the opportunity to smash it through their might could be substantially moderated to have legitimacy and become the order of the day? At the same time, when we look into the structure of Nepal's current political regime we find it at best as 'oligopolistic pluralism' or 'monopoly of non-democratic power', which has led to widespread inadequacies, inconsistencies, and altercations that have plunged the nation into a downward spiral affecting the society as a whole, not excluding non-democratic and exclusive states. Even if it were not damaging to democratic aspirations, it is unlikely to cultivate democratic norms and lawfulness. The want of credibility in society makes it more vulnerable to be overthrown. This can be problematic not because it would be unfair but illegitimate, although the repercussions may not be clear. The problem does not end there. Nepal's conflict-ridden transition is in dilemma under the leadership of sultanistic appetite of non-retiring leaders who are apparently linked with traditional clientele mechanism, but has an indomitable will to hang on to power as long as s/he can, no matter what. That precisely casts a perennial shadow over the prospects for democratic institutionalization. It is the environment that injects incentive to the populist politicians who promise to alleviate the suffering of the majority quickly in order to outbid their opponents. (Thapa, 2007)

A still more fundamental problem is due to what is called 'limited pluralism' or 'less democratic polity' while dwelling upon various types of political system. Although the Seven-Party Alliance[11] and the Maoists (SPAM)[11] recently have provided an opportunity for political reflection, now confined only to race/region politics and self-fulfilling prophecies, are high on rhetoric. They have forgotten the outlying areas, it is difficult to strengthen democracy. The fragility of the situation is characterized by the sluggish progress. In the case of Nepal, after a decade of deadly conflict, particularly following collapse of monarchy there still are several motivational or political forces at work, consisting of 'useful idiots' in Lenin's telling phrase. Nepal is having precious but limited amount of what is called 'rational space'–where everyone is on an equal footing to make choices in economic, political, or social sphere. The result is that Nepali democracy remains weak and shallow because of the mismatch between the formal political institutions and entrenched informal institutions of patronage politics that still govern behaviour. Although the ultimate claim to legitimacy, or for that matter to acceptability, of political rule lies in the type of consent expressed during the voting process, one may reasonably argue how democracy would work if the populace lack the resources to meet their basic needs. How can democracy work when most people live in poverty because the Iron Triangle of politicians, bureaucrats and businessmen appropriates the political, economic, and social space? While each case differs, some core questions are common. Yet, one would find that prevention of conflict is more difficult when the interests of major domestic actors are served more by perpetuation and intensification of the conflict than by its resolution. The central idea developed by Zartman and others is that there are points in the lifecycle of a conflict that are more conducive to possible resolution than others (Zartman, 2001). Yet, in practice it is discovered that ending a conflict is one thing, putting the shattered society back together is quite another.

There are some who claim that the current political situation is not the result of total revolution from which a new polity is born and has a clean state, and so problems have to be tackled while designing an appropriate political strategy during the transition period. Nonetheless, the ongoing process is a welcome change that could lay the foundation for development of a distinctive political system, although evidence suggests that consolidation of democracy involve divisions, obstacles, and reversals in the absence of favourable institutions. While it is true that it is not always possible to distinguish the form of democracy from its substantive content, but it is now nearly a year that new regime in power, still no strategy has been developed to kick at the problem to have a political settlement–in the belief that change could be accomplished through the ballot box. Obviously, Nepal's returning to normal politics has welcomed new entrants to the political process, but genuine control of the people over the political institutions is yet to begin. Such a situation ultimately helps conservative forces, and even 'browns' (monarchists) may return at some point and control over the policy agenda without convening a new constitution through CA such as the Nepali case shows, democracy for politicians meant jockeying for power and state resources, while unabated political and economic exclusion only worsened the pervasive self-deprecation, fatalism, conformism, and individualism.

Indeed CA could be viewed as a bottom-up model to invent a new way to engage citizens in the practice of democracy or for that matter, a process which fosters democratic constitutionalism compatible with consensual model of democracy to end violence and secure sustainable legitimacy to reduce the chances of any future reversal. While all polities must live with the harsh reality of group-fighting to establish supremacy, yet there is the need for the presence of individuals with special qualities and characteristics in enhancing mass politics and decreasing the influence of traditional stakeholders. While the democratic ideologies must gain wide and organized acceptance from all important sectors for a breakthrough of democracy, but if democracy is the rule of the people, then the assumption is that there is a clear demand in people's voices that they should be treated neither as beneficiaries of government programmes and schemes, nor as voters who elect their representatives occasionally, but as active citizens who participate in both public arenas and their own associations and communities.

It would be reasonable to assume that after a decade of Maoist insurgency and due to the defeat of one of the most repressive and ambitious royal regimes, one can see that the state apparatus is marked with the start of rather unexpected but remarkable process of reforms. More exactly, when we look into Nepal's political matrix, it cleared the way for the creation of a new constitution through CA that eliminated monarchy, it altogether and dismantled the traditional power structures antithetical to democracy, yet, the progressive transformation of the state and society based on a liberal constitution does not match the reality; for Nepal fail to critically appreciate the core problems mainly because the politics executed by the elites have made the people out of their reach. Although this would not be a quick or easy endeavour, yet, for the first time in Nepal's history, a serious alternative arena of political power and influence has arisen with so much vitality that has threatened the politics-as-usual. Certainly Nepal has a complex past yet the present development cannot be understood by a simple political or economic dichotomy, yet the outcome represent only a small portion of the population rather than have empowered the marginalized and muzzled people to participate in governance.

Understanding the nature of Nepali state and politics requires a detailed analysis of the socio-political system based on a fuller comprehension of the social structure. Nepal's difficulty perhaps is to put the personal differences and animosities aside, and find a way to work constructively for the common good. It would be right, then, to say that crumbling of authoritarianism is not synonymous with democratization. And that is not a point for debate. The most visible void at present is the absence of visionary political leadership who can genuinely swing public opinion in terms of the values being instilled and promoted to consolidate the essential features of democratic society–economic protection, social welfare, and liberal views. Another snag is that it is not enough for SPAM to merely proclaim that all is right. Others too must see it that way. Paradoxically, being democratic and claiming to be one are two different aspects. Again the problem with Nepali democracy is that Maoists continue to believe that an armed revolution can change everything.[12] Realistically too, democracy is essentially a public affair involving the exercise of political power and control in a situation where everyone can live in peace and harmony. But, deep socio-economic cleavages in no time turn into political wrangles with propensity to deteriorate and emergence of new dimensions in the conflict. While it is true that Nepal, fairly certainly, is a democratic state since the monarchy washed out with the demise of King Gyanendra, but it is a third-grade democracy in terms of Freedom House Index or a 'neopatrimonial state' (Kohli, 2004) or 'boss democracy' in which that an elite few actually hold sway over the country's economic and political life and resort to patronage, lack of a democratic mindset and negative image of political leadership corruption, fraud, and force to maintain their hold on wealth and power.

While we can reasonably expect that Nepal will foster a political culture that favours democracy and transforms social structure in which tolerance and compromise constitute order of the day, the nature of the problem involved here is whether political parties can indeed be inclusive as well as disciplined while trying to integrate all the social and ethno-cultural identities and interests and develop a political will that reflects the shift in preferences of Nepali society.[13] Since politics is complex, it would be useful to remind oneself that despite their claims that they are in the process of giving up demagoguery, or shows plausible tendency to evolve towards greater pluralism, nor the power structure of army has gained credibility from its commitment to become inclusive, egalitarian, and democratic. If the muscles to set-up democracy breakdown again, the culpability will solely lie on the incapability of politicians to respond to the issues of democratic consolidation. From the game theory perspective, if the institutions of Nepal's political system are increasingly seen as contributing directly to stagnation, the only gathering that can bring about changes is the people.

Although few Nepalese would deny even a state with democratic ambitions and modern technology cannot completely control all of its denizens all of the time, it seems that the current pace of events has not brought about sufficient condition for stability. The question is valid largely because once having pioneered a political change, the concerned political party gets bogged in its own traditional mechanisms and taboos. It is hard to predict how the party system would now evolve and perform in constitution-making process, but four years have shown rather conclusively that Nepal is a fragmented society and in the absence of consensual politics and relatively stable configuration of political institutions, the exercise would be too risky. Yet, of course, politics has been defined in many ways, from Laswell's famous dictum of 'who gets what, when, and how' (Cox, Ikenberry and Inoguchi, 1999) to the cynical Machiavellian notion that it is nothing more or less than competitive struggle for power conducted between those at the top who care little for ideals, and even less for the comfort of their fellow citizens. Such brutal realism apart, it was after all Churchill who evaluated democracy as the worst form of government of all, except for all the others. The problems of democracy are serious because there are social, economic and ideological differences among the people and the parties. Yet the current wave of transformation in Nepali politics has admirably welcomed a new era of political tensions to sustain peace, with visible differences between public opinion and party proclamations. What is beyond doubt is that the process of transition towards democracy would be complete when it acquires 'subjective political competence' with open contestation over the right to win control of the government through competitive elections which determine who governs and when a citizen feels that s/he is capable of influencing political decision-makers and can truly play a participatory role.

Nonetheless, one thing is clear: the end of royal autocracy may or may not be followed by a democratic regime. Even if we assume that *Jana Andolan II* was the manifestation of classic left-wing populism that persuades the government to play a role in organizing some form of social cohesion, often construed as welfare, and when monarchy has clinically been dead, it would be more pertinent to utilize its success in facilitating the transition towards multiparty democracy than to have qualms over institutionalization and quality of democracy. Equally important, Nepal's transition was achieved not through rupture of politically defeated monarchy but by agreement among key political actors, and there is ample reason to think that democracy is not 'the only game in town'. There exist groups of people, though insignificant in numbers that are willing to collaborate with the fallen regime and its abominable practices. In fact, political transformation in Nepal is still a struggle between forces that favour democracy and those that prefer *status quo*. Critics of such a view contend that those who accede to power never in fact rally themselves for radical changes and are unable to effectively challenge the power of traditional strongholds hostile to democracy which only further marginalize the millions that leads to a new bargain among elite political actors with no sensitivity for the masses. In somewhat parallel fashion, the overriding problem is that the conflict is in no way ripe for solution. Instead, there is a danger that Nepal could backslide into chaos since political institutions are weak and dependent on personalities that get toppled in a flash. Basing freedoms and rights on special traits or granting special rights to certain groups of citizens is the principle cause of powerlessness of individuals. But in a country where political, social and economic crisis, statism and stagnation had been the norm, the appearance of democracy is certainly a good beginning.

Not necessarily, all breakdowns of authoritarian regimes complete transition to democracy. It may stimulate mass mobilization, but a variety of contentious actions have often emerged even when authoritarian regimes have collapsed, democratic openings were not consolidated peacefully, immediately, and easily.[14] Whether Nepal becomes democratic is an interesting question with significant practical implications. It is interesting to discover that basically transitions "is a game–tug of war, so to speak–between those in power and those in opposition" (Przeworski, 1991:26; Huntington, 1991).[15] Thus, democratization can be both stabilizing and destabilizing. In

Nepal, with the halt of Maoist uprising, Nepal seems to have charted a different path away from violent conflict towards a new politics, intending to put in place the institutional means of civilian rule into the hands of a full-blown constitutional polity so as to end the crisis that began in February 1996 mainly because of cold crocodiles to devour democracy then and there, especially the monarchy which remains intact even if blunted. Looking into the case of Nepal after toppling of monarchic rule, whether it can substantially alter the organization and style of governance remains an open question. It would be useful to remind oneself that Nepal's honeymoon with democracy suffered cruel setbacks when it was nastily and swiftly slammed shut by the monarchy both in 1960 and 2005. Nepal's recent history is a crucial test of the claim that the rightist monarchy has always sought to undo democratic progress, ironically with the pretext that democracy has been weakened by the democrats themselves. The destiny of every state and its citizens relies mostly on the decisions of politicians; they can make or unmake a country.

The current Nepali political scene however tells us that it has become the perpetual victim of wrong political decisions. Logically, no one can claim that Nepal is a totalitarian state yet, but the problem is that the continued prevalence of clientelistic games in the political system suggests that totalitarian impulse has infected the body politic, which is likely to strengthen the power of anti-reform forces with new actors becoming more active and powerful to challenge the fundamental norms of democratic governance. This does not put an end to the matter. The puzzling fact is that the political parties have not yet established themselves as meaningful intermediary structures between the state and society. The parties and state are overcentralized and nurturing overparliamentarianism, particization, bureaucratization, and a new privileges class. It was not only developing a paternalistic approach towards the people, but also began anew to monopolize political power, state resources, public policies, and political decision-making with an intent to have hegemony over the lives and minds of the masses. While a clear break with the past may be necessary, yet we strongly believe that a multicultural society like Nepal can be held together by democratic culture, if the citizens not only have individual rights of political participation, but can also enjoy social and cultural rights, of which Habermas describes as 'constitutional patriotism' (Entreves, 1997). There is no god-sent framework for an ordered political life. But a good chance does stand now to dismantle the authoritarian structure and have democratic prowess.

Civic organizations have not been able to affect significantly the policy-making process from outside. Mass politics remains a toll for handful of ego-driven, short-sighted, and self-serving politicians who marvel at their short-term gains but inflict long-term damage. However, one might reasonably claim that the signing of the peace accord between the SPA-led government and Maoists on 21st November, 2006 was both an historic event and democratic achievement, a joyous celebration filled with emotions because for the past eleven years both of the signatories were fighting to kill one another. The beauty of the peace accord is that despite the gains on political and military fronts and their control over large parts of the country, the Maoists are obliged to adopt a strategy in conformity with the realities of changed international environment, as they too realize that the idea of revolution itself had lost its credibility by the end of 20th century due to the excesses of Leninism and Maoism. More exactly, one encouraging element is the transformation of political system in a consensual direction, especially in view of Maoists' unusual path to democracy: the ballot box as the new path to power in their quest for justice. It is not surprising, then, that a window has opened up and a change can be brought about by the ballot box. There is no question that no democracy can evolve unless the demos, the true legislators in whom power is collectively vested by the democratic form of government, can actively exercise the power. Yet in theory, it refers to the values of moderation and tolerance, which make conflicts less likely to arise and easier to resolve. Yet the challenges in the path to democracy cannot be met quickly unless the actors identify the consensual paradigms of political reality within the political discourse, if the real fight is indeed against authoritarianism.

While questions concerning the durability of democracy and real capabilities of the state ultimately depend on the charter of the democracy itself, the shift in perspective with each new wave in Nepal has been so great that one would think of a paradigm change at first glance. Nepal's current transition may never be completed unless there is unwavering commitment towards the accepted socio-political norms and preservation of the new order. More accurately, the absence of historical antecedents for democratic governance gives rise to suspicion of the troubles that lie ahead, even if the end of the 'people's war' demonstrates that Marx's deterministic view of history was grossly mistaken. Surely, it was a radical change in perspectives. But, to maintain stability and build democratic legitimacy, Nepal must discard confrontation and have consensus on basic rules of the game. The challenge is to assimilate democracy through performance, if Nepal to avoid yet another setback. One of the implorations is that building democracy is going to be arduous and messy unless those who matter have faith in the law. No one has doubt that ending the conflict essentially means moving it from the battlefield to the people's domain for contesting political power, particularly in a country polarized by insurgency in which many people were forced to take sides and have alliances to win, which might not be pertinent in times of peace.

Democracy does not mean that every citizen must believe in it. Nonetheless, it allows even antidemocrats to enjoy all legitimate non-violent activities. It is the duty of political parties and leaders and ultimately voters that they take it as a crucial innovation of the current wave of democratization. Yet a point to underscore here is that the declaration of Interim Constitution (IC) following the defeat of monarchy marked a decisive phase in Nepal's transition from monarchy to a republic—a political process of magnanimous creativity with enormous implications, not excluding avoidance of confrontational politics. The event would be appropriate to inform the people that Nepal has changed the political course, even if serious roadblocks have not been removed to set-up liberal democracy. One might reasonably claim that a text is understood in the light of certain presumptions. It would not be hyperbolic that IC sets an arranged marriage between SPA and Maoists, in which the consent has been passive and qualified. The logic is that until there is comparable level of economic development that might favour democracy, both rulers and the rules of the game are likely to come under attack and lose vital supporters. But, in order to advance towards its consolidation, they must at least endeavour to neutralize those who are unconditionally authoritarian, either by isolating them politically or by fragmenting them into insignificance that cannot threaten the new order. It will give a real chance to bring about an end to the traditional forces, especially monarchy—the number one enemy of democracy that until recently possessed unlimited powers sometimes in the name of democracy itself and sometimes ostensibly acting for the cause of the state.

One way to size up a regime and its political character, Nepali democracy has increasingly become the main feature of television and other media programmes, although it is still an interlude between one political regime and another. We tend to believe that this transition cannot be overcome until constitution is framed, free elections are held and a welfare state is set-up. The mechanism for restructuring of a state consists of complex, manifold and time-bound process that demands not merely technical skills but also reasonable vision and noble mission to attain it. Similarly, achieving democratic development and sustaining it over long-term requires a complex sequence of many contingent and interdependent factors. Admittedly, if any conclusion can be drawn from the experience of the past decade and half, they include politicians who won elections, took power, and then manipulated the mechanism of governance rather than bringing about demonstrative democracy with equalitarian economy and growth of citizens' talent. Phrased another way, democracy was gambled away by narrow-minded and incompetent politicians resulting in 'uncivil democracy'. There need be no illusion about that. As for the Maoists, although they are fuelled with outrage on their political exclusion and poverty enforced on the people by repression, their leadership nevertheless is made of counter elite who retains enough of Maoist ideology. With the toppling of royal autocracy, the brutal constraints that used to keep Nepalese silent have been removed something like what Fukuyama describes "moving beyond the conflicts and oppression of the past into an era of peace and freedom" (Fukuyama, 1991, 1995). Yet, the state is not at the service of the citizens; instead the citizen is at the mercy of the state.

Current Wave of Pessimism

A cursory look at the players in Nepali political game would reveal that despite SPAM success to defeat royal autocracy, the leadership of governing parties is obsessed with its own complexes and has failed to meet the challenges of tolerance and creativity that are the hallmarks of true leadership, which is all the more reason to be pessimistic. The leaders believe in traditional values rather than which would give the people the opportunity to determine their future for self-governing. More generally, perhaps, one could say that the extension of democracy in Nepal is not just a political citizenship, constitutional reform, or changes in the form of government but also realization of citizenship in the full sense of the term, which entails substantive social, cultural, and economic conditions. Nepal cannot be democratic unless important issues are decided by overwhelming majority that involves the entry of new actors into the polity, especially those who have been previously excluded such as women, indigenous people, and the Maoists who are the representatives of the responsive forces that stood against the repression of state authority.

The current pessimism about democracy is that some actors of international community hold significant sway in determining the course of Nepali state. More troubling is that there are numerous external factors and actors in Nepal attempting to influence the ongoing reconfiguration of the political order in the guise of working towards a new democratic order. These forces do not attempt to strengthen state structures and institutions, instead they work for their own benefit, often derailing or reversing the process. If we examine past six years Nepal's political history, we see they have been seeking to isolate Maoists by quietly supporting monarchy. Arguably, Maoists and their popularity may threaten democracy's long-term survival, but it is an axiom that in a democracy, the people's choice must be respected. Maoists, whether we like it or not, are seen as the most powerful political force in the Nepali politics. When it is so, the international community must be engaged with Maoists rather than try to isolate them. Engagement might not work, but the consequences of isolating a powerful political group which can garner a commanding share of the popular vote would probably be far worse. The real problem is not so much political cynicism but a failure by those who hold the banners of democracy to recognize that democracy can take several forms. comes in various shapes and sizes, and need not always be stamped with a 'made in USA' sign of authenticity.

Admirable though CA alone cannot create rules essential for democratic consolidation. Nepal's sustainable transition would require a complex interplay of many contingents such as cohesive political culture, strong civil institutions, professional bureaucracy, economic society, and common principle of order for there may be no other shared vision that might bind together a nation better. Apart from feudal-style politics, there has been erosion of the rule of law in its civil and political decisions. The potential scenario is disappointing: when legislators enact silly laws, executives enforce wise laws but foolishly, and the courts let go culprits wilfully, there is little point in negotiating a consensus in the first place. And clandestine deals do no good to a nation in the long run anyway. Since Nepal's democratization process is prone to get disturbed than being consolidated, politicians must act prudently to preclude worst-case reversals. Notwithstanding their shortcomings, they must behave statesmanlike. It would be naive to assume, however, that a new political order could resolve the conflicts without having ideological confluences.

Conclusion: Towards a New Constitutional Pathway

Studies on transition from an authoritarian set-up to a democratic order, which ideally demarcate the phases of liberalization, democratization, and consolidation, have shown that political turmoil invariably emanates from the rivalry for supremacy among contenders for power at extremities. This brings the very rules of the game under attack and the resultant loss of key supporters. This is presently the situation in Nepal where it is not possible even to guess where it is headed for, leave alone a wholesale adoption of a constitutional framework for democracy, since the overthrow of royal regime. In recent years, the rise of orthodox politics, especially the politics of terrorism, has posed an additional challenge to democratic societies and their governance. Multiethnic states have the additional challenge developing legitimate forms of interest representation and influence for significant, continuing structural reforms of the state that favour democratic consolidation. Moreover, even if democratic governments must simultaneously protect their citizens from violence and maintain their civil rights, today, many observe that representative democracy is in crisis, and decline of public in public institutions. Since democratic rule is based on the consent of the ruled, a secure and stable democracy cannot be established and maintained without broad-based popular endorsement, which is especially important for nascent newly democratic states, like Nepal.

A careful look of three political interregnums, one is after post-war in 1951 and after two Third Wave in 1990 and 2006 multiparty rule shows that elite dominated large-scale organizations and where politics was ultimately under the tutelage control of political parties what Michel says 'iron law of oligarchy' (Duverger, 1979). Progress has been slow in reforming the state apparatus by resolving the elitist clientelism, bringing the army under civilian authority or building a new support base for democracy. The most troubling aspect is the institutional disarray facing the state. It is hard to measure the content of democracy, whereas it is believed to have been consolidated when there are no political, military, or economic threats. Yet from people's perspective, a system is considered to have soundly consolidated when most of them begin to rely on it as the 'best way to govern the collective life in a society'.

No one has so far questioned the broad goals of an inclusive democracy that delivers good governance based on the principles of political pluralism, rule of law, constitutional supremacy, basic human rights and freedom, independent justice system, among others. Giving meaning to these basic concepts is where the problem starts. Given the bitter acrimony and wide divergence of opinion how they (political parties) are reconciled to agree on a draft that is accepted by cross-section of the Nepali society remains doubtful. This is particularly because the parliamentary parties, who want an Indian-style parliamentary democracy but failed to institutionalize the same since 1991, are pitted against the Maoists and other communist groups, who accuse the parliamentary parties for their failure in making democracy relevant to the needs of the people, want to establish communist regime under a 'people's republic.' The key question is not whether the basic law of the land is drafted by May 28, 2011 as stipulated in the amended interim constitution (originally that the new constitution should be declared on the date 28th May, 2010, and extended for a year) but whether the seventh constitution would last longer than all the previous six constitutions in the last six decades.

In a sense, the political parties are divided on the ideological orientation of the new constitution. It has not clearly spelled out its ideological commitment other than referring to the federal democratic republic based on pluralism, sovereignty of the people and representative form of government. Clearly, it intends to implement the aspirations reflected in the peaceful popular movement of April 2006 and the 12-point understanding between the parliamentary political parties and the Maoists reached in 2005 that brought the Maoist rebels into the peace process. This ideological ambiguity is shared by all non-communist political parties that want an Indian-style parliamentary democracy in Nepal. The biggest barrier to transform the institutional context to a culture of constitutionalism and democracy is the radical and militant attitude of a rapacious elite who want to maintain firm grip on power behind institutional façade. The argument is that a democracy without values easily turns into open or thinly disguised totalitarianism. Welcome to reality. It bites.

Another major difference is regarding the nature of regime, for example, Maoists call for a fundamental change in the system of governance by providing for direct elections for the President with full executive authority and combining all the three roles—the head of the state, the head of the army and the chief executive. The President, who could be removed only through impeachment, is to be assisted by a Prime Minister to be elected by the Legislature to look after the day to day administration. Both the President and the Prime Minister can serve for a maximum of two terms. This is not what the rest of the political parties want. The NC wants multi-party parliamentary system with the government headed by the Prime Minister with full executive authority and accountable to the Parliament. The CPN-UML endorses this system except that it wants direct election of the Prime Minister to address the anomalies of the multi-party regime such as unstable polity and unholy coalition governments Nepal experienced between the 1994 parliamentary elections and imposition of emergency in 2002. The third major difference is regarding the state structure. Ironically, there seems to be a consensus to break with the traditional unitary structure of the Nepali state into broadly a three-tiered federal structure consisting of a centre, autonomous provinces and districts. The consensus ends there. Specifically, that the Maoists are determined to use the opportunities offered by its victory at the CA elections for institutionalizing federal republic as a 'supreme means' for 'forward-looking restructuring of the state.' They pledges the 'right to ethnic or regional autonomous rule as well as the right to self-determination.' On the other hand, all Tarai (flatland) based parties want 'One Madhesh, One Province' which means they want the entire Tarai bordering India to be a single entity in the proposed federal structure with the right to self-determination, despite several ethnic groups indigenous to the Tarai including the Tharus, Dhimals, Rajbamsis and others who have launched an umbrella organization—the Federation of Indigenous and Ethnic People—are opposed to such a declaration.

Similarly, regarding the structure of the judiciary, despite most of political formations have pledged to uphold the independence of judiciary, how this is done remains to be seen, yet Maoist proposes a number of reforms to address that do not necessarily address the independence and fairness of the Nepali justice system. For example, they suggest the creation of 'people's courts' and reconciliation centres at the district and village level. Many suspect this could be an attempt to institutionalize the Maoist kangaroo courts known as 'people's courts' in areas where they continue to have their sway. There is a wide gap between the economic policy of the political parties as outlined in official party documents, manifestoes and policy statements and as practiced when they come to power. They have all been saying that now that democracy is being institutionalized, the next revolution should be economic. That is a tall order given the fragility of the peace and democracy building process. Still, the party documents are rich in rhetoric designed to please the voters while reflecting very poor research and weak policy formulation. For example, Maoist's 'new transitional economic policy' include implementing a revolutionary land reform policy to 'end feudal land-ownership by providing land to the tillers', promoting foreign direct investment in areas prioritized by periodic plans, encouraging public-private partnership, among others. Its main focus is to develop 'national industrial capitalism oriented towards socialism.'

The NC claims to adhere to 'democratic socialism' but supports liberal and competitive economy. The party during most of the period it was in power between 1991 and 2002 followed free market reforms that pleased the Western donors and the trading urban middle class that mainly benefited from such reforms while infuriating farmers and ordinary people for neglecting not only reforms in agriculture but also promising but not delivering social justice and social security. Most reforms were in the area of trade and foreign currency which came largely in response to wide-ranging economic reforms introduced by India. Likewise, the CPN-UML is admitting a mixed economic system by seeking to combine the market reforms and private sector growth with the process of redistribution of income and property in order to create a welfare society based on social justice. It argues for progress tax to reduce income disparity. It seeks partnership among the private public and cooperative sectors for the development of industry, trade, tourism and infrastructure development. It seeks to encourage foreign capital, foreign direct investment and technology. It stresses on developing agriculture, water resources and tourism to address issues of poverty and unemployment. Revolutionary land reforms programme would promote management, redistribution and productivity of land and encourage agricultural cooperatives. Similarly, there are several parties they want 'new Nepal' through radical social and economic reforms with their political leaders have the reputation of the merchants of dream. How they will sell the dream of now turning to 'economic revolution' remains to be seen. This is not the first time the Nepali people have been told about this dream however. Despite the differences on these key issues, all the political groups seem to agree on the need of a bicameral legislature. The CPN-UML wants the legislature consisting of a 'people's assembly' elected on the basis of mixed system combining both the First Past The Post (FPTP) and Proportional Representation (PR) systems.

While it is debatable whether Presidential system is less favourable for institutionalizing democracy than a parliamentary one, both background and foreground factors remind us that Nepal has been a case of notorious political development something like *Perestroika* and *Glasnost* which involved liberalization but not democratization of the post-autocracy central power structures. Surrounded with intense controversies, the political identities in Nepal are narrow, compounding, and often exclusive in which large sections of people often feel neglected, excluded, and exploited. The central question facing here is, therefore: What are the conditions under which democracy can survive and flourish here? It seems that Nepal's ruling cliques have fallen victim to a double whammy of lack of experimental knowledge of democracy and deliberate exclusion of any public debate that could have tempered their submissive views. We see there are pursuing parochial interests rather than to grab the opportunities to reconcile with divergent interests and create proper boundaries to overcome short-sighted bargains; they prefer to continue with the bickering and infighting. Both feed into the traditional traits of Nepali politics 'elitism and arrogance which exclude the populace from polity and the facade character of Nepali polity' focused on rituals and symbols rather than confronting and solving real-life problems. This has pervasively alienated the people from politics and public discourse. They are deeply cynical about their political leaders. If the above analysis is correct, then Nepal has not become democratic even after the toppling of royal regime but it remains a parliamentary oligarchic/oligopolistic state embossed as democracy in which a few of the elite actually hold sway over the country's political and economic life against the general will of the people.

Part of the problem, Nepal's experiences reveal, is that on the one hand, it glorify the impact of social movements while on the other, it fail to exercise critical judgment at the right moment. To be sure, if the state cannot channellize public demands, it is likely that the popular demands will be repoliticized, leading to a further realignment of partisan affiliation and alternative forms of representation and participation. Although competition is back with the end of direct involvement of monarchy in politics, it is very difficult to agree upon a model to resolve the differences on substantive issues. In the current Nepali context, there is no doubt that a large number of organizations are spending significant resources on undemocratic means to block the country into being a fully democratic state. Nepal has produced what might be termed a tentative, filtered and hybrid democracy with traces of authoritarianism, what Pridham calls negative consolidation of a regime whereby democratic procedures remains fragile and vulnerable to reversals (Pridham, 1991,1997 and 1998). The consolidation is deemed negative because the citizens believe that a certain constitutional structure is unfair and inadequate and an alternative system is more attractive to the influential actors in military, finance, big business, banks, trade unions and to the disgruntled citizens. Nevertheless, if the choice is the 'worst system of government' or 'no system of government', people may prefer the latter. Even if democratization typically creates a wide spectrum of politically significant groups with diverse and incompatible interests, there are indications of the existence of groups pressuring for non-democratic solution to the current crisis. Of particular concern is a violent conflict between the king and democratic forces, which has subsided for the time being but its recurrence cannot be ruled out. This also means that the monarchy can always make efforts to weed out the tender roots of democracy. Arguably, the outcomes of a revolution can be transformed into legal rights only when it has succeeded and the revolutionaries have been transformed as the founders of a new regime. Democratic consolidation after a popular opening is, therefore, far from a certainty.

If one believes in government by consent, one must believe that the people may, as a matter of fact, change their political system. Despite differing emphases of political parties, one of the main aims of *Jan Aandolan II* was meant to replace the overly bureaucratic, corrupt and statist regime, by creating as free, fair and formidable democratic society. Generally, a system of consolidated, responsive, and socially anchored parties strengthens political efficiency and effectiveness with regard to formulating and implementing policy.

There is neither a consensus on resolving all issues democratically, nor has the monarchy agreed to accept civilian authority. There are groups with vested interests who would like to jeopardize the process, and if those in power insist on monopolizing it and refuse to take care of public demand, the democratization process will surely be very rough. This reflects the absence of ideology competing with democracy. This, combined with problems of establishing a constitutional order, reorienting the authoritarian bureaucracy, and stabilizing political adjustments, the promotion of democracy in Nepal becomes an occasional sideshow which is not consistent with the realist expectations.

Unlike many other countries undergoing regime change, Nepal entered into the transition in a comparatively privileged position with respect to several variables, although the most important hardliners are not defeated, disgraced or jailed yet. What will happen next is impossible to predict reliably. But the democratic method is that institutional arrangement should decide by means of a people's vote and through a process of mutual understanding in what problem-solving theorists argue 'integrative bargaining.' (Thapa, 2006) Even if the interim legislature-parliament is often referred as facilitator of the process of change and its members, having been helpful to end the royal autocracy, always claiming that they represent the wishes and needs of the people, such claims are virtually illegitimate. In the Nepali context, most of the parliamentarians belong to the more privileged strata of society that believe in the importance of family ties. They are not only little educated and ill-informed about politics, but their political belief is more constrained than those of the people. Their understanding of public policy is determined not by coherent ideological stance but by primitive self-interests which support the political interest of institutionalizing monarchy.

One reason that the current legislators play no participatory role in mediating the impact of conflict is that they are selected not on the basis of their ties to constituency or the current political realities they ostensibly represent but on the basis of their clientele ties to party leaders. On the political knowledge dimension, what the political parties need to acknowledge is that ill-informed citizens can and do muddle through the political choices they have, that well-informed citizens can participate more effectively in defense of their values and interests in the political arena, and underneath the current monopoly of the Parliament lies a Hobson's choice for a state of anarchy subject to setbacks and even to the renewal of violent conflict. This does not put an end to the matter, however. In fact, the oligopolistic claims of SPAM leaders allowing the prolongation of Parliament, which is not a democratic way of conflict resolution. The problem is that every time a major political change occurs here, some segments of society would come up seeking access to public life through their organization. History makes it clear that each has demanded that the state respond to its particular interests, which means that parties have represented no more than fragmented interests. Despite the crucial change, the politics is dominated by a small number of elite actors who control the machinery in traditional clientele fashion.

While the role of institutions relies upon an implicit assumption that democracy is essentially a question of having the right type of constitution, but cataclysmic failure after World War I of the efforts to implant democracy in those European nations that had been governed by authoritarian regimes indicated that constitutional engineering by itself is not enough. For example, the Weimer Republic had been an ideal democracy on paper, but it failed to survive partly because its democratic institutions were inconsistent with an underlying authoritarian political culture. Hence, it must be noted that if the way of thinking does not change, even the best policy should be useless. Democracy failed in Nepal, in large part, because it lacked a participant political culture. No single set of institutions embodies democracy, even if, at a given moment in time, some particular country may seem to represent its 'best practice'. There is no question that CA is important not only because it is a venue for influencing political decisions but also because it transforms democratic rights into actual rights.

No doubt that peace is precious; it must be persistently promoted. Yet structured peace cannot be sustained when there is abject poverty and extreme inequality. Moreover, enhancing peace efforts based on the narrow definition of military and security terms would only be one-dimensional progress that could raise instability in the country. Regarding UN's involvement in Nepal's current peace process, it cannot throw its full weight behind one party, but its expertise and experience make it most helpful as a facilitator in the process. It can work with other nations to stop the flow of weapons into Nepal. Undoubtedly, the UN is often beholden to major powers like India, the US and China, which have their own interests in Nepal. They may not therefore act in unison to lighten world body's burden.[16] It can be perceived that the transition cannot be completed unless Nepal meets two requirements—a government is installed in office as the result of a free and popular vote and successful exercise of sovereign authority in formulating and implementing the policies without hindrance. It seems equally clear that the party system must survive and the democracy it has built be consolidated in future. Whether Nepal's traditional parties will be a positive force in this process and whether Nepal will make the transition from a besieged to a functional democracy remain to be seen.[17] Similarly, in civil-military theory, that a democratic pattern of civil-military relations is one in which there is low contestation by the military of the policies of the democratically elected government and where the military authorities accept that they have few prerogatives or reserved domain.

Nepal is still a long way from meeting the criteria liberal democracy because it is a country of family-based fiefdoms that determine the state objectives to suit their interests. Nepal does not have an elaborate anti-establishment political culture, but Nepal's political culture allows the politicians a great deal of autonomy in order to maximize their political flexibility that fosters personalism and clientelism. One reason is that the traditional Nepalese political parties have had, and still have very closed and weakly organized hierarchical organizations characterized by personalized leadership, undemocratic structure, and exclusionary approaches. Every democratic episode, whether successful or not, can be seen as a cycle of mobilization in which actors at both elite and mass levels take advantage of new expanded opportunities in both political and civil society. But the current standpoints of mainstream political parties of building democratic institutions especially on their hegemonic vocation and 'anything-goes' attitude to power and practices make democracy hard to sustain. The context is clear. Whatever their claims of modern characteristics, it is clear that the traditional dynamics in which political parties are more interested in capturing and distributing patronage than by constituting programmatically focused governments are still alive.

Over the past fifteen years, most academic writers and political scientists in Nepal have been spending their time in portraying the obvious phenomena comprising political parties, parliamentary debates and transition to and consolidation of democracy rather than assessing the relevance of federalism, proportional representation and presidentialism which are the fundamental institutional variables in alleviating ethnic and other social conflicts to achieve an enduring democracy in a pluralistic society. In our judgment, Nepali politics, it would seem, has shifted gears abruptly but we are still far from a consolidated nation-state which is structurally weak and incapable of accomplishing the tasks that a cohesive or competent nation should do. What we find here instead is a political change somewhat in Tocquevillean sense "a democratic regime change that has broadened the ideological spectrum of Nepali masses by freeing them from the right-wing extremism but still remains attached to the feudal monarchy which has at critical times been hostile to civil liberties and political rights and hence democratic political development." (Drury, Kriechaus and Lusztig, 2006; Ghandi and Przeworski, 2001). The most pertinent point to be made here is that the political parties have played a significant role to restart the democratic process but the main source of political power is still not the people. This is particularly true because political institutionalization has been far from adequate; adherence to the principle of rule of law is fundamentally lacking, which is a sturdy bulwark against the abuse of power. The political socialization theory maintains that democratic form of government is itself a social contract—an agreement among political forces to abide by a common set of rules that leads to resolving political conflict through a process of negotiation and compromise. Political change in Nepal reveals that the debate on feudal monarchy 'the greatest threat to democratic peace' is far from over. Since monarchy never had the kind of support of a significant segment of population it can be removed through a constituent assembly. It is in this sense that those who are personally affiliated to the monarchy and swear loyalty speak for even being content with lame-duck monarchy and ask the same of their followers, but if they ever became victorious, they would ultimately facilitate rightwing autocracy.

Thus, for those who believe that the end of royal regime has changed all the answers and all the questions, it is virtually impossible to contest unless a newly opened political forum gives space to the claims of democratic legitimacy to Maoists who have played a key role in its destruction. So far as the parliamentary declarations are concerned, we will not enter into a lengthy argument, as it has no legitimate power and authority to represent the people nor the capacity to restructure the polity. Thus, mere holding of parliamentary meetings does not prove that it is able to attain the kind of efficacy that is necessary to meet the general interests of the people. Obviously, even if the Parliament's decision are considered as progressive, it is distasteful and dangerous instrumentally, because it is institutionalizing the monarchy against the will of the people. This politics of self-legislation fatally undermines the autonomy on which all political freedoms depend. Nevertheless, the struggle for the first stage of democratic transition will be over when the parliament chooses to declare the election for CA. The first main argument for constituent assembly consists of two basic propositions: (a) all political decisions should be as legitimate as possible, and (b) the highest degree of legitimacy is achieved by decisions made by direct unmediated votes of the people. People may not trust the members of legislature, cabinet ministers, or even prime ministers, but they do trust themselves after all.

Let us consider, democracy is neither linear nor cumulative progress; instead it is a multilayered process in which there are some advances some of the time in some areas and having reversals in others. They usually go through a rocky transition in which mass politics transacts with authoritarian elite politics in a volatile way. One of Nepal's remarkable achievements is the Maoist commitment to political diversity and non-violent contest for power with a fair degree of democratic peace.[18] The continuing but gradually declining political violence indicates that there is a significant change in Maoists' behaviour, which may steer the peace process forward. But it is important to bear in mind that democratization can be particularly destabilizing in multiethnic societies where ethnic groups are uncertain about how fully their rights would be protected, especially when the state in transition is too weak to face the tyranny of violence in order to protect those rights. Violence is most likely to occur in the very early stages because democratization process brings new social groups with widely divergent interests into the political process at a time when the state lacks the institutional capacity to accommodate conflicting interests and respond to popular demands. While many factors account for the emergence of political change, democratic stability in Nepal would depend largely on what happens within the political realm itself comprising the leaders, the actions and the ideas.

Today Nepal's democratization is proceeding. From this point on Nepal's chances for democracy may be the strongest and should with some good fortune be able to focus on consolidating and improving its newly democratic regime, but the transition to democracy is a complex process in which the expectations of society are often in contradiction with the government discourse. From every point of view, the transition from a monarchy-dominated system to one where the democratic forces have control over the government provides a good opportunity to examine the prevalent attitudes, yet democratic exercise can be frustrating when control over public policy is divided between the different opposing groups. Any keen observer of Nepali politics can trace the undercurrents of the three political ideologies—'conservatism, liberalism and socialism.' But it would be a serious mistake to have failed to take the opportunity to create a truly secure Nepal. There are increasing doubts whether the SPAM can deliver lasting peace, much less democracy and justice because many believe that the leaders are prone to lie however their policy be revolutionary.

Not all disputes have neat solutions. Yet more explicitly, citizens feel that the political parties in the parliament do not represent their interests; these politicians are only out for their own enrichment at the public expense; and that once in power, they have failed to govern effectively. At this point, it would be fair to say that Nepal need fresh, talented, strong, and principled leadership to construct a nation with democratic values which can proudly live and prosper in the global society. The point here is not to argue whether the change in national sovereignty is a good thing or bad, but to recognize that focusing only on one's own interests alone ignores the political dimension of insurgency and thereby makes it more difficult to negotiate with the Maoists. It has been argued that no political system can enjoy 100 per cent trust from the people. Yet the governmental power is legitimate when it is conceived both by the rulers and the ruled as a trust. The argument is that the moment the rulers are found to have betrayed the trust, their power becomes illegitimate. Further, the claim is that all democracies are flawed to some degree but what quality of political delivery can Nepalis expect in the present circumstances? While democracy provides the instruments to solve the problems brought about by dictatorship and autocratic rule, simply eradicating oppression does not automatically solve Nepal's political problems. Surely, the responsibility of the transitional leadership is not to dictate solutions but to offer a mechanism for participatory resolution of the conflict.

Democracy must be inclusive but it cannot be so unless politically active segments of the population have a voice in the system. It would be foolish for the parliamentarians to put all the bets on a single horse. As noted above, even if the continuation of restored parliament is necessary, it also implies that backlash is probable from monarchy and other belligerent elements. This proposition creates a problem for peace because institutionalizing uncertainty may cause chaos. This is not a straightforward process, the outcome of which is built on a narrow political consensus. Since Nepal will not likely return to an absolute monarchy, every future political arrangement must focus on democratic federal republic with a power-sharing formula between a weaker central government and stronger autonomous regional bodies, in favour of a bottom-up approach that promotes a decentralized state consisting of regions that have extensive powers. The approach should be based on the belief that the best test of truth is the power of thought and self-determination. Obviously, a crisis is a time-sensitive threat to something of value that demands an immediate response.

In addition to structural changes, Nepal is in need of enlightened leaders who can help to guide the path to a truly deliberative democracy. Such leaders need not necessarily be perfect, but they must have the ability to continue learning; this is an essential skill of leadership. The weakness of the political leadership is that they seem to have compromised on every front. The credibility of political parties is so low that they are being driven by patron-client networks and egoistical leaders and their expression for societal interests takes place outside the formal political channel. In minimal sense, the catch-all tendency of pro-democracy groups during the protracted transition to democracy has provided for the emergence of unorganized and a relatively unstable party system. In the past, leaders like B.P. Koirala, Ganeshman Singh, Madan Bhandari, Man Mohan Adhikari, etc., who, by their incisive judgment and a sense of responsibility, guided the party. The leaders now on the scene, not only lack these qualities, but they are also formalistic, indecisive, espouse linear views of political development, and are overly-focused on material factors. These leaders have their own vision of democracy, which differs largely from the general consensus found throughout the international community. We are not suggesting here that all political actions must be committed to democracy, but if popular leaders are committed to democracy, and enjoy broad legitimacy in their organizations and movements, the prospects for democracy are better. There is a compelling need for the leaders and their parties to develop a framework that guides democratization and to create a system in which the leadership grows and the elected leader commands support up to the grass roots level. If democracy is to succeed, parties need to create their own *esprit de corps*, something like 'organizing of feelings on behalf of the movement'. Furthermore, they need to deal with the current crisis with decisive intervention and not treat it merely as a moment of fragmentation, dislocation or destruction.

At the same time, party leaders must remember that the citizenry should not be treated as a hindrance to political development. People often behave in one way because they see the alternatives as having worse consequences. Guerrilla warfare is not a new phenomenon and history is witness to its repeated occurrence. What is new, however, is its integration with social, economic, and political programmes that aimed to overthrow established authority and transform society through armed struggle. Above all, if political participation distanced itself from the input side, where the disadvantaged social groups have been weakened, where policy formulation is centralized, and where many of the largest reforms are passed without opportunity to debate, political unrest is inevitable. We can reasonably expect that Nepal will foster a political culture that favours democracy and transforms social structure in which tolerance and compromise constitute order of the day. Indeed, stability cannot be achieved unless Nepal is transformed from sleepy backwaters to a profound welfare state where the President would be chosen by the Parliament on the basis of post-electoral inter-party agreements something like Czech type 'parliamentarized presidentialism'. The Czech constitution created a dual executive in which an indirectly elected President plays an important role in the realm of foreign policy and performs symbolic and ceremonial functions, but the paramount powers of governance exercised by a Prime Minister who must have majority support in the Parliament. It may not be a final answer because every strategy in political science faces daunting obstacles, but this could be a progressive solution under which Nepal can manage to muster the political will overcoming the polarized and weak party system and adopt effective policies through stable government.

Although the peace agreement is itself a resource for sustaining the democratic compromise, yet the interminable struggles within the parties that often appear more driven by opportunism than ideological differences, culminating differences in schisms, scandal, and declining support. That is to say that in the present analysis, the political processes internal to many political parties is far from democratic control is centralized with little role for the party rank and file and there is little transparency. Some analysts see as central to the crisis of the political party system in Nepal is the absence of a strong centre party. A distinct argument concerning the political centre is made by William Barnes. (Wood, 2001) In reviewing the record of democracy building in Europe, he found that effective mass participation occurred historically because of the mass mobilization by centre-left parties characterized by serious commitment to reforming and regulating capitalism to make it more humane, more inclusive, more egalitarian, and more politically democratic. Clearly, if such parties do not emerge to carry out this function in Nepal, the country will remain an 'incomplete democracy'[19] or a 'hybrid regime' in which elections occur with regularity but without authentic mass citizenship and the effective institutionalization of norms of equal citizenship informing the rule of law.

Prior to that, consensus must be reached on large issues of social and economic policy involving rural development and distribution of income, which will in turn require the institutional development of responsive government and general strengthening of the state's democratic performance and legitimacy. Finally, a principal hypothesis is that despite significant advances in ideological pluralism and political tolerance, increasing political competition, and the gradual strengthening of the new institutions founded by the peace agreement to ensure democratic rule, democracy in Nepal is not consolidated but combines patterns of political competition with political disaffection and social exclusion that vary unevenly across sectors and areas. There is no single route to democratization, yet there are grounds for hope. The present freedom of expression and organization are absolutely without precedent, particularly in the countryside. Presuming that association stimulates political participation, Nepal's future depends on interlacing of the peace process, consensual and consociational democratic models, and a welfare-oriented economic system.

One would expect that the course of political matrix towards the structural changes is evident, especially in its attempts to solve fundamental political and social problems, including that of constitutional reform in terms of new politics and creation of new state institutions on the basis of rule of law, value system and democratic pluralism, although Nepal's politics is still dominated by a small number of elite actors who control the machinery in traditional clientele fashion. The simple fact may be that after the end of commissarial monarchy head-on political conflicts are now over. But, how the nation responds to attain a liberal ideal to succeed and manage the reform process properly to contribute to it success would be test of its democracy.

Notes

1. One problem is that the competitive elections is of a single dimension to measure democracy, because there are political systems with some democratic elements but also with limits on competition, participation, and liberties. Another way of thinking is that deliberative politics is firmly grounded in the idea of sovereignty. It seems that no single measure will do. See initially, the landmark study of Dahl, *Democracy and Its Critics*, 1989 and *On Democracy*, 1998.
2. It is confounding why Western political and economic aims are viewed not only with suspicion, but have consistently been hated by three categories of totalitarians: the 'reds' (Communists), the 'greens' (Islamists), and the 'browns' (Monarchists/Fascists). Moreover, democratic consolidation after a popular opening is far from a certainty: Iran after the overthrow of the Shah, Haiti after Papa Doc, and Nicaragua after Somaza had each a sultanate form in what Weber would call extreme partimonialism. Weimer democracy failed, as did Russia's February 1917 Revolution. The 1789 breakthrough in France was not consolidated for almost a century. The same was true for China's 1911 opening to democracy which was crushed within two years. The democratic system in Latin America and Africa after their independence had a trendy, sad, and short life.
3. Term 'Rana', used as an honorific personal name, signified strength in battle in the medieval north India, which was adopted by Jung Bahadur in 1850.
4. For example, Communist Party of Nepal-Marxist Leninist (CPN-ML), Communist Party of Nepal (Marxist), Nepal Workers and Peasants Party (NeWPP), CPN-MLM [Communist Party of Nepal (Marxist-Leninist-Maoist)] and three others which belonged to pro-Soviet communist parties.
5. Nepal had been united into its present form in the late 18th century through military conquests of the then principality of Gorkha. While it never was a Western colony like many other countries of South Asia and elsewhere, the successive regimes had been authoritarian

for centuries, but for the brief periods of 1950s and 1990s, and they exhibited arbitrariness of the rulers of different whims and were influenced by tradition and/or hierocratic sanction. Although insurgencies in Nepal have existed in latent form for over several decades, it burst into open for the first time on such a scale with the launch of the People's War on February 13, 1996 by the Communist Party of Nepal—Maoist (CPN-M). In fact, mere transformation of elite economic interests and emergence of structured compromise do not necessarily lead to political stability. The result was yet another royal coup in February 2005 which plunged Nepal into archetypical feudalism and extreme rightism, seriously affecting democratic transformation.

6. The Maoist uprising in Nepal is not a solitary event; it is the eruption of socio-economic contradictions of Nepali. It is an internal ideological war resulting from centuries of political neglect, divisive social system, and a long conflict-ridden Nepali history. Maoist insurgency according to European assessment 'only one eruption of general, deep popular dissatisfaction.' Countless latent conflicts, particularly caste and ethnic differences, could also escalate into armed conflict. The more noteworthy of the development is that a 12-point agreement was reached between Seven-Party Alliance and Maoists to topple King's autocratic rule. One reason why Maoist rebels were willing and able to accommodate themselves with Seven Party Alliances (SPA) is that their political demand for Constituent Assembly was secured. Another, less basic but still important, is a clear and uncompromising rejection of autocratic King Gyanendra and all-out changes in governance that are compatible with the socio-cultural and political realities of the country. This agreement was however made against Anglo-American (US, UK and India) interests who wanted SPA and monarchy work together to fight Maoists because they believe in a twin-pillar syndrome. This of course was a ideologically narrow mentality disconnected from the interests of the Nepalese. For a penetrating analysis of Maoist Insurgency, *see* Thapa, 2006.
7. This denotes to Royal Palace.
8. This refers to 19-days (April 2006) people's movement which cleared the way for the creation of a new constitution that could leave monarchy largely powerless or even eliminate altogether. It has created new space for public discussion for institutionalizing democracy.
9. An interesting feature of King Gyanendra's grotesque regime is that it is never satisfied to live and let live; it wants everyone to obey and to accept the validity of the rules of its game.

10. Nepal from 1769 to 1846 and also from 1960 to 1990, the kings of Nepal have ruled characterized as rule by peremptory command. In 1846, the power however was transformed to Rana family, a native clan that under which the succession of kings were mere figureheads continued up to the beginning of 1951. The Rana Regime was a semi-hereditary system. For the valuable discussion of Nepal's political history, *see* Rose and Joshi.
11. The seven party are: Nepali Congress, Nepali Congress (Democratic), Communist Party of Nepal-Unified Marxist-Leninist, Nepal Sadbhawana Party, Samyukta Jan Morcha, Nepal Workers and Peasants Party, and United Left Front.
12. Nepali politics is deficient in two key aspects. One problem is the monarchy which is clientelist, rent-seeking and self-serving. On the other hand, though Maoists are influenced by Marxism, their psyche is governed by Bolshevik activism. We are not surprised however to remember that Marx had a concept, fuzzy perhaps but still real, of what a comrade of the stateless society would be like or that Lenin, and later Stalin, tried to mould 'a new man' or that Mao acted in a similar fashion, though he several times changed his mind about precisely the sort of citizen he wanted to bloom or boom. Nor are we shocked that King Gyanendra wanted to construct a new Nepal which would function well with his authoritarian democracy. The blame may also be put on pro-democracy politicians, who have either become pariah among the population or are ineffective figureheads or both. The restructuring of politics after the February coup must have better-defined and comprehensive methods for representation so that the people are not ill-governed and neglected by democratic politics. Whether and to what extent political parties can successfully triumph are yet to be watched, but the questions concerning the real capabilities of political parties, possibility of institutional decay and downfall of dictatorial monarchy have become pertinent.
13. Democracy we do not mean to imply that will solve all the possible problems but unless institutions that are designed in such that in democratic games all the political actors and communities have a fair chance to win cannot be sustainable, but to lose.
14. That reform may or may not be 'democratic'.
15. The argument is, whenever and wherever there is poor governance, especially economic performance, rulers and the very rules of the game, for example, regime are likely to come under attack and lose the backing of key supporters.
16. In fact, the UN has succeeded in Namibia, El Salvador, Cambodia, Mozambique and Eastern Slovenia, but has been ineffective in many

situations because of clash of interests of powerful countries. In Cambodia, for example, China never wanted the Khmer Rouge eliminated, the USSR never wanted to do away with the State of Cambodia faction, and France and the US did not want to destroy FUNCINPEC. At best, the UN can act in Nepal as a 'supervisory authority.' Thus, no matter how much we wish it were so, UN is no panacea for the problems that arms control seeks to address in the absence of a clear mandate and different cultures agree on certain basic norms of behaviour, even though they may hold incompatible views regarding metaphysics and human nature.

17. Democracy says Przeworski, is a system of ruled open-endedness, or organized uncertainty. Uncertainty is such that in democratic games all the political actors must have a fair chance to win or conversely to lose. He views losing as more central to the definition of democracy which is 'a system in which parties lose elections', for losers must comply with the outcomes of political process in order for democracy to be self-sustainable. Democracy is consolidated when all the losers want to do is too try again within the same institutions. Similarly, Samuel P. Huntington, generalizes from a number of the third wave democratizations, claiming, 'Transitions were thus helped by the deradicalization of new participants. They were also helped if those who first came to power in the new regime were not far distant politically from the previous authoritarian rulers.' According to him, there have been three waves of democratization in the modern world and each of these waves was followed by a reverse wave in which some of the democracies reverted back to authoritarianism. There is an extensive literature of democratization but for a more detailed discussion, *see* Huntington, 1991; Diamond, 1999. Moreover, during the 1980s, many political scientists, especially Latin Americanists, were in favour of transition theory: creating typologies to explain why and how countries develop democratic regimes. And the scholarly contribution in this area is immense. O'Donnell and Schmitters's 'Transitions from Authoritarian Rule' and Diamond, Linz and Lipset's 'Democracy in Developing Countries', each in four volumes, are other major works in transition theory.
18. It was quite likely that Prachanda, the Maoist Party President and his comrades-in-arms would have been killed by the orders of Girija Prasad Koirala, the then Prime Minister, if he was permitted to use the army to contain insurgency by the late King Birendra.
19. A democracy must conform to the following: a government structure that preserves the rights and liberty of all individuals where all individuals are equal before law; the state machinery is limited,

transparent, and working for the protection of the rights of the individual; and where government elites are selected through merit.

References

Almond, Gabriel A. and Sidney Verba. 1965. *The Civic Culture*. Boston: Little Brown and Company.

Barber, Benjamin R. 2003. *Strong Democracy: Participatory Politics for a New Age*. Berkeley: University of California Press.

———. 1998. *A Passion for Democracy*. New Jersey: Princeton University Press.

Barker and Colin Mooers. 1994. "Theories of Revolution in the light of 1989 in Eastern Europe". *Contemporary Political Studies* 2: 987-1001.

Blaikie, Piers, John Cameron and David Seddon. 1980. *Nepal in Crisis: Growth and Stagnation at the Periphery*. Delhi: Oxford University Press.

Chadda, Maya. 2000. *Building Democracy in South Asia: India, Nepal, and Pakistan*. Colorado: Lynne Rienner Publishers.

Cox, Michael, G. John Ikenberry and Takashi Inoguchi. 1999. *American Democracy Promotion: Impulses, Strategies, and Impacts*. London: Oxford University Press.

Dahl, Robert. 1989. *Democracy and Its Critics*. New Haven: Yale University Press.

——. 1998. *On Democracy*. New Haven: Yale University Press.

——. 1971. *Polyarchy: Participation and Opposition*. New Haven: Yale University Press.

Diamond, Larry. 1999. *Developing Democracy Towards Consolidation*. Baltimore: John Hopkins University Press.

Drury A., Cooper A., Jonathan Krieckhaus, and Michael Lustig. 2006. "Corruption, Democracy, and Economic Growth". *International Political Science Review* 27(2):121-136.

D'Entreves, Maurizo Passerin. 1997. "Justice, Multiculturalism and Deliberative Democracy". *Contemporary Political Studies* 1: 384-391.

Duverger, Maurice. 1979 (Indian Edition translated by Barbara and Robert North). *Political Parties: Their Organization and Activity in the Modern State*. Delhi: B.I. Publications.

Elster, John. 1988. *Introduction to Constitutionalism and Democracy*. New York: Cambridge University Press.

Festenstein, Matthew. 1997. "Jurgen Habermas's Discourse Theory of Democracy". *Contemporary Political Studies* 1:373-383.

Fukuyama, Francis. 1992. *The End of History and the Last Man.* New York: Avon Books Inc.

——. 1995. *Trust: The Social Virtues and the Creation of Prosperity.* New York: Penguin.

Gunther, Richard, P. Nikiforos Diamandouros and Hans Jurgen Puhle. 1995. *The Politics of Democratic Consolidation: Southern Europe in Comparative Perspective.* Baltimore: John Hopkins University Press.

Gupta, Anirudha. 1993. *Politics in Nepal 1950-60.* Delhi: Kalinga.

Gutmann Amy and Dennis Thompson. 2004. *Why Deliberative Democracy*? New Jersey: Princeton University Press.

Ghandi, Jennifer and Adam Przeworski. 2001. 'Dictatorial Initiatives and Survival of Dictators' paper prepared for *Annual Meeting of American Political Science Association,* San Francisco, August 30-September 2.

Held, David. 1996. *Models of Democracy* (2nd Edition). California: Stanford University Press.

Huntington, Samuel P. 1991. *The Third Wave: Democratization in the late Twentieth Century.* Norman: University of Oklahoma Press.

——. 1997. *The Clash of Civilizations: Remaking of World Order.* New York: First Touchstone Edition.

—— and Lawrence E. Harrison, eds. 2000. *Culture Matters: How Values Shape Human Progress.* New York: Basic Books.

Joshi, Bhuvan Lal and Leo E. Rose Rose, 2004. *Democratic Innovations in Nepal: A Case Study of Political Acculturation* (reprint) Kathmandu: Mandala Book Point.

Kohli, Atul. 2004. *State-Directed Development: Political Power and Industrialization in the Global Periphery.* Cambridge: Cambridge University Press.

Lawoti, Mahendra. 2005. *Towards a Democratic Nepal: Inclusive Political Institutions for a Multicultural Society.* Delhi: Sage.

Lingle, Christopher. 2005. "Conflict in Nepal: Political debate should focus on freedom". *The Himalayan Times* (Kathmandu): 6.

Linz, Juan J. and Alfred Stepan. 1996. *Problems of Democratic Transition and Consolidation: Southern Europe, South America, and Post-Communist Europe.* Baltimore: The John Hopkins University Press.

Mainwaring, Scott and Timothy R. Scully.1995. *Building Democratic Institutions: Party Systems in Latin America.* California: Stanford University Press.

Mainwaring Scott, Guillermo O'Donnell, and J. Samuel Valenzuela, eds. 1992. *Issues in Democratic Consolidation: The New South American Democracies in Comparative Perspective.* Indiana: University of Notre Dame Press.

Mainwaring Scott and Timothy R. Scully. eds. 1995. *Building Democratic Institution: Party Systems in Latin America.* California: Stanford University Press.

Margolis, Michael. 1979. *Viable Democracy.* Penguin: Harmondsworth.

Biswarm Bhakta Mathema.1998. *Nepal Struggling for Democracy: Big Four the Martyrs, their Revolutionary Stand,* Kathmandu: Shakya Offset Press.

Mitchell, James. 1996. *Strategies for Self-Government.* Edinburgh: Polygon.

Newman, Saul. 2004. "The Place of Power in Political Discourse", *International Political Science Review* 25(2): 139-157.

O'Donnel Guillermo. 2006. "Crisis in Democracy". *Participation* 30(2): 5-8.

Powell, G. Bingham, Jr. 2000. *Elections as Instruments of Democracy: Majoritarian and Proportional Visions.* New Haven: Yale University Press.

Przeworski, Adam. 1991. *Democracy and the Market.* Cambridge; Cambridge University Press.

Pridham, Geoffrey, ed. 1991. *Encouraging Democracy: The International Context of Regime Transition in Southern Europe.* Leicester: Leicester University Press.

——. 1998. "Theorizing About Democratization and Lessons from Europe". *Annual Conference of the Japanese Political Science Association,* 2-4 October, Kyoto, Japan.

——. Herring, E. and G. Sanford, eds. 1997. *Building Democracy? The International Dimensions of Democratization in Eastern Europe.* Leicester: Leicester University Press.

Regmi, Mahesh Chandra. 1976. *Landownership in Nepal.* Berkeley: University of California Press.

Rose, Leo E. and Bhuvan Lal Joshi. 2004 (reprint). *Democratic Innovations in Nepal: A Case Study of Political Acculturation.* Kathmandu: Mandala Publications.

Rustow, Dankwart A.1999. "Transitions to Democracy: Toward a Dynamic Model". In *Transitions to Democracy,* edited by Lisa Anderson. New York: Columbia University Press.

Sanin, Francisco Gutierrez. 2005. "Fragile Democracy and Schizophrenic Liberalism: Exit, Voice and Loyalty in the Andes". *International Political Science Review* 26(1):125-139.

Shrestha, Anand P. and Hari Uprety. 2003. *Conflict Resolution and Governance in Nepal.* Kathmandu: Nepal Foundation for Advanced Studies.

Shrestha, Nanda R. 1997. *In the Name of Development: A Reflection on Nepal.* Kathmandu: Educational Enterprise.

Singh, Siva Bahadur. 2007. *Nepal: Struggle for Democracy*. Delhi: Adhyayan Publishers and Distributors.

Sorensen, Georg. 1998. *Democracy and Democratization: Processes and Prospects in a Changing World.* Colorado: Westview Press.

Thapa, Ganga Bahadur.1996. "Democracy: The Nepalese Experience". *Nepali Political Science and Politics, Annual Journal of Political Science Association of Nepal* (5): 1-27.

——. 1999. "Democracy in Transition". In *Decentralization and Good Governance in Nepal*, edited by Ganga Bahadur Thapa. Kathmandu: POLSAN, pp. 1-21.

——. 2006. "The Nepalese Dilemma: Conflict and Crisis in Democracy". *Readings on Governance and Development* VI: 42-61.

——. "Democratization Process: Taking a Wrong Approach to it". *The Himalayan Times* (Kathmandu), 6th February, 2007: 6.

——. "Embattled democracy: The Challenge is to find a way out." *The Himalayan Times* (Kathmandu), 19th September, 2006: 6.

Tornquist, Olle. 1999. *Politics and Development: A Critical Introduction.* London; Thousand Oaks, Sage.

Tulchi, Joseph S. and Gary Bland. 1992. *Is There a Transition to Democracy in El Salvador*. Colorado: Lynne Rienner Publishers.

Wood, Elisabeth Jean. 2000. *Forging Democracy from Below: Insurgent Transitions in South Africa and El Salvador*. Cambridge: Cambridge University Press.

——. 2001. "From Civil War to Political Democracy in El Salvador: Advances and Outstanding Challenges". Paper prepared for the Advances and Setbacks in the Third Wave of Democratization in Latin America conference held at the Kellogg Institute, University of Notre Dame, April 23-24.

Zartman, William. 2001. *Preventive Negotiation: Avoiding Conflict Escalation.* New York: Carnegie Commission on Preventing Deadly Conflict.

4
Federalism in Nepal: Issues and Challenges

B.C. Upreti

Introduction

The restructuring of state has come up in a prominent and in a big way in Nepal in the post-2006 phase, after the reinstallation of democracy with the successful *Jan Andolan 2006*. There had been three major issues involved in the restructuring of the state: abolition of the institution of monarchy and declaring Nepal a secular republication state; inclusive democracy and the federal structure of state. Nepal has made certain important headways with the formation of Constituent Assembly in April, 2008 and its subsequent decision on 26th May, 2008 to abolish the monarchy and declare Nepal a republican state. There has been an understanding that Nepal will have an inclusive democracy with a federal structure. However, these provisions along with detailed structural arrangements are supposed to come up in the new constitution of Nepal. Nevertheless, the issue of federalism has become a debatable issue in the country, particularly in terms of its forms and applicability.

Need for Devolution of Powers and Federalism

The devolution of powers and resources between communities and regions on the basis of equality and justice is essential for the growth and the sustenance of the democratic political order. In the multi-structured societies local governance and autonomy becomes a necessity in order to create a balance between the nationalist and the self or regional aspirations of the people. It has been observed in such societies that in the process of development certain regions and groups are left behind due to the majoritarian frame of governance or due to some other political reasons. But after a certain stages of modernization and development these communities and regions also become conscious about the discrimination and deprivation they have been facing and start raising voices against the discrimination and deprivation.

These deprived and discriminated communities and regions began to assert for autonomy. The demand for autonomy and its implications in the form of separatist movements would depend upon the response of the state by way of exercising devolution of powers and resources to these communities. Therefore, in multi-structured societies devolution of powers and resources is important in the context of nation-building. Federalism is considered to be the most viable means to attain the goals of devolution of powers and resources.

Federalism: Some Theoretical Considerations

There are two broad categories of the structure of state: unitary state and the federal state. Both are in practice depending upon the feasibility of the state, structure of the society and the size of the society. It is generally assumed that the unitary form of state is suitable in smaller states having a monolithic society.

In the multi-structured societies federalism has been one of the popular mechanisms to ensure participation of diverse groups, ethnicities and regions in the affairs of the state. Therefore, it has been emphasized by many scholars that federalism is not merely a power sharing device but it also provides a constitutional-legal framework for ensuring unity in diversity in multi-structured societies.[1] There are three aspects that have generally been emphasized in the context of a federal political order: federalism strengthens the foundation of participatory democracy; it contributes to the promotion of secular polity and federalism promote social justice.[2] One may say that federalism is a mechanism to build an open society.[3]

Federalism has been viewed in terms of shared rule and self-rule.[4] There is no doubt that federalism is an important device for conflict resolution and regional integration arising due to the question of accommodation of diverse social and regional identities within the political framework of a country.[5] It is thus clear that federalism can be an answer to the political complexities arising in multi-structured societies.[6]

Federalism should not only be viewed as a political philosophy but it provides a practical framework for the political integration of state by forging unity in diversity.[7] Federalism as a political mechanism seeks to diffuse powers between centre and units in such a way that the twin objectives of shared rule with specific self-rule are attained. As a socio-cultural theory it recognizes pluralism as a basis of peaceful coexistence.[8] As an administrative mechanism it provides a mechanism for the distribution of powers and also clarifies jurisdiction of various power-sharing units.

However, it has also to be understood that federalism is not a panacea for all problems and stresses occurring within a political system. The success of federalism depends upon the institutionalization of state authority and willingness of the ruling elite to share power with various groups and regions. In fact, it is within a process of democratic institutionalization that the ethno-regional conflicts can be resolved and federalism is the mechanism to resolve them. Therefore, democracy and federalism are interrelated. There are examples such as in Nigeria, Lebanon, Pakistan, etc. where federalisms could not be successful due to the failure of democracy. Therefore, in plural societies federal process can be successful only within a democratic set-up. In this sense, democracy and federalism has to go together. The federal polity cannot survive without a broad-based democratic order.

The federalism is not an end in itself. It provides a framework for sharing the powers of the state. But there are several complicated issues related with the federal process. The conflict between central and state units regarding power and resources and its consequences for centre-state relations is an important issue. The accommodation of ethnic diversities and regional identities within a federal structure may lead to further mobilization of such other identities and it may not be possible to accommodate all these rising identities. Hence, a balance has to be established between national and ethno-regional sentiments through certain well established parameters. It is a well established fact that the federal system works successfully when a proper equilibrium is maintained between the federal units.[9]

An equally important aspect of the federal process is the sharing of resources. In fact, it is rightly said that the economic factors play an important role in the evolution of federalism. The devolution of economies to the regional units is equally important.[10] It may be noted here that the demand for regional autonomy is at times based upon unequal distribution of resources and discrimination and deprivation in the process of development. It is also possible that certain regions are unequal in size, resource endowment, agriculture potential, etc. It is quite natural in such cases that they lag behind in the process of development. It becomes a source of tensions and conflicts. These conflicts become more acute if the regional identity coincides with the ethno-cultural identity. The point is that the regional economic disparities have been posing a threat to federal politics in many countries such as India, Canada, Belgium, Spain, Nigeria, etc. Therefore, equitable sharing of resources is an essential component of the federal process.

Federalism has acquired different shapes in different countries and it has been characterized differently in different countries such as centralized federations, quasi-federations, cooperative federalism, etc. Broadly speaking there are parliamentary federations and there are presidential federations. There are a large number of countries that have developed distinct models of federal governments in one way or the other, such as the United States of America, India, Canada, Switzerland, Germany, Ethiopia, Belgium, Australia, etc. On the basis of the experiences of numerous federations, one may argue that there cannot be an ideal model of federalism. In fact, the local conditions are significant in devising a formula for federal governance.

Federalism in South Asia: A Note

In the context of the demand for federal state structure in Nepal it would be useful to briefly look into the process of federalism in South Asia. In South Asia, India has the most successful federal structure because in such a diverse country federalism alone would have worked. India has The Indian Federalism based on ethno-linguistic, geographical and development oriented considerations. India has fairly succeeded in addressing the issues of autonomy, separatist movements and the development based discrepancies. It is true that there are dissatisfied groups and regions but it is a fact that the Indian Federalism has shown enough resilience in dealing with autonomy demands. There are problems and issues of Centre-State relations and all that but there are constitutional-political mechanism as well to deal with such issues and problems. The Indian federalism has been characterized as quasi-federalism, cooperative federalism, etc.

Pakistan emerged as a separate state on the basis of religious autonomy. The independent state of Pakistan accepted the formula of a federal state structure but it never complied to the notion of federalism. It is true that the two wings of Pakistan; East Pakistan and West Pakistan were based on the principle of federalism but all powers were concentrated on West Pakistan that actually became a bone of contention for the people of East Pakistan and it led to the disintegration of Pakistan. Pakistan is still faced with several ethno-regional movements but has failed in finding an amicable solution. The emergence of Bangladesh as an independent state is an important example to make it expressive that the suppression of autonomy movements based on certain valid grounds may backfire in the form of disintegration of the state itself.[11]

Sri Lanka has also rejected the principle of federal state which indeed alienated the Tamils and the country has been faced with a serious ethnic crisis over the years. There are many who would believe that federalism may provide an answer to the Sri Lankan crisis.

The South Asian experiences clearly indicate that the autonomy demand based on ethno-regional issues need to be addressed properly.

II

State in Nepal: The Backdrop

The issue of federalism has come up in Nepal recently though there has been demand for regional autonomy earlier as well. The demands for ethno-linguistic or regional autonomy arising in any society always have a historical context. Therefore, in order to understand these issues in a proper perspective it is necessary to look into the historical foundations of the Nepalese state and society.

The founders of the kingdom of Nepal envisaged a highly centralized and authoritarian state. The Hindu philosophy of kingship was made basis of the Nepalese state and society. The king was incarnated as the representative (*Avtar*) of Lord Vishnu and the masses were viewed as state subjects. The society was organized in accordance with the four tier system (*chaturvarna*). The upper caste people enjoyed power and social status. It also led to the concentration of economic resources in the hands of the upper caste people. They developed a vested interest in the perpetuation of the royal authority and a centralized state. It paved a way for the growth of a feudal social structure.

The king tried to contain social diversities through power and authority. Efforts were made to bring all non-Hindu communities within the fold of Hinduism through a process of Hinduization. The regime consolidation was the prime motive behind pursuing these policies. It naturally led to deprivation and alienation of the non-Hindu tribal communities. Thus, a myth of a monolithic state was created that continued till there remained a strong centralized authority.

One another important feature of the process of social consolidation in Nepal was the homogenisation of the society according to Parbate culture.[12] Identification with the hill culture consequently became an essential prerequisite for entering to the politico-administrative structures of the country. It resulted in a strong discontent among the people of Tarai region which owned a different socio-cultural background. The people of Tarai were called Madheshi—a derogatory term used for people belonging to hot climate. Thus, the unitary state of Nepal alienated both non-Hindu ethnic groups and the people of Tarai.

This kind of situation continued even after the dawn of democracy in the country in 1950 due to a number of reasons.

Continuation of the monarchy as centre of power became a major factor. Even in democratic regimes monarchy was considered as the most powerful institutions that determined the dynamics of politics in the country. The political supremacy of the monarchy also helped in retaining the upper caste domination over politico-administrative structures of the country and the feudalistic order of the society.

The monarchy came to centre stage of politics under the panchayat system that once again established authoritarian power structure in the county. It also provided a strong basis for the perpetuation of the traditional bases of power and authority and also the feudal socio-economic order. As a result of the highly centralized and authoritarian power structure that a strong foundation of the exclusive political order was laid down. It was so strong and there were such vested political interests that even the post-1990 democratic regimes failed in altering this situation. Similarly, the exclusion of the people of Tarai from the politico-administrative framework also continued despite democratic governance after 1990. Exclusion of the Madheshi people not only sowed seeds of discontent but it also exposed the character of the democratic governance and the nature of state in Nepal. The ruling elite of Nepal created a myth of superiority of the hill culture and it being the repository of the Nepali culture. They had a vested interest in it as it barred the Madheshi people from entering into higher political and administrative positions.

The unitary state of Nepal was characterized by:

- Monarchic Supremacy
- Hindu State
- Authoritarianism
- Feudalism
- Dominance of Nepali as the language of the nation
- Dominance of upper caste people—hill Brahmins, Chettri and Newaris.
- Hill cultural supremacy
- Patron-client relations
- Negligence of Tarai

The people of Tarai resented against the exclusive nature of the state. Demand for the autonomy of the Tarai region was raised during the fifties.[13] But Tarai remained excluded. The authoritarian nature of the political system during the panchayat phase did not provide any opportunity to the people of Tarai to assert for autonomy and inclusion.

The panchayat system faced a strong resentment from various outlawed political groups and students towards the end of the decade of the seventies. The Mongolian ethnic groups took advantage of the emerging discontent against the panchayat rule and began to assert for their inclusion within the power structure in an organized way. The Mongol National Organization was formed in 1979. The patterns of political representation did not change much after the 1980 referendum which had gone in favour of the continuation of the panchayat system.

The socio-political mobilization among the Mongolian groups did reflect a concern among the ethnic groups towards the exclusive nature of the Nepali state. The various ethnic groups and the people of Tarai gave their support to the 1990 democratic movement. Some change in the nature and characteristics of the Nepali state in terms of popular representation was obvious after the installation of democracy in the country in 1990.[14]

However, it was not inclusive in the real sense of the term. The hill and the high caste domination prevailed to a large extent. Moreover, the political mobilization of the ethnic groups was weak, fragile and fragmented as the 1990 constitution did not permit formation of political parties on the basis of ethnicity, culture and religion.

In the post-1990 phase there was some assertion by the ethnic and regional groups and the democratic order also provided scope for their mobilization and assertion. However, it was more in the form of demands for larger political space instead of conceptualizing the demand in the framework of autonomy and federalism. The Mongolian ethnic groups raised the issue of autonomy and suggested to create autonomous regions on the basis of the historical occupancy of different regions by these ethnic groups. The Maoists for the first time raised the question of autonomy within a federal state structure.

Bases of Federalism in Nepal

Nepal has a plural society and geographical diversities, which provides a strong basis for ethno-regional federalism. It may be pointed out here that the issues relating to ethnic identity and the quest for cultural rights can be best addressed within the framework of an ethnic federalism. It reduces the possibilities of ethnic resurgence and conflicts that are bound to erupt in a plural society after a certain stage of development. Nepal has 4 racial groups: Caucasoid, Mongoloid, Austroloid and Dravidian.

There are 59 ethnic groups that constitute about 37 per cent of the total population. Out of this 18 groups are in the Mountains, 24 in the hills and 17 groups in Tarai. Magar (19.2%), Newar (14.7%), Tharu (18.1%), Tamang (15.2%), etc. constitute the major ethnic groups. There are 93 linguistic groups in Nepal. Nearly 35 per cent population is Nepali speaking. The Hindu religion (80.62%) has predominance in Nepal. Other religious groups are Buddhist (10.7%), Muslims (4.20%), Kiranti (3.60%), Sikh (0.03%), Jain (0.02%), Bahai (0.01%) and Christian (0.45%).

It is significant to note here that the Mongolian groups and the Madheshi had been resenting the domination of Brahmin—Chettri and Newar for a long time. The Madheshi on the other hand have been resenting against their marginalized status. The Maoists took advantage of the resentment among these ethno-regional identities and sought their support by raising their cause. Obviously, these groups have been socially and politically mobilized during the insurgency and it is now difficult to satisfy them within the existing framework of a unitary state. They have been demanding autonomy and devolution of powers. The violent movement in the Tarai during 2007-08 in the post-insurgency phase clearly explains the quest for autonomy and identity among the people of Tarai. The rise of regional political groups in Tarai during the last two years also shows the level of political mobilization in that region. Therefore, these groups and regions can be satisfied only within the framework of a federal state.

In geographical terms Nepal is divided into three distinct regions: the mountains, the hills and the Tarai. These distinct geographic regions also represent distinct patterns of life, culture and resources. The mountains are scarcely populated due to harsh climatic conditions and it is a resource poor region. The hills are also poor in infrastructure, agriculture and industrial development except the valleys, which form the main centres of economic activities and population concentration. The Tarai region forms the main industrial and agriculture belt of the country. Therefore, there is larger concentration of population in this region. However, the people of Tarai have been marginalized in politico-administrative structures of the country. They have lesser control over the resources of the Tarai in comparison to the people of the hills who had been absentee landlords traditionally and also control other resources of the region.

There are sharp inequalities in terms of distribution of resources in Nepal–between communities and regions. The feudalistic orientation of the economy is strongly prevalent in Nepal. The traditional power elite and the upper castes have a strong hold over economic resources.

Federalism is not only a process of devolution of political power but is also a process of devolution of resources. In fact, economic factors play an important role in the evolution of federalism. Unequal development of communities and regions is a serious bottleneck to the federal process. The generally assumed notion in many of the Third World countries that the problem of disparities and unequal development will be resolved by rapid overall economic growth has not proved to be true. Therefore, the federal process has to incorporate economic federalism as an integral part.[15] Economic issues that are significant in the context of economic federalism are: equitable access to resources and their benefits, rights upon natural resources, agriculture and industrial growth, infrastructure development, revenues, banking, etc.

The Maoist Federal Model

The Maoist gave sufficient thought to seek support from various dissatisfied ethnic groups and regions.[16] In September 2001, they formed a United People's Revolutionary Council under the convenership of Babu Ram Bhattarai. They constituted caste and ethnic based frontier organizations in order to mobilize them such as Magarant National Liberation Front, Tamang National Liberation Front, Tamuwan National Liberation Front, Limbuwan National Liberation Front, Nepal Dalit Liberation Front, Tharuwan National Liberation Front, Madheshi National Liberation Front, Karnali National Liberation Front, Thami Liberation Front, Majhi National Liberation Front and Newa Khoal.[17]

Further, they divided the country into 9 autonomous regions as following:

1.	Kirat autonomous region	Hill areas of Mechi, Kosi and Sagarmatha
2.	Tambasaling autonomous	Hill areas of Bagmati (excluding region Kathmandu) Narayami and Janakpur Zones
3.	Newar autonomous region	Kathmandu valley
4.	Tamuwan autonomous	Hill areas between Kali Gandaki region Budi Gandaki
5.	Margarat autonomous	Hill areas from west of Kali region Gandaki to Dhantagiri; Rapti and Lumbini zones
6.	Tharuwan autonomous	Western Tarai area from Rapti to region Mahakali zones
7.	Madheshi autonomous	Tarai of Awadhi, Bhojpuri and region Mathili speaking areas
8.	Bheri-Karmali	Hill areas of Bheri-Karmali autonomous region zones
9.	Seti-Mahakali	Hill areas of Seti and Mahakali autonomous region zones

These autonomous regions form the major part of the Maoist model of federal structure of Nepal. No other political parties have so far submitted any other model of federal structure. So whether

Nepal is going to adopt this model or follow a different one is not yet clear.

The federal process in Nepal has so far passed through 4 steps:

I. SPA-CPN (M) agreed in negotiation with the Madheshi People's Rights Forum and Nepal Federation of Indigenous Nationalities to declare Nepal a federal state.
II. Nepal was formally declared a federal republic through the second amendment to the constitution in early 2007.
III. The Constitutent Assembly in its meeting approved the declaration of Nepal as republican state.

It is now for the Constituent Assembly to devise the structure of federalism in the new constitution of Nepal.

Issues and Challenges

It appears that in the present context of the Nepalese politics a federal structure has become a necessity. There cannot be any denial of the fact that the Tarai region and the ethnic groups have been marginalized and discriminated within the unitary state of Nepal. Both the people of Tarai and the ethnic groups have been politically mobilized over the last one decade. The questions of autonomy and inclusiveness have become highly significant. As such federalism has become a major instrument of conflict resolution, peace and stability in Nepal. Therefore, federalism is inescapable. At the moment the Maoist model of dividing Nepal into different autonomous units is the only formula available for a wider consideration. It is not clear if there is a national consensus over this model. Or that the Constituent Assembly is going to incorporate this model in the new constitution framework of federalism is also not clear. It is also not clear if Nepal is going to draw from the other models of federalism available in various parts of the world. So far, generally two types of arguments have been put forward among the academic circles—one is ethnic federalism. There seems to be lot of favour to ethnic federalism particularly among the Mongolian communities. It is true that they have been marginalized and hence should be given autonomy within a federal structure. Some autonomous regions based on ethnic identity have already been outlined.[18] But, the problem is as indicated in some writings. Out of 75 districts of the country none of the ethnic groups enjoy majority in 61 districts. Therefore, the ethnic federations have to be caste carefully in a long terms perspective. But, it is more important to note that ethnic federalism is a sensitive issue as it is related to inter-community relations. It is full of challenges because it also opens doors for politicization of ethnicities and identity politics, thereby opening rooms for rise of ethnic conflicts. If the problem of smaller ethnic groups is not properly addressed, it may lead to identity politics.

The territorial or geographical federalism has been more expressive in the context of Tarai. Tarai has strong geographic features to become an autonomous region. The people of Tarai have been talking in terms of 'One Madhesh One Pradesh'. But there are distinct ethnic identities within Tarai that have been aspiring for autonomy. Here the more important issue is whether or not the ruling elite of Nepal would accept Tarai as a single federal unit for historical-political reasons at large? There are also problems of development in the mountain region but the people of this region are not politically motivated compared to Tarai. It appears that in the Nepalese conditions there would be a need to take into consideration both ethnic and territorial federalism.

The problem of equitable distribution of resources is also important.[19] The proper balance has to be created between the communities and the regions. On the whole, the issue of federalism is significant but challenging as well. It has to be dealt with a long-term perspective. The sharing of natural resources, food security, land reforms are important issues that need to be properly addressed to in a federal structure.

It has also to be noted that federalism is not an end itself. It is only a mechanism and a process not in itself a remedy to all ills. One may also be reminded of the fact that federalism resolves problems but generates more problems if not addressed properly.

Nepal's main problems today are low level of development, regional imbalances and disparities, exclusion and centralization. Therefore, what has to be ensured is development, inclusion, equity and justice and devolution of powers and resources? Mere creation of federal units would not help unless proper policy measures are taken in this regard and their implementation is ensured. The local self-governance is considered as the third layer of federalism. Devolution of powers and resources to the grass roots level is key to the success of federalism. Lastly, federalism is a political phenomenon. It would require a wider and long-term perspective.

The historical foundations of the Nepali state and the contemporary realities of its society have to be taken into consideration while evolving a long-term perspective on federalism.

Notes

1. Azam, Kousar J. 1998. "Federalism and Contemporary Discourses". In *Dimensions of Federal Nation-Building*, edited by Abdulrahim P. Vijapuri: 26. New Delhi: Manak.
2. Pant, Nalini "A Discourse on Multiculturism and Indian Federalism". In *Dimensions of Federal Nation-Building*, edited by Abdulrahim P. Vijapuri: 21. New Delhi: Manak.
3. Khan, Rasheeduddin. 1997. "Federalism in India: A Quest for New Identity". In *Rethinking Indian Federalism,* edited by Rasheeduddin Khan. Shimla: IIAS.
4. See, Elazer, Daniel J. 1987. *Exploring Federalism*. Tuscaloosa: University of Albama Press. For other similar explanations see, Burgers, Michael and Alain G. Gagnon, eds. 1993. *Comparative Federalism and Federation.* Harvester Wheatsheaf; Watts, A.L. 1996. *New Federation: Experiments in the Commonwealth.* Oxford: Clarendon Press; Scheiber, HN, ed. 1987. *Perspectives on Federalism*. Berkeley: University of California Press.
5. Saxena, Rekha. 2006. *Situating Federalism, Mechanism of Inter-governmental Relations in Canada and India:* 27. New Delhi: Manohar.
6. Mazid, Aktar. 2008. "Federal Idea and its Relevance for Diverse Societies". *Indian Journal of Federal Studies* 1: 12.
7. Watts, Ronal L. 2008. "Federal Idea and its Contemporary Relevance". *Indian Journal of Federal Studies* 12: 2.
8. Khan, Rasheeduddin, ed. 1997. *Rethinking Indian Federalism.* Shimla: IIAS.
9. Shreekumar, S.S. 2007. "Social Bases of Indian Federalism: Challenges and Prospects". In *Federal System and Coalition Government in India,* edited by D. Sunder Ram: 244. New Delhi: Kanishka.
10. Mozoomdar, Ajit. 2007. "The Political Economy of Modern Federalism". In *Federal System and Coalition Government in India,* edited by D. Sunder Ram: 244. New Delhi: Kanishka.
11. See for some instances in different contexts, Abdulrahim P. Vijaypuri n.1.
12. See, Upreti, B.C. 2007. "State and Society in Nepal: The Emerging Issues of Their Restructuring and Transformations". *Indian Journal of Nepalese Studies* XIII: 33-44.

13. See, Gaigc, Fredrick H. 1975. *Regionalism and National Unity in Nepal*, Berkeley: California University Press. Also see, Upreti, B.C. 2007. "Regional Movements and Madheshi Politics in Nepal". *Nepali Journal of Contemporary Studies* III (1): 76-36.
14. For details see, Upreti, B.C. 2006. *Nepal, Democracy at Cross Roads, Post-1990 Dynamics, Issues and Challenges.* New Delhi: Kanishka Publishers, Distributors.
15. Boadway, R. and F. Flalters. 1982. *Equalization in a Federal State: An Economic Analysis.* Ottawa: Economic Council of Canada.
16. For details see, Upreti, B.C. 2008. *Maoists in Nepal: From Insurgency to Political Mainstream.* New Delhi: Kalpaz Publications.
17. Pyakurel, Uddhab P. 2007. *Maoist Movement in Nepal: A Sociological Perspective.* New Delhi: Adroit.
18. Sharma, Pitamber. 2008. *Unravelling the Mosaic: Spatial Aspects of Ethnicity in Nepal.* Lalitpur: Social Science Baha. Quoted in Tuk Bahadur Thapa Magar, September. 2008. "Ethnic Federalism in Nepal: Challenges and Opportunities". *Nepali Journal of Contemporary Studies* III (1). For more detailed references of federal issues in this regard see: Mahendra Lawoti. 2010. *Federal State Building, Challenges in Framing the Nepali Constitution.* Kathmandu: Bhricuti.
19. Magar, Tuk Bahadur Thapa. September. 2008. "Ethnic Federalism in Nepal: Challenges and Opportunities". *Nepali Journal of Contemporary Studies* III (1): 22-23.

5
Restructuring State and Society in Nepal: Post-Accord Challenges

Anjoo Sharan Upadhyaya

Introduction

The post-Accord Nepal is agog with transformative ideas and discussions as how to restructure its state and society to meet the political and socio-economic imperatives of 'new Nepal'. However, the tracks of democratic reforms and peace-building are still not on firm grounds. Despite a Comprehensive Peace Agreement (CPA), the peace process is moving at tardy pace and there is no dearth of premonitions and uncertainties. The political upheavals and instability has not expectedly delayed, if not derailed, the constitution making process.

However, it would be unwise to be pessimistic about the post-CPA gains. For sure the continued discussions and negotiations among the stake have led to tangible progress toward settling certain critical issues like citizenship, ethnic harmony, equal sharing of development benefits, political inclusion, recognition of Tarai languages and promotion of gender equity. Nonetheless, some basic issues regarding the restructuring of political institutions and process still remain contested. For instance, there is no consensus about the appropriate form of the Government; Presidential or Parliamentary, Federal or Unitary. The initial maturity displayed by the various warring political leadership to favour a pragmatic and consensual politics has been challenged seemingly by parochial and short-term interest. The ensuing faultlines in interpreting and implementing the spirit of agreements has obviously engendered anxiety among the stakeholders and Nepal watchers. The present paper attempts to present a broad-brush view of the politics of contestation and challenges that lie ahead.

By all reckonings, the peaceful political transition in Nepal from assertive monarchy to a multi-party democracy signified a new era in Nepal. The Comprehensive Peace Agreement (CPA) which put an end to the decade long cycle of violence was thus welcomed as a benchmark for a peaceful and democratic new Nepal. However, the path of consensus building beyond the ouster of Monarchy was never easy. The promised elections to the Constituent Assembly could only be held after prolonged delays in April 2008 and now the task of completing and giving her a new constitution is nowhere near completion. Despite four changes of prime ministers and three extensions of the deadline of constitution making the uncertainties continue unabated.

Soon after the CPA was signed, negotiation between the dominant Communist Party of Nepal Maoist [CPN (M)] and the Seven Party Alliance (SPA) that had cobbled together a Government in Kathmandu contestations began. This unravelled in day to day developments. For instance, the Maoist Chairman, Push Kamal Dahal (Prachanda), impatient with the delay in the Constituent Assembly election, wanted the country to be declared a republic by a two-third majority of the members of the interim parliament; while the UML sought a referendum on Monarchy and the National Congress remained cagey on both the ideas. The jostling was not simply over the power-sharing arrangements or election mode for the Constituent Assembly; there were fundamental discords on the very character of the state and citizenship, nature of development and economy and Nepal's external policies. However, despite the strident disaffections, the negotiating parties remained determined to save the eight party agreements and to carry out the CPA mandate.

The CPA, in fact, raised exemplary promises. To begin with it brought the Maoist party having resorted to communist models of armed offensive as a facilitator in quest of democracy? Indeed the expeditious and complex events leading to the successful assertion of *Jana Andolan* in April 2006 hardly allowed a critical evaluation of how the Maoist impulse could fuse with the other democratic actors in the country. There is no doubt that the democratic transference of

Prachand Path, an evolutionary and homegrown fusion of Maoism, has been a rare phenomenon whose political ramifications were to take long time to be reckoned in practical terms. Ostensibly, while retaining its objective as a People's Republic, the Maoists tactically acquiesced in the bourgeoisie democracy to "fuse class war, mass movement, diplomatic efforts and peace talk". It was then felt that the idea was to gain grounds to campaign for a socialist democratic republic, revolutionary land reforms, decentralization and federal structure, foreign direct investment in only employment generating sectors, transformation of the rural economy into an industrial one, education for all etc.

Clearly, the repeated postponement of the dates for the election of the Constituent Assembly was a tactic to not give away the political salience achieved through the 'barrel of the gun', till they were sure to secure a formidable salience in the democratic dispersion. Their initial opposition to permit the relocation of police posts and village development committees was an early manifestation of such bargaining streak. On the other hand, the constituent elements of the SPA leadership, full of acrimonies and divides, did not have political clout and moral groundings to resist Maoist political prescriptions. In any case, much depended on the way Maoists and the SPA found common grounds for collaborative action. However, the pressure of public constituencies and political maturity of political leaders ensured an eventual consensus on a final date for the elections to take place and also held a promise which is likely to hold at least till the proximate future.

Recent Unfolding of Party Politics

However, much before the elections for the making of a new constitution were held there were challenges to the acceptance of the Interim Constitution arrangement as was manifest in the dubbing of the Interim Constitution (IC) 'exclusionary' as it was prepared in the interest of only eight parties by the Rastriya Prajatantra Party (RPP), Rastriya Janashakti Party (RJP) and Rastriya Prajatantra Party Nepal (RPP-Nepal). The Federation of Indigenous Peoples opposed the Interim Constitution (IC) on the grounds that it had ignored their demands for federalism, ethnic autonomy and local self-determination. Nepal Workers and Peasants Party (NeWPP) and Jana Morcha Nepal (JMN) opposed the provision to give citizenship to all born in Nepal after 1990. Nepal Bar Association and Supreme Court judges also opposed the IC, arguing that it subordinated the judiciary to the executive, made the Premier all powerful which undermined the system of checks and balances of power. The IC barred those political parties which held opposite views against the spirit of the constitution, recognized only 8 incumbent parties, allowed a party to be registered only if it could submit 10,000 signatures to the Election Commission (EC) and allowed the government to sign treaties with any foreign country without any parliamentary approval.

No sooner that the CPA was brought in place were there exultations about forthcoming elections and how to go about it. The elections that took place for the CA returned the Maoist's party as the largest party and soon enough the elected representatives were faced up with contestations of leadership. Seeing no option but to forge a stable and meaningful government that works with a vision and offers practical gains for the common masses the second largest party in the Legislative Assembly namely the Nepali Congress decided to stay away from the wheeling and dealing of the new representatives in the CA. The Constituent Assembly that doubles itself as the Legislative Assembly has the massive mandate of not only of framing a new constitution but also of governing the country as a representative legal body. It was natural for this body to have an acrimonious start. The representatives that were to frame the constitution with consensus were the same who were debating over minor issues of governance with competitive spirit. Consequences were that the task of governance with all its perks took precedence over constitution making. In such circumstances occupying a prestigious political office took precedence over the mighty task of framing a new democratic constitution.

The task of reconstructing the society along with the imperatives of catering to the basic human needs to reduce poverty, illiteracy and unemployment and to provide clean, transparent and good government loomed large before the CA. The task of reconstruction and rehabilitation was no less urgent to compensate the enormous loss in human and material resources incurred during the decade long violence. With nearly 13 thousand people killed, 270 thousand displaced and 1.5 million forced to migrate, this was to be an arduous endeavour.

One of the critical agenda of the CPA and later the CA was to end the suffering of the common people and their needs for lasting peace and the respect for human rights. The major source of strength for Nepal was the overwhelming surge of democratic aspiration of almost all the diverse segments of Nepali society. This was amply manifest in the *Jan Andolan II* of April 2006. This movement that lasted for nearly three weeks was unprecedented. They occurred throughout the country and the method in which they were organized was extremely mature. The leaders could direct the protests without being visible themselves, and thus avoided being arrested, causing any setback to the movement. The tacit understanding between the CPN-M and the SPA was also a major step in political maturity. The Nepalese political parties were also extremely vibrant and their commitment to an accountable, responsive and all-inclusive government substantially undermined the autocratic, non-responsive and monarchical identity of Nepal. However, they too have their own downsides. There is an inhérent lack of inner party democracy that is typical of the South Asian political scenario. There is also the generation gap that exists within these parties.

There is a need to bring about stability and real democracy in Nepal. However, the nonchalance of Maoists as well as the State on the recent spate of violence and human rights abuse does not hold out bright prospects for human governance. In any case, at this point there are evident faultlines between the growing expectations and assertions of public demands by civil society, media and people's groups and the diminished ability of the worn out state to fulfil them. The report of human rights violation amid strident protests of disaffected groups including Dalits, Madheshis for greater political space is symptomatic of fragile and incapacitated governance. Indeed the post-conflict peace building entails important human rights challenges including the fate of over hundred thousand Bhutanese refugees of Nepalese origin who have been left in an indeterminate state. The culture of impunity continues to prevail in Nepal with what seems an unholy consensus between the former governmental agencies and rebels, by which there is a total avoidance of bringing to books those who violated the law of the land by indulging in extra judicial killings or forcibly appropriating property of the rich or the landed people.

One of the major promises that Nepal holds today comes from the Nepali journalists who played a key role in the overthrow of the autocratic rule and the restoration of democracy in the Himalayan homeland. The Federation of Nepalese Journalists (FNJ) condemned the royal takeover (February 2005) and even as the army and the government attempted to suppress the press, the journalists made full use of the electronic media, mainly the internet, to communicate with the world on various issues concerning Nepal. They also succeeded in developing an awareness of the denial of their rights of freedom of expression. Consequently, the Committee to Protect Journalists (CPJ), Reporters Without Borders, International Federation of Journalists (IFJ) and other international media groups expressed concern about the threat to freedom of press in Nepal. The journalists continued to voice their concerns on suppression of free press. Thus, the press exhibited an extraordinary resilience and courage and can be counted as one of the major assets that Nepali society could count on in its journey of transformation from autocracy to democracy. The press of Nepal thus has become a very effective player in the entire dynamic of bringing about real democracy in Nepal.

Nepal and for that matter the entire South Asian region is in the grip of a crisis of governance wherein corruption, continued political instability and social conflict have caused the failure of public institutions and delayed in achieving the targets of social justice and development. In addition to promote livelihood support and to carry out local development activities, the reconstruction has to accord a high priority to a massive expansion of basic social services. There are also voices that some of the infrastructure projects could also be taken up on a war footing to generate extensive employment opportunities and to boost the languishing economy. These may include the hydropower and irrigation projects, construction of Broad Gauze Railway Line, development of Software Parks and tourist spots at appropriate locations in the *Terai* and in the Hills.

Expectedly, Nepal with its long legacy of autocratic rule is taking time to adapt to the recent political transformation. It has not thrown up many ideas on how to alleviate the chronic poverty and sufferings of the common people. If expeditious steps are not taken up in this direction the rhetoric of April revolution is likely to rebound and permanently impair the democratic impulse. The government still inflicted by incapacitating processes and culture cannot accomplish this task alone. The non-state actors could help in transforming attitude and reinforcing effective informal institutions in districts/villages/ communities for harnessing local resources, knowledge for effective implementation of development endeavours only to a certain limited extent. Ultimately, it is the people and policies of Nepal that will have to gain enough maturity to stabilize democracy and accountable government.

Global Community

Nepal over these years has shown a tremendous amount of faith in the International community. The call of the Maoists to the United Nations to set-up a mission in Nepal was readily accepted and along with came the ready support from the international community for Nepal. However, the decade long domestic upheavals have tarnished the international image of Nepal and led to a steep decline in foreign aid. Despite recovery efforts by the international aid agencies, positive indications of actual increment on foreign direct investment were hard to come by. According to some estimates alarming foreign loans and declining development expenditure might move the country in a debt-trap situation.

The major donors–India, EU, UK, USA, China and Japan along with the international financial institutions came forward to help bail out Nepal's sinking economy. The European Union upgraded its office in Nepal in 2002 to become the Delegation of the European Commission to Nepal. Four projects were implemented by the EU: To support sustainable livelihood for vulnerable populations in the mid-western Nepal; Economic empowerment to the vulnerable communities in eastern Nepal (Bhutanese refugee camps neighbourhood); develop radio programmes on conflict management and assure a continuous analysis of the conflict at the local level. The Presidency of the EU on behalf of the EU welcomed the recognition that in Nepal sovereignty belonged to the people and the EU fully supported the Nepalese people in their aspiration for peace and democracy. The World Bank approved a $25m grant to be utilized for the benefit of the rural poor and vulnerable groups in Nepal. German Government has provided half a million Euros to the World Food Programme. The British Government stood at 62.7 million pound sterling and the US development package notwithstanding its skepticism about the Maoist intent, at $45 million.

India being the prime trade partner of Nepal has a major role in helping out its neighbour in need. India offered a soft credit of Rs. 7.5 billion for the execution of infrastructure development projects and enhanced its aid to Nepal budget from Rs. 1.4 billion to Rs. 2.4 billion.

additionally; it provided a grant of Rs. 1.3b to build unified, modern check posts along the Nepal-India border and Rs. 1.08b for the establishment of a trauma centre. On March 31, 2007, the Indo-Nepal-transit treaty was renewed for seven years and of the 15 transit points, seven were agreed for the transportation of goods under sensitive list. Very recently India also agreed to develop priority projects in Nepal and also extended a grant assistance of Rs. 1875 crores for goitre control in Nepal. Agreement on Promotion and Protection of Investments, Agreement for Dollar credit line of US $250 million between Government of Nepal and Export-Import Bank of India was also reached. On its part Nepal also offered to serve as a "transit state" between India and China. Nepal and China (March 16) signed an agreement on duty free access for all Nepalese goods to the Chinese market. China has provided Rs. 180 million to invest in "mutually agreed" projects in Nepal. Nepalese goods will be exported to three major Chinese markets–Tibet, Mainland China and Hong Kong.

Displacement and Migration

The eleven-year old conflict has displaced about 3,00,000 people and has intensely affected Nepal's social progress. Nepal's total fertility rate is 3.5 children per couple while infant mortality rate is 64.4 per 1000 live birth. 6,000 mothers die each year in child-birth. Two-thirds of the babies die within 28 days, which equates to over 30,000 neonatal deaths annually. The main reason for this condition is lack of post-natal care. Despite government ban on child marriage and the law for punishing brides and bridegrooms who ask for or offer dowry, the system has not been abolished due to poor law-enforcing mechanism. There are 75,000 cases of people living with HIV/AIDS. Among these 16,000 are women (ages 15-49). Health facilities for the people of rural areas are declining due to declining investment, low motivation of the doctors and poor infrastructural condition. Medical equipment at district hospitals and health centres are dysfunctional. The facilities need to be improved. Only 67 per cent of the people have safe drinking water facilities.

An estimated 2 million people are believed to have been internally displaced. Largely from rural communities, they have fled from targeted attacks, violence and increased economic hardship. The majority of these people live with relatives in temporary abode, or on abandoned plots in district or regional towns, or in the capital. Few statistics are available, not least because most displaced people would not want to attract the attention of the security forces. Up to 2 million people are thought to have left, migrating to India or beyond.

Women displaced by conflict were especially vulnerable. Human trafficking across the border with India had also increased, according to a local NGO monitoring movement of girls.

Gender

Nepal's Gender Development Index (GDI) value is 97.3 per cent of its Human Development Index (HDI) value. Out of the 136 countries with both HDI and GDI values, 119 countries have a better ratio than Nepal's. Despite implementing in the CA, a quota of 33 per cent of seats for women and a further commitment by the political leadership to provide women 50 per cent of seats in the institutions of governance, gender disparity persists in every aspect of life. Though women have become reasonably visible, severe disparities continue to exist in area such as politics, formal labour market, education and empowerment measures. Women's organizations and international community have been actively working in Nepal towards making Nepal a more inclusive society and polity and are pushing for a more gender responsive governance.

The successful consolidation and assertion of civil society in Nepal, like in other fledgling democracies, is a *sine qua non* to steer the country from the throe of an unresponsive autocratic rule to a pro-people democratic, secular state.

Reconstruction of the state has never been a smooth easy quick task. It has mostly been a challenging and time taking long drawn process. Nepal is not likely to be an exception. However, as long as there are no serious setbacks, there is a ray of hope for a stabilization of the democratic transference of Nepal. Patience has to be exercised in any analysis of Nepal after the conflict.

With the reins of governance coming in the hands of Baburam Bhattarai, there are once again high hopes that the constitution drafting would now be a top priority. The recently concluded visit of the Nepalese Prime Minister to India evidence his resolve to do so. Expectedly, the Indian leadership expressed full support for efforts the peace process and constitution drafting to pave way for Nepal's transition to an inclusive, multiparty democracy in Nepal.[1]

Note

1. http://www.indembkwt.org/Recent%20Statements/view.php?id=121

References

Acharya, Meena. 2005. *Efforts at Promotion of Women in Nepal.* Kathmandu. Friedrich-Ebert-Stiftung.

Baral, Lok Raj (ed.). 2006. *Nepal: Facets of Maoist Insurgency.* New Delhi. Adroit Publishers.

Bennet, Lynn, 2006. *Unequal Citizens Gender, Caste and Ethnic Exclusion in Nepal,* Kathmandu, Department for International Development and World Bank.

Karki, Arjun and David Seddon. 2003. *The Peoples War in Nepal Left Perspectives.* New Delhi. Adroit Publishers.

Kumar, Dhruba and Hari Sharma. 2005. *Security Sector Reform in Nepal: Challenges and Opportunities.* Kathmandu. Friends for Peace.

Pathak, Bishnu. 2006. *Politics of People's War and Human Rights in Nepal.* Kathmandu. BIMIPA.

6

Civil-Military Relations in Nepal

Bishnu Pathak

Introduction

Civil-Military Relations are the relationships between state-civil society, citizenry and military organization(s). It is a politico-legal concept initiated by western democratic nations/societies and developed alongside the progress of democracy, particularly after the end of the World War II and the establishment of the United Nations.

Samuel P. Huntington writes that the 'slogan of civilian control' over the military was the invention of democratic parliamentarians as a way of increasing their power *vis-à-vis* the British Crown during the 17th and 18th centuries (Pathak and Uprety, March 7th, 2010). He writes, "The CMR is one aspect of National Security Policy. The aim of the National Security Policy (NSP) enhances the safety of nation's social, cultural and political institutions against threats arising from other independent states" (1957:1). The CMR encompasses the entire range of relationships between the military and society at every level (Feaver, 1999) that started with Sun Tzu and Carl von Clausewitz. Beside Huntington, Morris Janowitz effectively initiated a CMR into scholarly debate in modern democratic society. The CMR broadens the focus beyond democratic control to include other dimensions and levels of analysis (Bruneau *et al.*, October 19th, 2009).

The principal aim of the study is to enhance the level of understanding and to commence a debate and discussion on CMR among the concerned actors such as civil, military, combatants of the Maoist Army (MA) and citizenry in Nepal.

Civil-Military Relations: Theoretical Debates

The CMR has relation of a trinity (three legs), namely, Democratic Civilian Control (DCC), effectiveness, and efficiency. Putting accountability at a top priority, the DCC (leg I) that exists if it is grounded in, and exercised through, institutions ranging from natural laws that empower the Ministry of Defense, oversight committees, and executive bodies such as military, police forces and intelligence agencies (Bruneau, 2006) including the National Security Council (NSC). Two classic works, Samuel Huntington's *The Soldier and the State* (1957) and Morris Janowitz's *The Professional Soldier* (1960), address military effectiveness and civilian control (Nielsen, 2005).

The second leg of the trinity is the measure of effectiveness which is particularly focused on the fulfilment of the assigned roles and missions of the military, security forces and/or armed forces. The third leg is efficiency that centres on the utilization of resources to accomplish assigned roles and missions.

Besides, the DCC, effectiveness and efficiency, the CMR is a dynamic instrument that functions through objective, subjective, vertical and horizontal control theories. Huntington's theory of objective control developed during the Cold War era focusing on maximization of military professionalism and neutral actor keeping the military outside political affairs (Born, 2000:2). However, Janowitz tried to minimize the difference between objective and subjective control defending military effectiveness and DCC for checks and balances and power separation (Haltiner, 2000:2). Karl W. Haltiner developed the theory to reduce/abolish the numbers of universal conscription "citizen-soldiers" on the basis of civil, military and citizenry dimensions less-emphasizing the *en masse* military service (Haltiner, 2003:361).

The Swiss model of CMR applies DDC as subjective control. Switzerland recognizes as the oldest democracy and civil society federalist state in Europe, has no standing army, but it has the largest 2,20,200 militia in the world (Pathak, August 29, 2009) and people mobilizes as a voluntary army in the case of crises (Born, 2000:2). Vertical control exercises the civilian supremacy through government, bureaucracy, parliament, constitution, political measures, etc. to enhance the civil authority in the nation (Lambert, June 2005:17). It is one kind of chain of command and its command control mechanism. Horizontal control integrates military/armed combatants within civil society on the broad concept of DCC. It assesses the practical and additional usefulness to play promotion of security awareness, monitoring of the military, rule of law, publicly scrutinizing bureaucracies, types of forces among others. Such measures are to be conducted by the external actors, media, civilian experts, NGOs etc. (Born, January 2001).

Communist countries, namely, China and Vietnam talk the CMR by a different institutional mechanism, the Political Commissioner System (PCS), appointing directly from the government/party. It means the People's Liberation Army (PLA) of China and Vietnam People's Army (VPA) of Vietnam are influenced by the intervention in politics (Kamphausen *et al.*, September 2007). The particular objective of the PLA is to view its core responsibility for its contribution to the People's Republic of China (PRC)'s large national development goals (Finkelstein, September 2007). The military strategy guidelines the strategy of economic development coordinated for their nation's economy, politics, military, diplomacy, and culture developments (Cooper III, September 2007). The tasks of the VPA are 'to maintain combat readiness for safeguarding the socialist homeland and marking a contribution to the cause of national construction' (Thayer, August 23, 2009).

The CMR functions smoothly without any military-political conflicts due to single party rule in China and Vietnam. However, civilian authoritarian regime in Taiwan has started democratization in recent years. In Taiwan, the political commissioner has been replaced to ensure de-politicization of its armed forces for the sake of civilian control.

In both China and Vietnam, the hierarchy of military officers is paralleled by the hierarchy of political officers representing the Communist Party (Shambaugh, 1991). Such parallel authority is reinforced by the high level of military officer membership in the Communist Party (CP). About 70 per cent high-ranking and mid-level security officers in Vietnam are from the governing party (Trinkunas, 1999). In communist system, two military committees such as Military Committee (MC) and Communist Party Military Committee (CPMC) have developed as a parallel organization. For example, the chairman of the PRC heads both the Central Committee and Central CPMC putting him supreme commander of party and the PLA. Besides, the political commissariat monitors party's indoctrination into the PLA and VPA.

In 1969, during the Cultural Revolution (1966-1976), the PLA officer membership in the CP central community rose nearly half 45 per cent, but dropped to 19 per cent in 1987 (Shambaugh, 1991) along with the rise of Deng Xiaoping's free-market economy with the policy of "hide your strength, bide your time" (Pillsbury, 2000).

The expansive explanation of military's role has been amalgamated by the decision of the party leadership in both China and Vietnam to moderately *byaparikaran* (marketize) the budget of the military or armed forces. In the case of Vietnam, 20 per cent budget of their armed forces for 1989 was internally generated and 12 per cent of military official participated directly in economic activities till 1994 (Thayer, 1994). Due to PLA's willingness to continue support the rule of the Chinese Communist Party and to obey directives from top party leaders, the PLA's influence also increased on the selection of China's top civilian leaders that enhances the PLA's ability to shape the domestic political environment. China's Communist Party Central Committee ended on October 18, 2010 elevating Vice-President XI Jinping (June 1953-), Vice President of the Central Military Commission as successor of the President Hu Jintao from 2012 (Richburg, October 18, 2010).

Civil-Military Relations: History to Present

The long history of the CMR seems asymmetrical in Nepal, initiated with the *Dibya Upadesh* of Prithvi Narayan Shah, 242 years ago. His *Upadesh* "Nepal is yam between two colossal rocks" still relevant in Nepal (Wagle, August 30, 2010). The Nepali military has been consistently used for personal interest of the Ranas and monarchs in general, neglecting the national interest and people. It means people have a conception that Nepal Army (NA) develops along the patron of feudal forces for their own protection in the name of country. Even after the announcement of the republican Nepal, people look NA suspiciously in the lack of CMR. The principal reason of that many prominent rank-and-file in the NA has still been occupied by near and dear of feudal forces.

The first Commander-in-Chief (C-in-C) Bhimsen Thapa (1806-37) started to recruit his brothers into the senior positions in the military for his stronghold in the military. The Rana misused their power categorizing such as A, B and C divisions. Misusing state power, Jung Bahadur Kunwar transformed his family name to Rana. He introduced *Shree Tin* to Ranas likely to His Majesty (*Shree Five*) monarchy. He distributed all major posts of the army to his brothers, sons and relatives, and promoted them to pursue the aim of consolidation of power as well as (preserving) his own and his family's rule (Adhikari, 2005).

The current debate on the civilian supremacy or DCC is a part of its controversial history. Professor Dhurba Kumar says, "The army-monarchy relationship was further consolidated by King Mahendra with the adoption of the Military Act, 1959, and deepened further when the 'Act on Right, Duty, Function and Terms of the service of the Commander-in Chief 1969' made the Chief of the Army Staff (CoAS) responsible and accountable to his majesty rather than the Government (2009)". Along with crushing the democratic government, banning the multi-party democracy and putting the democratic leaders into the jail in the name of protection of national interest and sovereignty, the then Nepal Army formally transformed into Royal Nepal Army (RNA) under the Mahendra's active regime and military strength shifted from Singha Darbar to Narayanhity Darbar (Pathak and Uprety, March 7, 2010).

Mahendra captured state power in the name of nationalism compromising with national interest and security; signed a controversial Arms Assistance Agreement with India in 1965 that compelled Nepal to put under its security umbrella on the course to supply arms, ammunition and equipment for the army. He sometimes used China and sometimes India cards without any concrete *Rashtriya Mul Neeti* (National Security Policy). He signed the controversial Kalapani treaty with India (to please Indian power and politics) among others.

During the Panchayat era, the entire security system including the military was employed by confidents of king pursuing the slogan of *Rajbhakti, Hamro Shakti* (loyalty to the king is the power of the army). The Chief of Army Staff, Pyar Jung Thapa, gave a keynote speech to the graduate officer cadets at the 11th convocation of the Command and Staff College of the RNA on May 14, 2004. The keynote speech reads:

> "The crown is the symbol of our identity and the Kinships is the progenitor and guardian of the Royal Nepal Army along with the unalterable symbol of Nepali nationalism and national unity. The faith, devotion and the trust of the people towards the Crown have remained the essence of Nepali nationalism since time immemorial. All Nepalese should therefore be united towards preserving the symbol of our identity along with the fundamentals of our national interests" (Kumar *et al.*, 2005).

The popular democratic movements I (March-April 1990) and II (April 2006) have changed the political landscape; Nepal became a multi-party democratic to republican country abolishing constitutional monarchy and power has transferred from the king to civilian supremacy. However, national security was still the exclusive domain of the palace (Wagle, 2009). An unpublished report on Understanding NSP of Nepal says, "Nepal does not have NSP even after such massive democratic changes taken place" (Pathak, September 12, 2010).

The civilian supremacy *versus* military supremacy has been the confrontational issue since the inception of peace process in Nepal. When the NA did not accept the orders of the Prime Minister, Puspa Kamal Dahal (Maoist), he fired the then Army Chief, but reinstated by the first republican President on the support of 22-parties in the Constituent Assembly. It resulted in lingering of peace process for a long as the constitution could not be drafted on stipulated time on May 28, 2010, and integration and rehabilitation of the combatants of the Maoist Army have standstill. Due to the extreme pressure of the NA and the caretaker government, United Nations Mission in Nepal (UNMIN) shall be withdrawn from mid-January 2011 leaving half-way the Nepal's peace process.

The concept of CMR is a new phenomenon in Nepal. The discussion of CMR initiated while the House of Representatives transformed the then Royal Nepal Army to Nepal Army dissociating for the first ever from the monarch under democratic civilian control on May 16, 2006.

Civil-Military Relations in Mainstream Parties

There have been sharp differences among the mainstream political parties such as UCPN (Maoist), Nepali Congress and CPN (UML) on CMR stated at their election manifestos in the last Constituent

Assembly (CA) elections 2008. The Maoists focused for the presence of two armies, i.e., Nepal army and the Maoist army and put forward professionalizatior of the PLA and democratization to the Nepal Army. They demanded to construct a High Level Security Commission to restructure the security mechanism in the present context making NA inclusive. They also proposed the concept to establish the specialized security forces for border, industry, forest, highway, rural areas, etc. (Nepal Communist Party-Maoist, Falgun 2064 BS).

The Nepali Congress (NC) focused to set-up the NSP to protect national border and geographical/territorial integrity, natural resources, and life and property of the people, promote social harmony. The policy should imply security not only to the army but also to the citizens. It demands of democratization, inclusive and professional to NA. The Armed Police, Nepal Police and National Investigation Department shall be transformed as per the federal structure (Election Manifesto of Nepali Congress, 2064 BS).

The UML proposes similar agendas of NC. The UML says that the NSP shall develop to benefit security of national border providing protection to geographical integrity, life and natural resources, and social harmony. The NSP includes both NA and the people and NA shall mobilize for constructive works. Integration and management of Maoist combatants shall be carried out in consensus (Election Manifesto of the UML, 2064 BS).

Civil-Military Relations in Understandings and Agreements

The understanding, agreements and peace accord signed between the Seven Party Alliance (SPA)-led Government and the Maoist enhance CMR and DCC to both NA and MA. The article 3 of the 12-point understanding signed in New Delhi on November 22, 2005 stated that an understanding has been made to keep the Maoists armed force and the RNA under the United Nations or a reliable international supervision during the process of the election of CA to conduct it in a free and fair manner.

Article 144.1 of the Interim Constitution (IC) has stated on the provisions of the NA and appointment of the Army Chief under the Article 144.2. Besides, the Council of Ministers shall control, mobilize, democratize and manage the NA with the consent of the political parties (Article 144.3). The democratic structure and inclusive character shall be developed following the norms and values of democracy and human rights (Article 144.4). There shall be a National Defense Council (NDC) headed by Prime Minister, Defense, Home and three ministers (Article 145.1) for mobilization, operation and use of the NA. The Secretary of the Ministry of Defense shall work as the Secretary of the NSC (Article 145.4). Except in case of mobilization in natural calamities, the Army shall have to be presented to the special committee prescribed by the parliament within a month of decision, and be approved accordingly (Article 145.5).

Prior to the promulgation of the IC, the name "Royal Nepal Army" has changed to Nepal Army (Article 3.1) under the House of Representatives proclamation on May 18, 2006. The Army Chief of the NA for the first time managed to appoint by the Council of Ministers (Article 3.3) revoking Supreme Commander of the NA (Article 3.4).

The transitional provision to the Maoist army of the IC 2007 said, "The Council of Minister shall form a special committee to supervise, integrate and rehabilitate the combatants of the Maoist Army, and the functions, duties and powers of the committee shall be as determined by the Council of Ministers" (Article 146). The management and monitoring of the arms and the army shall be carried out in accordance with the "Comprehensive Peace Accord" (CPA) concluded on November 21, 2006 and the agreement regarding the 'Monitoring of Arms and Army Management' reached on December 8, 2006 (Article 147).

The 10-point CPA concluded between the Government and the Maoist party stated to hold the CA election free and fair (Article 4) confining the MA into seven main cantonments at Kailali, Surkhet, Rolpa, Nawalparasi, Chitwan, Sindhuli and Ilam (Article 4.1).

All arms and ammunition except those required for the security of the cantonments shall securely be stored in the iron containers at each cantonment and the keys shall be kept by the head of the concerned party after installing a lock. A device with a siren and a camera along with technical details for the monitoring by the UN for its record shall be assembled in the presence of the concerned party (NA/MA), Government and UN (Article 4.2).

Similarly, the NA shall be confined within the barracks. It shall be guaranteed that their arms are not used for or against anyone. Equal numbers to that of Maoists stored shall be kept into the iron containers and shall be sealed with a single-lock and the key shall be kept by the concerned party stalling a siren and camera for UN' record and monitoring (Article 4.6).

While the MA stays in the temporary cantonments, the Government of Nepal shall provide rations and other necessary arrangements (Article 4.3) and security provisions for the Maoist leaders shall be made through an understanding with the Government (Article 4.5).

Both sides agree to allow the UN and Donor Agencies based in Nepal, I/NGOs, press, human rights activists, election observers and foreign tourists for unrestricted movement in Nepal (Article 5.1.12). NA performances like border and conservation areas security, protected parks, banks, airports, power houses, telephone towers, central secretariat and security of VIPs shall be continued (Article 4.8).

Following provisions (reached an Agreement on Monitoring of the Management of Arms and Armies (AMMAA) shall proclaim violation of human rights.

- Unauthorized troop movements, recruitment, conscription or mobilization,
- Unauthorized replenishment of military equipment,
- Violation of human rights, humanitarian law or obstruction of freedom of movement of people, goods and services,
- Espionage, sabotage, air surveillance and acts of subversion, and
- Military flights, or military flights utilizing civilian aircraft, over cantonment sites without 48-hour notification to the parties and the UN Mission, except in emergency situations or medical evacuations (Article 5.3)

Those agreements, understanding and peace accord shall be revised at any time with the consent of both parties. For this, both parties agree to provide each other prior written information if they wish to make any change or amendment.

Civil-Military Relations and Army (Re)integration

(Re)integration of the NA and MA into the National Army is not a first-hand experience in Nepalese history. On April 10, 1951, ten thousand *Jana Mukti Sena* (People's Liberation Army)—the former combatants of the Nepali Congress who had been able to capture seven major cities in eastern Nepal (Basnett, March 2009) and mid-western region—were unanimously converted into *Rakshya Dal* (Defense Force) recognizing them as a Para-Military Force (similar to present Armed Police Force) of Nepal by the then coalition Government led by Mohan Shamsher Jung Bahadur Rana. The intention behind the integration was to bring them under the control of the conventional army (Pathak, December 21, 2008).

PM, Matrika Prasad Koirala united to the *Jana Mukti Sena* again in the name of *Rakshya Dal* and Gyan Bahadur Subba Yakthumba had been made its commander (Tamang: 2063). The government reintegrated some personnel of *Rakshya Dal* into the Nepal Police and Subba was made DIG and later IGP during the Prime Ministership of Matrika Prasad Koirala. D.B. Lama—one of the members of *Jana Mukti Sena*, became the IGP during the last phase of the Panchayat era. The remaining *Rakshya Dal* force was finally transformed into Home Guard Brigade (HGB) and then Bardabahadur Battalion in 1960.

Conclusion

In five years period of peace process, many agreements were signed, but the issues of (re)integration, rehabilitation, professionalization, democratization and right sizing of the NA could not be achieved except to discharge the disqualified MA. It happened in the lack of confidence building measures, radical change *vs.* conservative interests, parties' affiliation with two extreme lines of thoughts—disorderly undergoverned liberal democracy of India and the orderly, overgoverned, controlled democracy of contemporary China. While 3,500 km Sino-Indian borders have been tightened by both sides, transitional Nepal has been an epicentre of both adopting string of pearls strategy (informally initiating the Cold War) between Indo-US-West allies and Sino-Confucianism-Muslims allies (Pathak, manuscript).

In a bid to derail the ongoing peace process, the Indian Embassy in Kathmandu has sent comments on *Global Practices of DDR-SSR: SSR in Nepal* (Situation Update 87) produced by the present Peace and Conflict Study Centre (PCS Centre), formally known as Conflict Study Centre (CS Centre). The comments recommended that the Maoist fighters should not be integrated into top position in the NA and should not be included about the unit or sub-unit level of the army. Terming the integration as rehabilitation, the Indian embassy suggested rehabilitating fighters in the civil society. It also suggested integrating Maoist fighters into army only after integrating them in industrial security force, border security force and government office (more see Annex I). It is to be remarkable of that the deadlock on integration and rehabilitation of the MA ended on August 31, 2009 when Embassy's comments published in *Janadisha* national daily newspaper on August 29, 2009.

In Nepal, the CMR has been a crucial issue. The trinity theory does not apply to both armies in Nepal due to un-accomplishment of peace owing to differences on fundamental principles of a drafting of a new constitution, state restructuration and army integration. Among the objective control (maximization of professionalism), subjective control (autonomous military institution), vertical control (politico-civilian supremacy) and horizontal control (society-military link) theories, former two are outdated, but later two shall be the best assets. Besides, trinity and control theories, identity theory shall also be the best options for the CMR in socio-cultural colourful mosaic in Nepal. Civil-Military-Citizenry-Bureaucratic (CMCB) relations shall be the best asset in this transitional Nepal.

The success of the CMR depends on vested security interest of India and China. In 1950, the Nepali Congress armies (re)integrated into state security forces following the desire of India. In present transition Nepal, India has its reservation of the MA (re)integration into security forces until and unless the Maoists surrendered in front of India's power and politics likely to other mainstream parties. On the other, China informally backs the Maoists politics and (re)integration of the MA into security forces. The movements of China substantially increased in recent years in Nepal suspiciously watching Indo-US civilian nuclear deal of February 2, 2009.

The CMR is a DCC that ends the culture of impunity enhancing accountability, inclusiveness and revitalizing ownership. First, the CMR is a civil supremacy over military, ex-combatants and other (legitimate and illegitimate) armed forces; second, it is a direct coup against military or armed forces regime or those with the hold of power; third, it is a silent coup over military or armed forces supported political parties' autocratic regime; and fourth, it is a overthrow of one political party controlled and politically trained military; and finally, it is a government under civilian control.

References

Adhikari, Indra. 2005. *Nepal: Trends of Militarization (1996-2005)* Available at http://www.nccs.org.np/journal08-2/Indra.pdf

Agreement on Monitoring of the Management of Arms and Armies. December 8, 2006. Kathmandu: Nepal Government-Maoist Party.

Basnett, Yurendra. 2009. *From Politicization to Grievances to Political Violence: An Analysis of the Maoist Movement in Nepal*. London: London School of Economics and Political Science. Working Paper Series No. 07-78. March.

Born, Hans *et al.* 2000. "Models of democratic control of the armed forces". A paper presented at ERGOMAS Interim Meeting of Working Group 'Democratic Control of Armed Forces', 4th ISF Conference, Geneva: DECAF. November.

Born, Hans. 2001. *Criteria for Democratic Civilian Control of the Armed Forces*. Unpublished Working Paper. Geneva: DCAF. January.

Bruneau, Thomas C. *et al.* eds. 2006. *Who Guards the Guardians and How: Democratic Civil-Military Relations*. Austin: University of Texas Press.

Bruneau, Thomas C. *et al.* 2009. "National Security Councils: Their Potential Functions in Democratic Civil-Military Relations". *Defense and Security Analysis* 25(3). October 19.

Code of Conduct for Ceasefire. 2006. Kathmandu: Government and the Maoists. May 25.

Comprehensive Peace Accord (CPA). 2006. Kathmandu: SPAM. November 22.

Cooper III, Cortez A. 2007. "Preserving the State": Modernizing and Task-Organizing a "Hybrid" Plan Group Force. In *Right Sizing the People's Liberation Army: Exploring the Contours of China's Military*, edited by Roy and Andrew Scobell. September. Available on http://www.strategicstudiesinstitute.army.mil/pdffiles/pub784.pdf

Eight-point SPA-Maoists Agreement. 2006. Kathmandu: SPAM. June 16.

Election Manifesto of Nepali Congress. 2064 BS. Kathmandu.

Election Manifesto of UML. 2064 BS. Kathmandu.

Feaver, Peter D. 1999. "Civil-Military Relations". *Annual Reviews Political Science*. 2(211):7.

Finkelstein, David M. 2007. "China's National Military Strategy: An Overview of the Military Strategic Guidelines". In *Right Sizing the People's Liberation Army: Exploring the Contours of China's Military*, edited by Roy and Andrew Scobell. September. Available on http://www.strategicstudiesinstitute.army.mil/pdffiles/pub784.pdf

Haltiner, Karl W. 2003. "The Decline of the European Mass Armies". In *Handbook of the Sociology of the Military*, edited by Giuseppe Caforio. New York: Kluwer-Plenum Publishers.

Haltiner, Karl W. 2000. "Democratic Control of Armed Forces: Renaissance of an Old Issue?" Paper presented at the 4th ISF conference Geneva: DECAF. November.

Haltiner, Karl, W. 1998. "The Definite End of the Mass Army in the Western Europe". *Armed Forces and Society* 25(1).

Huntington, Samuel P. 1957. *The Soldier and the State: The Theory and Politics of Civil-Military Relations*. Cambridge: Belknap Press of Harvard University Press.

Interim Constitution of Nepal. 2007. Kathmandu.

Janadesh. 2009. *Sena Samayojanbare Bharatia Dutabasko Gopya Sujhab (A Secret Suggestions of Indian Embassy on Army Integration)*. Kathmandu. August 29.

Janowitz, Morris. 1960. *The Professional Soldier: A Social and Political Portrait*. Glencoe Illinois: Free Press.

Kamphausen, Roy and Andrew Scobell, eds. 2007. *Right Sizing the People's Liberation Army: Exploring the Contours of China's Military*. USA. September. Available on http://www.strategicstudiesinstitute.army.mil/pdffiles/pub784.pdf

Kumar, Dhruba and Hari Sharma. 2005. *Security Sector Reform in Nepal: Challenges and Opportunities*. Kathmandu: Friends for Peace.

Kumar, Dhruba. 2009. *Democratic Control of Security Force July 8, 2008: Left Parties in India withdraw support to Government*. Kathmandu: Nepal Institute for Policy Studies and SAFERWORLD.

Lambert, Alexandre. 2005. *Categorization of Democratic Civilian Control (DDC)*. Geneva: DCAF. Working paper 164. June.

Nepal Communist Party (Maoist). 2064 BS. *Election Manifesto (New Ideology and New Leadership for a New Nepal: Commitment Paper of the CPN-Maoist for the Constituent Assembly Election)*. Kathmandu. Falgun.

Pathak, Bishnu and Devendra Uprety. 2010. *Disarmament Demobilization and Reintegration and Security Sector Reform in Nepal: A Preliminary Sociological Observation*. Basel: TRANSCEND Media Service. March 7.

Pathak, Bishnu. 2008. *Modelling the Integration of the Maoist Combatants: DDR or SSR?* Kathmandu: Conflict Study Centre. December 21. Situation Update: 80. Available at http://www.internationalpeaceandconflict.org/forum/topics/modelling-the-integration-of

Pathak, Bishnu. 2005. *Politics of People's War and Human Rights in Nepal*. Kathmandu: Bimipa Publications.

Pathak, Bishnu. 2009. *Global Practices of DDR-SSR: SSR in Nepal*. Basel: Transcend Media Service. August 29.

Pathak, Bishnu. Manuscript. "Nepal at the Verge of Sino-Indian Battleground". *Conflict, Peace and Development.*

Pathak, Bishnu. 2010. *Assessing Maoists Janaandolan III in Theory*. Basel: TRANSCEND Media Service. May 27. Available at http://www.transcend.org/tms/2010/05/assessing-maoists-janaandolan-iii-in-theory/

Pathak, Bishnu. 2010. An Unpublished Report on *Understanding National Security Policy in Nepal*. Kathmandu: Nepal Institute for Strategic Studies. September 12.

Pathak, Bishnu. 2009. *Federalism: Lessons from India*. Basel: TRANSCEND Media Service. June 24.

Pillsbury, Michael. 2000. *China Debates the Future Security Environment*. Washington DC: National Defence University Press.

Richburg, Keith. 2010. "China's Vice President on Track to become next Leader". *Washington Post*. October 18.

Shambaugh, David. 1991. "The State and the Soldier in China. The Political Work System in People's Republic of Nepal". *China Quarterly* 127. September.

Sharma, Bala Nanda. Undated. *Civil Military Relation: Strengthening Democracy in Nepal*. Available at http://www.fesnepal.org/reports/2009/seminar_reports/papers/Article...Balananda%20Sharma.pdf

Six-point SPA-Maoists Agreement. 2006. Kathmandu: SPAM. November 8.

Tamang, Shyam Kumar. 2063. *Jana Mukti Sena: Aauta Nalekhiyako Ethihas*. Kathmandu: Akata Prakashan.

Thayer, Carlyle A. 1994. *The Vietnam People's Army under Dai Moi*. Singapore: Institute for South-East Asian Studies. Pacific Strategic paper 7.

Thayer, Carlyle A. August 23, 2009. *Vietnam People's Army: Development and Modernization*. Ministry of Defence: Sultan Haji Bolkiah Institute of Defence and Strategic Studies.

Trinkunas, Harold A. 1999. *Ensuring Democratic Control of the Armed Forces in Asia*. Washington: East West Centre. Political and Security Series 1.

Twelve-Point Understandings. 2005. New Delhi: SPAM. November 22.

Wagle, Geja Sharma. 2009. "National Security Policy and Role of National

Council". In *Changing Security Dynamics in Nepal,* edited by Bhattarai Rajan and Rosy Cave. Kathmandu: Nepal Institute for Policy Studies and SAFERWORLD.

Wagle, Geja., 2010. "Challenges and Principles for National Security of Nepal". Paper presented at the Seminar on Understanding National Security Policy of Nepal, Kathmandu. August 30.

7
Media Contribution in Transfer of Power in Nepal

Binod C. Agrawal

Introduction

Landlocked Himalayan Kingdom of Nepal was known for relative isolation and state controlled media access and exposure until late twentieth century. The limited print and electronic media produced and distributed within the kingdom was fairly restrictive though newspapers and magazines, radio and television signals were received without much restrictions from the neighbouring countries particularly from India. Other countries like China also broadcast Nepal focused information and news. On the turn of the twenty-first century, Nepal's cultural and political scene have taken revolutionary path in which kingship has been replaced by democratic order. The aim of the paper is to discuss and analyze the contribution of media in achieving transfer of power to people. The paper is based on the first-hand interaction with Nepal media persons and available secondary data on the growth and development of media in Nepal and political events. Radio broadcast in Nepal started in April 1951. At that time, radio coverage was small and limited to Kathmandu—the capital and surrounding valley. Radio Nepal since then has grown both in terms of infrastructure and broadcasting time. Added to it has been expansion of "community radio" often used for political campaigns. Television arrived in mid-eighties in Kathmandu and rapidly expended its coverage. In spite of several political upheavals and turmoil gradually private entrepreneurs took over media within Nepal. Youth within Nepal and emigrants to other parts of Asia provided continuous information that contributed to influence the struggle for democratic power to people.

> "The achievement of Nepal's citizen's radio in establishing community broadcasting and then depending it from a dictatorial regime in 2005 has become a model for public radio in other parts of the region" (Dixit, 2009:12).

Political Communication in Nepal: A Theoretical Perspective

Norris (1999) identified three main schools of thought on political communication developed over a period of several decades in twentieth century mostly in Euro-American democratic context. These included "mass propaganda", "partisan reinforcement" and "recent theories of cognitive, agenda setting and persuasion effects…" (Norris *et al.*, 1999:2). Habermas (2006) reported impressive increase in the volume of political communication in Euro-American democratic countries—a phenomenon quite visible in the South Asian countries including Nepal to-day. The political communication is dominated by mediated communication "that lacks the defining features of deliberation" (Habermas, 2006:414). At the same time, power of political communication shapes presentation of messages… in multiple ways tempered by political and social power of the ruling elite. The political communication contributes in agenda setting and also legitimating of democratic process (Habermas, 2006:415). Such political communication helps in the formation of a plurality of public opinion that would "…yield non-arbitrary standards for the identification of the courses of communication pathologies" (Habermas, 2006:416).

Media especially radio in the context of Nepal, manifested "…itself in the choice of information and format, in the shape and style of programmes …and framing of issues" (Challaghan and Schnell, 2005 as reported by Habermas, 2006:419). Nepal's political communication was reinforced by Maoist insurgents spread over large part of the country at a time when King had largely lost his legitimacy to rule and kingdom was inflicted with corruption and indifferent administration. Concurrent media development saw withering of State monopoly of radio and television especially on the periphery of Nepal's boundaries.

The contribution of FM radio in achieving democracy must be examined in this frame of political communication for "partisan reinforcement" between King and Maoist insurgents. A similar role of media can be found in case of Iran where cassette recorders were used for convening the message to overthrow the Shah of Iran (Tehranian, 1984).

Data

In last three years, the author has had direct interaction and exchange of views with several prominent Nepali journalists, researchers and radio broadcasters like Radio Sangramatha, Nepal's first non-government independent radio station. In addition, the author could interview several Nepali men working in India. The views expressed are based on limited observations on day to day reporting of Nepal television and Indian English newspapers.

Aim

The aim of the paper is to find out the contribution made by FM radio in achieving transfer of power to people in Nepal from monarchy.

Geopolitical Position of Nepal

Landlocked Hindu Himalayan Kingdom of Nepal was known for relative isolation and State controlled Media Nepal a SAARC (South Asian Association for Regional Cooperation) member country is predominantly mountainous having physical and cultural diversity. In spite of linguistic and dialect diversity, Nepali language is widely spoken and remains a major means of communication. Often Nepal is considered as "a yam between two boundaries" and sandwiched between two Asian giants—India and China" (Kasajoo, 2008a and 2008b).

Nepal is divided into three regions—Himalayan, Hill and Terai. Snow covered mountains are cold and largely barren. Himalayan region covers little over one-third of the land mass. Mount Everest is situated in this region along with other world's highest peaks.

Important valleys are situated in the Hill region of Nepal covering over 40 per cent of the landmass. Kathmandu, the capital city, is situated in Hill region. It is densely populated and continues to dominate the political scene of Nepal. The productive Tarai region or plain area of Nepal covers little over 20 per cent of the country land mass and runs along the northern border of India. Almost half of the country's over 25 million humans live in Tarai region. These geo-physical differences in three regions have played significant historical role in the past leading to the present political changes in Nepal.

Monarchy, Maoists and Media

In South Asia, the non-colonized countries include Nepal and Bhutan which have had age old monarchy. They both are going through the process of democratization. (http//news.rediff.com/column/2010/may/24/nepalise-woes-require-indian-support.html). In this process, China and India have been playing an invisible role. Tiwari (2001) believed that Maoist movement in Nepal must be viewed in the background of Naxalite movement in India and Maoism in China. Over a period of time, Communists of Nepal, like in other parts of South Asia, divided and formed as much 19 Communist parties while political movement for democracy continued. The main enemy remained King and/or Nepali Congress for most of the Maoists. In case of Nepali Congress, Maoists believed that they were supported by "...expansionist India and imperialists America..." (Tiwari, 2001:3). Many others believed that China supported Maoists in Nepal. Nepal journalists give no credence to the view that China gave covert or overt support to the struggle.

No evidence of direct or indirect media support from India or China is available in the struggle for democracy. The same is asserted by many Nepali journalists and communication researchers who do not even mention name of any country which supported Maoists during armed conflict. Tiwari (2001:4) believed that Maoists did not have ".... advantage of geographical continuity from India" and "...ideological support from Radio Beijing" (Tiwari, 2001:4). However, Singh (2009) asserted that "The Maoist have close links with China have received material and moral support from it during their 10 years of armed struggle".

Aditya Man Shrestha (2009:5), a senior journalist of Nepal observed, "The experience of media during armed conflict in Nepal have testified that the media was sandwiched between conflicting parties... The partisan role they played unfairly dominated the whole media world".

"People who have been suppressed, exploited and marginalized for political, social, cultural and economic rights continue to strive for its transformation into a modern democratic country" (Kasajoo, 2008a:83). During political struggle period, constitutional monarchy was questioned and challenged by Nepal Communist Party (Maoist) by way of sporadic but regular insurgency across country. "People's War" was supported by men and women together (it was estimated that about 30 per cent guerrillas were women).

Radio and Roots of Democracy

Among all electronic media, radio broadcasting has had several ups and downs but steady growth and development in Nepal over half a century dating back to 1951. Even in its infancy, radio was utilized "....to broadcast revolutionary messages...". (Kasajoo, 2008a:341). "Similarly, the revolutionaries started Prajatantra Radio Nepal from Biratnagar, the eastern city in Terai in early 1951" (Kasajoo, 2008a:341). According to Kasajoo (2008a) an eminent Nepali journalist, the seed of democracy was sowed in Nepal more than half a century ago in which media especially radio played an important role in challenging and attempting to throw monarchy.

Several attempts since then have been made to have a democratic Nepal by introducing multi-party democratic system to start with, which survived for a short period of 10 years till 1960. Two years later in 1962, King Mahendra introduced the *Panchayat* system which was viewed by Nepali people and other observers as direct and autocratic rule. Almost thirty years later, due to popular people's demand for democracy in 1990, King Birendra introduced constitutional monarchy and a multi-party democratic rule. The short-lived multi-party democratic system could not fulfil the aspirations of Nepali people.

After 1996, radio in Nepal grew and spread throughout the country in "Short Wave", "Medium Wave" and FM from 10 watts to 10,000 watts radio stations both in public and private sectors. Radio expansion was with or without the label of community radio since no distinction was made between commercial and community radio in Nepal (Kasajoo, 2008a). FM radio was last to arrive on scene but with a bang having over 290 licensed FM radio stations in August 2009. (See current status http://www.nepalradio.org/p2_information.htm)

State owned Radio Nepal was used as a mouthpiece of the Government and Public Service Broadcasting. On the other hand, the Community Radio reached to the remotest part with the messages of change in social and political order. Technical skill training and financial support for the expansion of radio in Nepal was received from various parts of the world having explicit and implicit ideological and political agenda.

Bhattarai (2007:137) reported "In March 2006, the Royal Nepalese Army said it had been licensed to run six FM stations. At the same time, the Maoists who have been engaged in a violent insurgency since February 1996 claims to be operating five clandestine FM stations".

FM Radio has been most preferred source of information though Indian radio is also listened too especially by shopkeepers and housewives in a low literacy and mountainous country. FM Community Radio dotted across Nepal influenced listeners in far-flung and remote areas starved of information and news. The public opinion stated getting influence directly by enabling radio listeners to hear what was happening in Kathmandu the capital and in the rest of the country while experiencing bullets of Maoists, disappearance of near and dear or killing of informers or loyalists of King.

"People's war" or arm struggle against King by Communist Party of Nepal (Maoist) who was called: "Maoist insurgents" by royal regime and radio broadcast started around the same time. The wild fire of insurgency engulfed almost all parts of the country except some parts of Kathmandu valley. The arm struggle was carried out by men and women together (it was estimated that about 30 per cent guerrillas were women). The toll of violent conflict was estimated to be 12,000 to 13,000 lives which included police, insurgents (Maoist guerrillas) and alleged informers of police and innocent civilians.

The demand for democracy was accentuated after King Gyanendra declared a State of Emergency on February 1, 2005 and assumed direct power. The political struggle took a dramatic turn within a short span of time. The end result was declaration of Nepal as Federal Democratic Republic by the Parliament rectified after national election 2008 and removal of King without clear majority in the parliament by any political party. Even after five rounds of parliamentary election for Prime Minister of Nepal no one has been elected (Chandrasekharan, 2010). An experience of parliamentary democracy of Nepal is no different than experiences of many multi-party democratic countries. The struggle for bringing multi-party parliamentary democratic system of governance in Nepal continues.

Interviews of Nepali men working in India, who visit Nepal at least once a year for an extended period, indicated that radio listening gained popularity over a period of time. These men also listened radio broadcast carrying Maoist messages and CDs were distributed and sold in the marketplace. Some of these CDs were sold in the border cities and towns of India and were available in New Delhi having large Nepali working population.

Bhattarai (2007) described in detail alternative media's contribution in early days of political transition from monarchy to democracy. Apart from community radio according to Bhattarai (2007:150-158), other media included community towers, community telephone centres, audio-cassettes, regional/district newspapers, wall newspapers, alternative theatre and video. Bhattarai (2007:172) reported that "the alternative media forms in Nepal has been successful largely due to the open environment. But long-term success even these efforts would [be] possible in a democratic polity".

Radio especially FM Radio in last ten years it seems helped to achieve democracy. Its role must be seen in the long drawn political struggle from the grass roots in the frame of "agenda setting" and "partisan reinforcement". The cumulative radio effects of political communication have brought about major changes in opinion of an average Nepali men and women who began to despise the King Gyanendra. So much so that King lost his "God like image" that was taken for granted not long time ago.

The transition from monarchy rule of the King to total democracy has been somewhat a novel and exalting experience to the citizens of Nepal. In this context, Rashmi (2009:1) observed, "As Nepal continues in its transition of defining its political destiny a new born republic, what remains certain is the fact that the Radio assumes an indispensable role in shaping the opinion of the people; and hence the fate of its future.... Indeed, the Radio has been a central pathway of connecting and empowering the diverse people of Nepal as a dynamic political entity". Based on brief analysis, it is concluded that FM Community radio in Nepal played a significant role in achieving transfer of power to people from monarchy.

References

Anonymous. 2010. Current Status. Broadcasting and wireless operation Frequencies Issued by Frequency Division, Ministry of Information & Communication, Government of Nepal. http://www.nepalradio.org./p2_information.htm

Bhattarai, Binod. 2007. "Nepal: Picking up Steam, but Political Bottlenecks Ahead". In *Media Pluralism in Asia. The Role and Impact of Alternate Media,* edited by Kalinga Seneviratne: 132-175. Singapore: AMIC and Kim Wee School of Communication and Information NTU.

Chandrasekharan, S. 2010. Nepal: Wrestling for Prime Minister's Crown: update No. 228, July 27, 2010 Note No. 592. http://www.southasiananalysis.org./papers

Dixit, Kunda. 2010. "View Point: Media is the Message: The Media must Help Restore and Protect Democracy to Ensure Development". *Media Asia* 37(1): 10-12.

Habermas, Jurgen. 2006. "Political Communication in Media Society: Does Democracy still Enjoy an Epistemic Dimension? The Impact of Normative Theory on Empirical Research". *Communication Theory* 16: 411-426 doi:10.1111/j. 1468=2885.2006.0028O4.x

Kasajoo, Vinaya. 2008a. "Nepal". In *Asian Communication Handbook 2008*, edited by Indrajit Banerjee and Stephen Longan: 335-368. Singapore: AMIC and WKWSCI-NTU.

_____. 2008b. "Nepal: Proliferation of Community Radio set to Change Communication Patterns". In *Community and Mainstream Media: Partnering to Promote Millennium Development Goals*, edited by Kalinga Senevirantne: 81-107 Singapore: AMIC. (CD).

Noorris, Pippa, *et al.* 1999. *Theories of Political Communication.* London: Sage Publications.

Rashmi. 2009. *State of Radio in Nepal* (Term Paper). Saturday, June 27, 2009. Posted in Rashmi Blog.

Shrestha, Aditya Man. 2009. "Role of Media in Conflict Revolution in Nepal". Paper submitted to Seminar on "Building Bridges for Peace in Nepal" organized by Centre for Economic and Technical Studies (CETS) in Cooperation with Friedrich Ebert Stiftung (FES), October 17, 2009. http://telegraphnepal.com/test/new-det.php?new

Singh, Harbhajan. 2009. "Maoist Government in Nepal: Ramifications for India". Article No. 1234 dated January 13. http://www.claws.in/index/php?action=detils&mid=236&u id=71

Tiwari, Clintra K. 2001. *Maoist Insurgency in Nepal: Internal Dimensions.* http://www.southasiaanalysis.org/paper2/paper187.htm

Tehranian, Majid. 1984. "Dependency and Communication Dualism in the Third World with Special Reference to the case of Iran". In *Continuity and Change in Communication Systems: An Asian Perspective*, edited by G. Wang and W. Disanayake. Norwood, NJ: Ablex Press.

8

Role of State for the Development of Microfinance Sector in Nepal

Ms. Yashmita Awasthi

Introduction

More than subsidies poor need access to credit. Absence of formal employment make them non-'bankable'. This forces them to borrow from local moneylenders at exorbitant interest rates. Many innovative institutional mechanisms have been developed across the world to enhance credit to poor even in the absence of formal mortgage, therefore, Microfinance has become, in recent years, a fulcrum for development initiatives for the poor, particularly in the Third World countries. It has been practiced in varying forms in different countries and has come to be regarded as an important tool for poverty alleviation. Although MF could possibly include a range of financial services targeted to the poor.

This paper discusses the role of state on developing microfinance sector to enhance access to financial services to a majority of un-served and underserved poor and low income households with emphasis on two aspects: sustainable financial services and enhancing access to financial services to un-reached. In this paper, a review of different schools of thoughts on this subject is done and state's role are discussed considering country context, realities and environment within which existing financial market operates. Further, this paper emphasizes sustainability and mass outreach at the outset in cognizance of significance of the debate for financial sector development and the fact that often policy makers' concerned on providing services to poor tend to ignore issues relating to permanency of services.

In 21st century poverty, unemployment and terrorism are the most crucial problems that the world community has to eradicate for promoting peace and harmony on this planet. The two later problems revolve around the central problem, i.e. poverty. Poverty is not just curse but it is central problems which give birth to several other problems such as unemployment, illiteracy, low living standard etc. The stress should be on the central problem so that one can control on other hindrances of a developed society. Microfinance has become, in recent years, a fulcrum for development initiatives for the poor, particularly in the Third World countries. It has been practiced in varying forms in different countries and has come to be regarded as an important tool for poverty alleviation. Although MF could possibly include a range of financial services targeted to the poor, in common parlance, however, micro-credit and MF are often used interchangeably with emphasis on provision of credit to the poor. Microfinance can be an effective tool in making this planet free from the curse of poverty. Microfinance is not a recent development. Every developed country and some developing countries, particularly in Asia, have a long history of microfinance.

Over a period of time a significant growth can be observed in the development of microfinance services in Nepal which is evidenced by emergence and growth of a large number of Micro Finance Institutions (MFIs) and microfinance programmes over time. Micro Finance Institutions (MFIs) allow thousands of households, usually deprived from the commercial and development banking sector, to access financial services and thereby address poverty problems. Ironically, much of the literatures on this subject are lopsided on addressing issues related to commercial finance and there have been limited discussions on issues related to financial services for the poor. The enormity of poor people's demand for a variety of financial services and potentials of sustainable financial institutions to meet such demand is a relatively new area of concern in microfinance literature. It is in this context that the role of the state in developing microfinance sector has received attention in recent years. This subject has added significance in view that proper state interventions influence involvement of stakeholders, social welfare and lay foundations for a sound microfinancial system while making a positive contribution to industrial growth.

Literature on role of the state in developing microfinance sector generally provide a standard list of measures that state should do to promote microfinance. These recommendations, among other, include improving enabling policy environment; developing a legal, regulatory and supervisory framework, and eliminating provision of directed credit at subsidized interest rates. Such policy prescriptions have limited significance to both policy-makers and practitioners as they need to be tailored consistent to country context and realities.

Objective of the Study

The paper discusses the role of state on developing microfinance sector to enhance access to financial services to a majority of un-served and disadvantaged poor and low-income households with emphasis on two aspects: sustainable financial services and enhancing access to financial services to the unreached.

Research Methodology

The information required for this paper is gathered from secondary sources through a review of available literature on enhancing access to financial services for the poor and disadvantaged groups.

1. Review of Literature

Available literatures on the role of the state on developing microfinance sector are reviewed and findings of the review are synthesized to include: (i) different schools of thoughts on role of state and (ii) fundamental considerations to define the role of state in developing microfinance sector.

1.1 School of Thoughts: Close scrutiny and synthesis of available literatures reveals that there are at least three different schools of thought on role of the state on developing microfinance sector.

Laissez-faire School

This school of thought emphasizes that the state should maintain macroeconomic stability and entrust the private and non-government sector with the responsibility to enhance access to financial services and sustainable microfinance development. This school of thought underlines that the more state involvement in microfinance sector, the less will be its contribution to sustainable development. According to this view, state's main contribution to microfinance sector would be to stay out of the way by closing the state owned commercial, development and microfinance banks and avoiding directives.

Interventionist School

This school holds the notion that involvement of the state to enhance access to financial services and microfinance development is a must due to market failure. A majority of the poor are out of the frontier of formal finance owing to failure of financial market. The state has a major role to play in expanding frontier including provision of services by different types of government-owned organizations owing to realities that traditional commercial banks are not interested in microfinance market for various reasons including high transaction cost and credit risk and private risk capital is unlikely to flow in those areas because of difficulties to achieve essential triangles of microfinance (outreach, sustainability and impact) in these areas. While experts in this camp admit the possibilities of "state failure", they believe on the potential positive contributions of the state on expanding frontier of financial services.

Moderate Interventionist School

This school of thought combines fundamentals of laissez-faire school and interventionist school. Believer of this school of thought emphasize that the state should not only maintain macroeconomic stability but also provide enabling policy environment and essential financial infrastructure. However, this school does not support direct interventions by the state in providing financial services.

1.2 Fundamental Considerations

Fundamental considerations that determines the role of state include, but are not limited to level of macroeconomic stability; stage of development of banking system; stage of development of microfinance sector; size of potential microfinance market; geographical diversity; and population density. These fundamentals are discussed hereunder.

Macroeconomic Instability

Ensuring macroeconomic stability is one of the most important tasks for the state. Macroeconomic instability adversely affects overall economic growth and limits productive economic opportunities and potential for expanding sustainable access to financial services. High inflation in particular erodes capital of financial institutions and makes it difficult to mobilize resources to expand services. As a matter of fact, macroeconomic instability increases volatility of interest rates, exchange rates and relative prices and imposes additional costs and risks on financial institutions and their existing and potential clients. High inflation creates difficulties to harness full benefits of supportive measures and state must be accountable on controlling inflation.

Banking System

Growth and development of microfinance sector essentially depends on stages of banking system development. Basic banking services are essential for developing sustainable microfinance although traditional banking institutions may not provide microfinance services directly. On the absence of sound banking system, MFIs experience difficulties in selecting a safe place to park their deposits and manage loanable fund for on-lending to their clients. MFIs will lack confidence on security for their deposits in poorly managed and performing banks where they also have to incur high transaction costs in withdrawing deposits. A less developed banking system also makes it difficult and more costly for MFIs to access funds from banking system, while a more developed banking system can be a significant source of support. Thus, state has an important role in developing efficient banking system to facilitate development of microfinance sector.

Stage of Development and Structure of Microfinance Sector

Stage of development and structure of microfinance sector determines the role of state on developing microfinance sector. State has to play crucial role if the microfinance sector is matured and complex to ensure prudent growth and development of sector. Regulation and supervision of MFIs has received much attention in recent years in the literature. The microfinance industry has a relatively large potential market and is characterized by too many small-scale suppliers although institutional diversity is generally an important characteristic of a robust microfinance industry, institutional proliferation cannot necessarily be considered good for healthy growth and development of microfinance industry. A majority of small-scale service providers are unable to diversify their risks adequately across space and activities that they finance. They also run greater risks of being subject to liquidity problems that in turn affect their service quality and reliability.

Most of these small operators have neither adequate capital nor human resources to use new Information and Communication Technologies (ICT) to expand their operations to realize economies of scale.

Size of the Potential Microfinance Market

The size of the potential market matters in defining appropriate role for the state in developing microfinance sector. Geographical aspects and population density influences the size of potential market and significantly determines the role of the state. Enhancing access to sustainable microfinance services is a complex proposition in remote areas with difficult terrain and low population density where prospects for commercial operations are questionable with available financial technology. In such areas, state can promote either community based operations through NGOs or even offer smart-subsidies for example either on auctioned basis or on the basis of the number of clients reached to commercially oriented suppliers to operate in those areas.

Rural Infrastructure

Access to rural infrastructure plays an important role for developing microfinance sector. Microfinance sector grow better quantitatively and qualitatively if basic rural infrastructure deficiencies such as better rural roads, bridges, irrigation facilities, market facilities, primary health care and education facilities are addressed and economic opportunities for rural population are increased and basic financial services are productively used.

2. Findings and Discussions

2.1 State and Microfinance Nexus

The Microfinance industry in Nepal has evolved through strategies implemented by the Government of Nepal, the bilateral and multilateral development partners, and private sector. Today, the industry reaches around 1.2 m clients mainly in Tarai regions and accessible hills. The diversity of retail MFIs is a key feature of Nepalese microfinance industry. Regulated microfinance development banks, cooperatives, financial NGOs, and community-based savings groups provide a wide range of microfinance services.

History of microfinance is relatively short but eventful in Nepal marked by costly process of trial and errors. Access to financial services is regarded as one of the essential services to address poverty problems in Nepal since the advent of planned development efforts in mid-fifties. The cooperative movement became the first vehicle of Nepalese microfinance industry as 13 cooperatives provided access to financial services to flood victims resettled in Chitwan district. Following the success of these self-help concepts, more societies were promoted in other parts of the country. In parallel, rural finance institutions were established such as the Agricultural Development Bank of Nepal (ADBN), which aimed at providing credit and marketing support to agriculture modernization and development.

In 1974, the two state-owned commercial banks, Nepal Bank Ltd. (NBL) and Rastriya Banijya Bank (RBB) were directed by NRB to invest at least a portion (first 5% to increase as high as 12%) of their deposit liabilities in the 'small sector'. This marked the beginning of the directed credit system in Nepal. In 1976, the scope of the small sector was broadened to include agriculture, cottage industry and services, and has since then been called the 'priority sector'. The credit didn't reach the poor, as only influential and well-connected people, with collateral, were able to access financial services linked to these programmes. This led to the development of targeted initiatives, such as the Intensive Banking Programme (IBP) in 1981, initiated by government and NRB, through partnerships with commercial banks.

Starting in 1975, the Small Farmers' Development Programme (SFDP), implemented by the ADBN, mobilized farmers groups using a credit plus approach, and as a first experience of group-based lending. Unfortunately, it failed due to political pressure for a fast expansion, overemphasis on credit, high delinquency levels and the overall not satisfactory performance of the system.

In 1982, the Cottage and Small Industries (CSI) Project and the Production Credit for Rural Women (PCRW) provided new directions to priority sector lending, focusing on project viability rather than collateral, and therefore provided a financing window to the poor through commercial banks collaborating with local development organizations.

In 1990, the Government of Nepal established Rural Self-Reliance Fund (RSRF), with the objective of providing wholesale loans to NGOs, cooperatives and financial intermediaries for on lending to the poor. The Microfinance Department of Nepal Rastra Bank (NRB) acted as the secretariat of the RSRF and management committee headed by the NRB Deputy Governor oversees the fund.

In 1992, the Government of Nepal on the recommendation of the NRB, established Regional Grameen Bikas Banks (RGBBs) in each of the five development regions of Nepal, modelled on the Grameen Bank methodology, while other private commercial banks have small equity stakes. During the same period, private initiatives led by NGOs, such as Nirdhan and the Centre for Self-help Development, also used the Grameen Bank methodology, resulting in a generally more efficient and successful replication. Other NGOs also gradually opted their participation and involvement in microfinance sector.

In the 1990s, with technical assistance from GTZ, local branches of the ADBN under the SFDP, started to be reorganized into federations of small farmers groups and transformation of SFDB Sub-Project offices (SPs) at VDC level into Small Farmers' Cooperative Limited (SFCL); each operating as an autonomous cooperative.

With the promulgation of Development Bank Act in 1995, Nirdhan was the first NGO (1998) to transfer its microfinance portfolio into an autonomous microfinance rural bank namely Nirdhan Utthan Development Bank. Since 2000, three other microfinance rural banks were created through the same process first initiated by Nirdhan, with DEPROSC Development Bank (DDB) in 2000, Swabalamban Bikas Bank (SBB) Ltd. and Chhimek Bikas Bank (CBB) in 2001. Acknowledging poor performance of RRDBs under public ownership, NRB started a restructuring programme. As of December 2009, four of the five RGGs located in eastern, central, western and mid-western development regions are privatized. The post-privatization performance of these RGBBs is yet to be seen.

With a view to provide a source of wholesale fund to be regulated MFIs, government facilitated the establishment of the Rural Microfinance Development Centre (RMDC) which later on opened its lending to other microfinance service providers. Further, in order to create assured financing window to SFCLs, the government further facilitated the establishment of the Sana Kisan Bikas Bank (SKBB) under the Development Bank Act. The SKBB provides wholesale funds to SFCLs.

Important initiatives in the microfinance sector implemented by the Government are:

- Credit co-operatives established in the 1950s.
- Co-operative bank established in 1963.
- SFDP established under ADBN (1975).
- Commercial banks required following priority sector lending directives (1974).
- The IBP involved commercial banks in microcredit (1981).
- Gender based micro-credit—Production Credit for Rural Women (1982).
- Setting up of Rural Self-Reliance Fund (1991).
- Gender programmes refined involving NGOs—Microcredit Project for Women (1994).
- Replication of Grameen banking model (1992).
- Co-operative Act promulgated to support the credit cooperatives (1992).
- Government-run MF programmes banking with the poor, Bisheswor with the Poor, Jagriti, Youth Self-Employment, etc.

Microfinance regulation is mainly under the Banking and Finance Institutions Act (BAFIA) and the Financial Intermediary Act. MFIs are categorized as 'D' type financial institutions under BAFIA and the prudential norms are designed in line with normal financial institutions. Capital requirement is lower for MFIs. 13 microfinance banks, 2 wholesale MFIs and 16 credit co-operatives are regulated under this Act. The Financial Intermediary Act is designed to accommodate Non-Governmental Organizations under regulation. Even though prudential norms have been designed, follow-up procedures are very weak. The Nepal Rastra Bank has not taken any action for non-submission of reports or non-compliance of regulations and 45 financial NGOs are licensed under the Act.

Government of Nepal announced National Microfinance policy 2064 on May 4, 2008 and prior to that there was no formal policy as such. But informally or in scattered way government and NRB used to have various policy that governs microfinance operation such as Deprived Sector Lending (DSL) promoting MF by government itself by way of establishing Grameen Banks or emphasis on co-operative development, etc. The policy seeks to assist in poverty reduction through sustainable, simplified and access oriented microfinance services. The objectives of the policy are: increase the access of microfinance services for poor and weak financial status family and women group and conducting income generating and employment generation work, make microfinance service reliable and accessible through MFIs, help microfinance service supplying organizations to develop required capacity to be established in sustainable and self-capable manner, formulate required law related to microfinance, and develop appropriate institutional mechanism to increase the microfinance service and to make such service disciplined.

2.2 Role of the Government

Protector Role

State should play a protective role for developing microfinance sector. Legal and regulatory environment is the main tool for the state to demonstrate the protective role. Regulation becomes a necessity with development of microfinance sector in order to protect savers, allow MFIs to mobilize external resources and offer them an official recognition against their informal and sometimes unfair competitors. Regulation must strengthen microfinance movement and should not impede its development with rigid rules. Regulation should encourage innovation providing flexibility for institutional forms. Compared to commercial banks, transparency in financial accounting and objectives of sustainability should be the same among MFIs, but some aspects like liquidity requirements may be stricter given the seasonality of demand, dependency on donors' undo or short-term liabilities. Further, some rules may be more flexible such as recognizing concept of solidarity group as a guarantee and approval of uncollateralized loans.

Proper functioning of the protector role of the state is most essential, because it builds trust and addresses imbalances between customers and financial institutions. The protection role of the state will be more challenging with the introduction of new products and services such as home mortgages, consumer loans, etc., delivery channels such as branchless banking, and players such as non-bank finance companies, telecommunication companies, retailers, etc.

Provider Role

In certain circumstances state should be engaged as a Provider of financial services to the poor and disadvantaged groups. Given that the performance of state-owned financial institutions and programmes varies, there are cases where state has engaged as a direct Provider of financial services, especially subsidized credit, as one of the least efficient policy interventions for sustainable access. Such a role combines both financial and policy objectives. Although state-owned microfinance services providers typically are expected to at least break even, they often do not because of policy objective challenges. Such institutions tend to perform relatively better on outreach than profitability. They require massive periodic recapitalizations, demanding extensive public funding that could have served other policy purposes such as health or education or created incentives and support for private institutions to deliver pro-poor finance. Those institutions with stronger outreach often perform better financially. Having the state act as provider of financial services also may create unfair competition by offering subsidized credit and erode payment culture if collections are more relaxed. The state backed institutions can play a more positive role in providing payment or savings services than subsidized credit.

Promotional Role

State has many options to serve as promoter of financial inclusion. The model of integration of microfinance within public sector enables expansion of outreach among rural population. The development of MFIs as an alternative to deficient role of the state and market incurs lots of constraints that may limit their outreach. Under such circumstances, role of the state can be to invest in network building: a minimum banking structure can facilitate development of a rural financial system where complimentarily between institutions increases outreach and sustainability. In terms of depth of outreach, neither integrated/complementary, nor alternative model of microfinance *vis-à-vis* the public sector adequately reach the poorest of the poor. This may arise from inherent limitations of microfinance as a tool to reduce extreme poverty. In this case, financial interventions are just part of a range of choices for development assistance seeking to reduce poverty.

For adopting innovations, model that integrates microfinance within public sector can help support its adoption as a public good. The state could play a role in implementing innovations such as microfinance services to agriculture or insurance services. Further, a balance of power must be created between state, local authorities and financial institutions through external control to avoid political intrusion while ensuring a dynamic adoption of innovation and sound financial practices. Global best practices indicate that MFIs require subsidies for start-up investment and network building and for other innovations such as micro-insurance schemes. Further, addressing extreme poverty requires complementary services such as infrastructure, education, health, etc. that can be offered through NGOs or state services, but independently from financial services.

2.3 State's Priorities in Microfinance Sector

A discussion on some of the priorities of the state on developing microfinance sector follows hereunder. Complete phase out of directed credit programmes. While it is generally assumed that the old directed credit paradigm is out and the new paradigm of financial system development is dominant and widely accepted, Nepal continue to have significant directed credit programmes or have re-introduced in one form or other (Youth Employment Programme) to channel credit on sectors considered important for addressing poverty problems. Budgetary funds are used and part of the deprived sector lending resources is diverted on such purposes. Since, these programmes insist on loan disbursement and are not very serious about loan recoveries, there is likelihood that the scheme may weaken financial institutions. They also damage potential for sustainable development of microfinance market primarily through weakening of financial discipline among borrowers and reducing incentives for operations by commercially oriented service providers. Therefore, it is essential for the governments to phase out such programmes where they exist and stay away from those in future as a policy. The rush to substitute short-cuts for building sustainable microfinance systems is most likely to reduce social welfare of the poor in the long-term.

Support ICT Development in Rural Areas

State's interventions are needed to support use of new Information and Communication Technology (ICT) in rural areas because these cannot only expand size of potential markets but also reduce transaction costs and risks for both clients and service providers. Supportive policies by governments are required to deal with emerging "digital divide" between urban and rural areas and enable rural financial institutions to take advantage of ICTs.

Allow More Room for Foreign Equity Participation

The state can also make a significant contribution to microfinance industry by liberalizing foreign investments in the industry. In general, most Nepalese MFIs still do not have a capacity to bear foreign exchange risk associated with borrowing in foreign currency. On the other hand, many social investors are interested in investing their funds in microfinance industry but are unable to make equity investments in MFIs because of restrictions imposed by the state. If government can initially allow and facilitate equity investments by foreign social investors, this market could be more dynamic. The experience of equity investments of such social investors may be used to determine whether microfinance market liberalization should be deepened to include commercial investors.

Reform State-owned Rural Financial Institutions

Nepal has taken effective measures to reform state-owned rural financial institutions and contributed significantly to sustainable development of microfinance industry. A notable example is the Agriculture Development Bank, two state-owned commercial banks (NBL and RBB), SKBB and GGBBs. Notwithstanding these, Nepal continue to rely on state-owned rural financial institutions that adopt old paradigm of subsidized credit and continue to undermine potential for sustainable microfinance. There is a need to take a fresh look at these institutions with a view to either reforming or liquidating them. Emerging evidence appears to suggest that their physical infrastructure can be effectively used to provide financial services for rural population including the poor, provided that state is willing and committed to introduce and implement essential reforms. The state has mobilized financial and technical support for such reforms from multilateral financial institutions such as Asian Development Bank, World Bank, etc.

Microfinance and Poverty Reduction

There has been substantial progress over the last three decades or so in design and delivery of financial services to the poor on a sustainable basis. The clients' loan repayment capacity is a prerequisite for any microfinance services to implement well. Clients must have the capacity to repay the loan under the terms by which it is provided. Otherwise, clients may not be able to benefit from credit and rather it will risk them being pushed into debt problems. This sounds obvious, but microcredit is viewed by some as "one size fits all". Instead, microcredit should be carefully evaluated against the alternatives when choosing the most appropriate intervention tool for a specific situation. In general, microfinance services assist the poor to break the vicious cycle of poverty. However, there exist evidences that microcredit is an inappropriate intervention in situations where conditions pose severe challenges to standard microcredit methodologies. In populations that are geographically dispersed or nomadic; with a high incidence of debilitating illnesses (e.g., HIV/AIDS), depending on a single economic activity or single agricultural crop or reliance on barter rather than cash transactions, etc. are not suitable microfinance candidates. The presence of hyperinflation or absence of law and order may stress the ability of microfinance to operate. Microcredit is also much more difficult when laws and regulations create significant barriers (e.g. by mandating interest-rate caps) to sustainability of MFIs. Only the strong and innovative MFIs are able to operate even in extremely challenging circumstances. These providers uphold two prerequisites of successful microcredit: discipline both for clients (timely repayment) and institutions (business practices that lead to sustainability); and no subsidization of interest rates. There could be some alternatives to microcredit that can assist poor to break the poverty trap.

Role of Regulation and Supervision in Microfinance

All the commercial MFIs are regulated to protect their depositors and prevent risks to financial system. Best practices principles has been that credit-only MFIs do not take deposits from public and are too small to pose much risk for financial system, hence, should not be regulated. Regulation by financial authorities is needed for MFIs that take deposits. In effect, only the savings-based financial cooperatives or credit-based MFIs that want to start taking deposits to finance their growth are to be regulated. This is not the case. In Nepal all the registered MFIs have been brought under the purview of regulations and supervision. As a matter of fact, MFIs that do not take deposits do not need intensive regulation and supervision, but they do need a certain minimum regulatory structure in order to operate.

Conclusion

The status of the microfinance market clearly shows that the state has an important role to play in developing a sustainable microfinance industry. The outcome of involvement of the state on developing microfinance sector is mixed and suggested optimal roles state can play to foster permanent financial access for the poor and recommend that the states' role should be confined as an enabler and not as a direct provider of financial services. State could develop a vision of integrating microfinance into broader financial sector and articulating complimentarily between private and public roles in building inclusive access to finance. The vision being developed could explore ways to promote expanded access to commercial financing. Such a vision should be anchored in a solid understanding of the stage of financial-sector development and key access gaps and obstacles, so that state can tailor interventions accordingly. A good diagnostic assessment that identifies barriers and institutional capacity should always precede selection of appropriate interventions. State should play an important role in setting a supportive policy environment that stimulates expansion of financial services in remote areas while protecting poor people's savings and suggest that the state's involvement should concentrate at maintaining macroeconomic stability, avoiding interest-rate caps, and refraining from distorting market with unsustainable subsidized and high-delinquency loan programmes. State can also support financial services for the poor by improving business environment for entrepreneurs, clamping down on corruption and improving access to markets and infrastructure. At the most, in a very much specialized situation. state funding for sound and independent microfinance institutions in remote areas may be warranted when other funds are lacking and where enhancing access to financial services is one of the challenges for improved livelihood situation of the poor and disadvantaged groups.

References

Report of Nara Hari Dhakal entitled "Role of the State for the Development of the Microfinance Sector".

ADB. 2000. "Finance for the Poor: Microfinance Development Strategy". Available at http://www.adb.org

ADB, Manila and NRB, Kathmandu. 1994. "Nepal Rural Credit Review Final Report Volume 1 (Summary Report)", Kathmandu.

Charitonenko, S. and S.M. Rahman. 2002. "Commercialization of Microfinance: Bangladesh". Manila: Asian Development Bank. September.

Charitonenko, S. and D. de Silva. 2002. "Commercialization of Microfinance: Sri Lanka (Draft)". Manila: Asian Development Bank. December.

Development Project Service Center, Nepal and J. Ledgerwood. 1997. "Critical Issues in Nepalese Microfinance Circumstances". Maryland: IRIS Centre.

Dhakal, N.H. 2007. "Towards Expanding the Frontier of Microfinance Services in Nepal" a paper presented in an International Conference on Rural Finance Research: Bringing Research into Policy and Practices, organized jointly by FAO, IFAD and Ford Foundation during 19-21 March, 2007 in FAO Headquarters in Rome, Italy.

Dingcong, C.G. and L.M. Joyas. 1998. "Profile of Philippine Microfinance NGOs: A Nationwide Survey". Microfinance Coalition for Standards, Manila. August.

Fernando, N.A. 2001. "Proliferation of Microfinance Institutions", *Finance for the Poor* 2(3). September.

Gonzales-Vega 1997. "The New Development Finance", *Economics and Sociology*. Occasional Paper No. 2398, The Ohio State University. October.

Long, M. 1999. "A 1999 Perspective on Finance and Development: Development Report 1989". A presentation made at the Third Annual Seminar on new Development Finance at Frankfurt, Germany. September.

Meyer, R.L. and G. Nagarajan. 2001. *Rural Financial Markets in Asia: Policies, Paradigms, and Performance*. Hong Kong: Oxford University Press.

Rhyne, E. 2001. *Mainstreaming Microfinance: How Lending to the Poor Began, Grew, and Came of Age in Bolivia.* West Hartford, Connecticut: Kumarian Press.

Robinson, M.S. 2001. *The Microfinance Revolution. Sustainable Finance for the Poor.* Washington DC.: The World Bank.

Sharma, S.R. and V. Nepal. 1997. *Strengthening of Credit Institutions/ Programmes for Rural Poverty Alleviation in Nepal.* Bangkok: ESCAP.

Sinha, S. 2000. "Nepal Country Study in Asian Development Bank 2000". In *The Role of Central Banks in Microfinance in Asia and the Pacific.* Manila: ADB.

9

Economic Development Imperatives and Impact of Globalization in Nepal

Sujit Ranjan Prasad and *Raman Ranjan*

Introduction

The world is under the transitory phase of evolutionary transformation into the "Borderless world" as conceived by Kenechi Ohmae. Global trade environment has changed due to the changes in trading framework. The process of Globalization was initiated with the inception of GATT (General Agreement on Tariffs and Trade) in 1948. Its arduous task confronted many hindrances opposition and culminated in the institutional transition to WTO (World Trade Organization).

Though Nepal has pursued open trading system since 1951, Government regulated the market and intervened in every sphere of the economy, which ultimately deteriorated the condition. Apart from this, lack of mineral resources, inhospitable terrain, lack of adequate infrastructure, reliance on foreign aid, majority of agrarian population, illiteracy, poor health care facilities, shortage of safe drinking water, political instability and Maoist violence are some of the drawbacks which Nepal has confronted since it started Economic Planning in 1956. Though fiscal conditions remained satisfactory for a long period of time it could not be maintained due to the growing external and internal instability. In 1980s, fiscal deficit was reported, which grew over the years. Balance of Payments (BOP) also showed negative trend. As a consequence, Nepal agreed to IMF Structural Adjustment Programme (SAP). Reforms were initiated as a preliminary measure with deregulation, liberalization and privatization, in several spheres of the economy.

These measures were met with opposition and criticism. Despite the hindrances, differing perceptions and opposition to Globalization, there has been unequivocal acceptance of its developmental imperatives. This paper examines the conditions, contributions, change, and challenges that Globalization had on economic development imperatives in Nepal.

The world is under the transitory phase of evolutionary transformation into the "Borderless World" as conceived by Kenechi Ohmae. Global Trade environment has changed due to the changes in trading framework. Globalization has played an important role in sustaining the economic expansion of Global economy. After initial reluctance, developing countries and LDCs opted for globalization as a perquisite for GATT membership, WTO commitments and under pressure from International financial institutions.

Until 1980s, Nepal remained an Agrarian economy with respect to output and employment. Although economic planning started with the introduction of First Five Year Plan in 1956, Nepal closely followed the economic policies of India. It followed the import substitution industrialization policy. In this process agriculture, industry and commerce sectors could not grow and modernize. Government regulated the markets and interfered in every sphere of the economy, resulting in subdued productive capacity, and macro-economic and structural imbalances. Moreover, there was political instability, mass protest and Maoist violence [from 1996 onwards]. The combined effect of these events was increased budgetary, trade, current account and Balance Of Payment (BOP) deficit. From 1982-83 to 1984-85 there was constant BOP deficit. Thus, Nepal promptly accepted the developmental prescription of IMF and World Bank and implemented economic stabilization programme and structural adjustment programme.

The primary objective of this paper is to assess the impact of globalization on economic development imperatives of Nepal. Such assessment is necessary for review of achievement and further policy intervention. This paper is divided into seven sections. Section 2 describes the country profile. Section 3 enumerates the economic development imperatives and their status under various five year plans. Section 4 defines and discusses various aspects of globalization concisely Section 5 details the process of globalization in Nepal. Section 6 assess the impact of globalization on economic development imperatives in Nepal. Section 7 ends the paper by discussing the conclusions.

Country Profile

The Himalayan Kingdom as Nepal is referred to, is situated in South Asia, along the southern slopes of the Himalayan mountain range. It is like an irregular rectangle and lies between 80°4′ to 88°12′ East longitudes and 26°22′North to 30°27′North latitude. The landlocked country is about 885 kms. long and 201 kms. wide. Its neighbours are China in the North and India in the South. The international border with China is 1078 kms. long and that with India is 1593 kms. The total land area is 1,41,499 sq. kms.

Nepal can be divided into 3 major physical regions that runs parallel to one another from east to west.

(i) The Tarai, which is an extension of great Gangetic Plain of India, lies south of the "Siwalik Range" (sometimes known as Churia Hills). Its average width is 16 kms. to 25 kms. and extends along the boundary with India.

(ii) The inner Tarai, situated between the Siwalik Range and "Mahabharat Lekh", consists of hills and broad basins. Kathmandu valley is a circular basin and lies in this region.

(iii) The mountain region stretching from Mahabharat Lekh to the Great Himalaya including lesser Himalayas and covers 65 per cent of the total area. (Encyclopedia Americana, 2006)

Entire country is drained by 3 river systems which drain from north to south cutting through various ranges that divide the country. These river systems are: (a) Gogra (Karnali), (b) Gandak (Narayani), and (c) Sapt Kosi.

Population of Nepal is estimated at 25.3 million (ADB, 2006) with per capita income of $310 (US$). Large majority of people live in 29,120 villages (Shukla, 1993). 91 per cent of the people are Hindu, 8 per cent Buddhist and 1 per cent Muslim. Christian missionaries are admitted but conversion is forbidden.

About 90 per cent of the country's workforce is engaged in agriculture. 42 per cent of people are below poverty line. The main crops are rice, maize, millet, wheat, potatoes, oilseeds, sugarcane, tobacco, jute, fruits and vegetables.

Manufacturing plays an important role in Nepal. However, a few medium scale industry and a large number of small scale industries exist. Most of them are connected with the processing of food and other agricultural products.

Nepal emphasized its development programmes in a series of Five Year Plans. In the beginning primary emphasis of plans was infrastructure development. Agriculture development was addressed from Fifth Five Year Plan. From Sixth Five Year Plan poverty alleviation was taken on priority basis.

The constitution of 1959 provided for a bicameral legislature, but the Government was dismissed by King Mahendra. In December 1962, another constitution was promulgated which provided for the Panchyat system of governance. In 1990, a new constitution was promulgated which provided for the multiparty parliamentary system of Government. From 1996 onwards when Communist Party of Nepal (Maoist) [CPN (M)] was formed, violence and unrest increased. King Gyanendra suspended the Government in 2002. In May 2006, seven party-CPN (M) alliance formed the government and proclaimed Nepal to be a Sovereign Republic.

Economic Development Imperatives

Quest for economic development in Nepal started with the end of Rana regime in 1951. Owing to unique geographical location, size, topography and LDC status, Nepal's economic development imperatives include infrastructure development, lowering population growth, poverty reduction, human capital formation, raising employment and lowering underemployment, tapping hydroelectric power potential, reducing overdependence on agriculture, directing labour towards secondary and tertiary sector, increasing agricultural productivity, strengthening tourism industry, developing market oriented private sector, devising industrial growth, developing foreign trade, developing and diversifying exports, establishing administrative and public services institution to support economic development, and attaining economic stability.

With these economic development imperatives, economic planning began in 1956 with the introduction of First Five Year Plan. The series of five year plans pronounced Government's development imperatives and strategy. Each plan had different developmental priorities but the resource allocation did not always reflect these priorities. Each of the plans depended heavily on foreign assistance in the form of grants and loans. First Four Five Year Plans (FYP) concentrated on infrastructure development in order to facilitate the movement of goods and services.

The First Five Year Plan (1956-1961) allocated about Rs. 576 million for development expenditure. 36 per cent of budget expenditure was allocated to transport and communication and 20 per cent was provided to agriculture, including village development and irrigation. This plan also focused in statistical data collection and resulted in actual expenditure of about Rs. 382.9 million. In most cases together were missed by wide margin.

The Second Five Year Plan (1962-65) was introduced in 1962 and covered only 3 years had an expenditure of Rs. 615 million. 39 per cent of the budget expenditure was allocated to transport and communication. Industry, tourism and social services was second priority. This plan made some improvement in industrial production, road construction, telephone installation, irrigation and education. These two five year plans were developed with minimal database and both depended on foreign aid.

The Third Five Year Plan (1965-70) gave priority to transport and communication, industrial and agricultural development. Total expenditure was Rs. 1.6 billion. The priority of Fourth Five Year Plan (1970-75) too was transport and communication with 41.2 per cent of budget allocation. Whereas agriculture was allocated 26 per cent of the budget. The Third and Fourth Five Year Plans increased involvement of Panchayats in development process.

The Fifth Five Year Plan (1975-80) addressed the problem of poverty for the first time. Top priority was given to agricultural development and emphasis was on increasing food production and cash crops. Increased industrial production, social services and controlling population growth was on priority agenda. Agriculture remained top priority of the Sixth Five Year Plan (1980-85). Social service received second priority and budget allocation to transport and communication was less than the previous plans.

The Seventh Five Year Plan (1985-90) encouraged private sector and local Government participation in the economy. The plan also targeted increasing productivity in all sectors, expanding opportunity for employment and fulfilling basic need of the people. The availability of food, clothing, fuel, wood, drinking water, primary healthcare, sanitation, primary and skill based education and minimum transport facilities was emphasized.

The Sixth and Seventh Five Year Plans were successful in achieving targets but due to stagnant exports and high increase in imports, there was trade deficit and negative Balance of Payments (BoP).

The Eighth Five Year Plan (1992-97) made provisions for privatization and liberalization. Major objective of this plan was sustainable economic growth, poverty alleviation, reduction of regional imbalances and employment generation.

Ninth Five Year Plan (1997-2000), laid emphasis on investments in agriculture and hydroelectric power and carried forward the agenda of liberalization and privatization. This plan also adopted a long-term approach to poverty reduction by 10 per cent by 2017.

Under the Tenth Five Year Plan (2002-2007) priorities have shifted to security and poverty reduction, but with renewed emphasis on privatization and efforts to encourage private investment.

The developmental priorities of various five year plans were outcome of the Government's policies. The paradigm shift in Government's policies owing to Globalization was reflected in the Budget. The next section briefly discusses the concept of globalization.

Globalization

Free flow of goods and services, technology capital and even labour or human capital across borders is termed globalization (Datt and Sundaram). Kenechi Ohmae (2005) view globalization as the liberalization of the individual, consumers and corporations and regions from the legacy of the nation state in which they belong. It is described as the process of increasing economic and non-economic linkages across nations of the world. Combination of deregulation, liberalization and privatization denotes globalization (ILO, 200 4b).

It has been widely accepted that globalization has 3 components viz. (i) Liberalization of international trade, (ii) Expansion of FDI, and (iii) The emergence of massive cross-border financial flows. (WCSDG, ILO 2004a)

Developed countries limit the definition to these 3 components only and insist on developed countries to accept their definition and conduct debate on globalization within the parameters set by them. But from the point of view of developing countries, the definition of globalization is incomplete without the addition of the fourth component viz. (iv) Unrestricted flow of labour (Datt & Sundram, 2006). The debate at various international forums, blacks out "Labour flow" as an essential component of globalization.

In spite of the fact that earlier episodes of globalization involved massive cross-border movement of people, but the current process restricts this (WCSDG, ILO, 2004a). Labour component along with various issues are being negotiated at the WTO ministerial meet, nevertheless deadlock continues.

Despite the presence of GATT from 1948 onwards, globalization did not start on its own and even faced resistance from nations on its implementation. Several revolutionary changes witnessed during the period 1980 to 1995, viz. fall of socialism across Europe and Asia, balance of payment crisis by nations, world oil crisis due to Gulf War in 1990, and formation of WTO in 1995, acted as catalytic precursor for globalization across nation. Presence of some underlying factors too were responsible for its implementation and adoption, such as: (i) policy decisions to reduce national barriers to international economic transactions, (ii) impact of new technology especially Information and Communication Technology (ICT), (iii) increasing openness and growing influence of global market forces (WL SDG, ILO, 2004a), and (iv) Economic stabilization and Structural Adjustment Programme (SAP) of international financial institution.

Proponents of globalization view it as delivering economic prosperity to people across the world. They suggest that it promotes open societies and economics and encourage unhindered exchange of goods, ideas, services and knowledge. It also propagates innovation, creativity and entrepreneurship, enhance awareness about human rights, enable social movements, mobilize opinion and strengthen democratic accountability. It has also contributed in raising sensitivity, inequality, poverty, gender discrimination, child labour and environmental degradation, wherever they may occur (WCSDG, ILO, 2004a).

Whereas Kiely (1998) view the actual process of globalization to be intrinsically uneven, unequal, and unstable, opponents also cite the example of growing exclusion and poverty in certain regions of the world. Many people have been dislocated from their traditional livelihood and local communities, cultural diversity and environmental balance have been threatened.

Globalization in Nepal

Imperial Government of Nepal was dogmatic and reluctant to globalization and free trade initiative by GATT and other international financial institutions. Though, King Birendra had realized the impediments of political system in the rapid economic growth and initiated reforms in early 1980s, but it was restricted to political system. There was a series of compelling circumstances which necessitated the adoption of economic reforms.

Nepal was mostly an agrarian economy till 1980s with respect to output, employment and social relations. Due to this, neither agriculture nor industrial and commercial sectors of the economy could grow and modernize.

Nepal's fiscal balance was maintained in the budgetary operations for a long period of time, but could not be sustained due to the growing internal and external instability. In the Financial Year (FY) 1980-81 the domestic borrowing was about 4 per cent of the total developmental expenditure. But in early 1980s, developmental activities had to be increased mostly financed by foreign aid as per capita income stagnated and agricultural production declined (ILO, 2004b). Despite increase in foreign aid, foreign exchange reserves fell down due to the lower level of mobilization. There was a deficit in balance of payments for three consecutive years from 1982-85. This situation increased the deficit financing. The domestic borrowing for development expenditure ratio increased from 4 per cent in Financial Year 1980-81 to 25.7 per cent in Financial Year (FY) 1981-82. Inflation rate increased to 14.2 per cent of GDP, growth fell to 3.8 per cent from 8.3 per cent and became negative by 3 per cent in Financial Year (FY) 1982-83. Government continued budgetary deficit financing through, the domestic borrowing and strategic revenue mobilization remained neglected. Apart from this, Government regulated the markets and intervened in every sphere of the economy and maintained an inefficient centralized public management of foreign exchange, agricultural inputs and industrial investment. These policy measures resulted in the deterioration of more economic situation in Nepal.

These precursor activities necessitated the Government to adopt economic stabilization programme, under the Stand by Credit facilities of the International Monetary Fund (IMF) in Dec. 1985. Again in 1986-87, the Structural Adjustment Programme (SAP) was commenced for 3 years, under the Structural Adjustment Facility (SAF) of the IMF and Structural Adjustment Loan (SAL) programme of the World Bank. Thus, the process of liberalization was initiated in Nepal. This phase of liberalization is termed as 1st generation reforms or standard reforms or orthodox reforms, in the international financial literature. (UNCTAD, LDC Report-2006). Some additional elements were added to the standard reforms, which came to be known as "Washington Consensus" [Williamson (1990) in UNCTAD LDC Report-2006] was taken up in 1990s.

The reform process was further accelerated by the formation of parliamentary multi-party system of Governance in 1990. Due to the increased global economic integration, Nepal became a member of GATT in 1989 and applied for WTO membership in 1997. It joined WTO on 23rd April, 2004 and become 147th member. Nepal is the second least developed country after Cambodia to join WTO. The policy reforms taken by Nepal in 1980s and 1990s were strongly influenced by international financial institutions, which emphasized stabilization, liberalization and privatization programme. Since 2000, second generation reforms have been taken up by various countries of the world. In 2002, Nepal started its *Comprehensive Economic Reforms Programme*, to strengthen its reforms process (WTO, 2005). This programme is a second generation reform.

Policy Reform

In 1990, Nepal intensified the liberal economic policy regime. The shift in economic policy regime was from inward looking. Import Substitution Industrialization (ISI) to outward looking Export orientation. The dimensional shift focused on economic globalization, liberalization and privatization. The reform in economic policy initiated in early 1990s was under the framework of *Enhanced Structural Adjustment Facility (ESAF)* of the IMF.

In the beginning emphasis of the economic reforms was on the fiscal side. Later on external sector and financial sector reforms were carried out.

The major components of the 1990 reforms were:

- Elimination of quantitative restrictions.
- Rationalization of tariff structure by drastic reduction of the average rate of tariff and the number of tariff slabs.
- Sharp reduction, though not elimination of discrimination against exports.
- Introduction of partial current account convertibility of Nepalese Rupees (NR).
- A broad range of measures to attract Foreign Direct Investment (FDI) including guarantee for repatriation of return on investment in convertible currency, tax incentives and a rise in the proportion of stocks of companies that can be owned by foreigners.

In the reform process all types of subsidies including fertilizer, irrigation, food transportation and interest were completely withdrawn. The impact of these reforms and consequently globalization is discussed in the next section.

Impact of Globalization in Nepal

Isolating the effects of any given set of policies from combination of events is difficult. In assessing the impact of Globalization, data sources from ILO, UNCTAD and IMF and their publication have been used.

With the implementation of liberalized policies under globalization former inward looking, import substitution and state intervention was abandoned. A new approach was put into place, which was based on market oriented, open, outward looking liberalized policy with the aim of achieving higher sustainable growth and poverty reduction.

Changes in Macro-economic indicators

Due to changes in macro-economic policies there were some changes in the macro-economic indicators. After the initiation of globalization, the GDP growth rate had averaged to around 4.4 per cent per annum as compared to 4.2 per cent per annum before liberalization. Average savings rate increased from 10.64 per cent, in 1980s to 13.8 per cent in 1990s. Average investment increased by 23.6 per cent per annum as compared to 19.1 per cent in pre-liberalization period.

Agriculture

Agriculture is the principal economic activity of the people of Nepal. Agricultural land constitutes 28 per cent of the total area, which is about 96,00,000 acres of the total 3,49,64,402 acres. This constitutes about 0.3 hectares per capita (Shukla, 1993:199). Due to the dependency on the monsoon, agricultural production has not improved properly which contributes to its lower growth and ultimately no changes in the living standard of rural people. About 93 per cent of labour force is employed in agricultural sector with productivity ratio of 207 (UNCTAD LDC Report 2006). (see Table 9.1)

There has been a change in agriculture after globalization. Diversification of crop has taken place. Fruits, vegetables and cash crops are replacing cereals due to high cash returns, which indicate the change in agricultural practices. The share of agriculture in GDP has declined from 51 per cent in 1990 to 39 per cent in 2001.

There was no substantial increase in price of major agricultural products. The raised cost of agricultural inputs due to the withdrawal of subsidy from fertilizers and irrigation (shallow tubewells) was not favourable to farmers as the price of output did not increase. The low food prices also created low income to farmers. Despite this food

Table 9.1: Sectoral Distribution of Labour Force and Inter-sectoral Labour Productivity in Nepal

Labour force[a] in agriculture (% of total labour force)		*Labour productivity[b]*					
		In Agriculture		*In non-agriculture*		*Economy wide*	
1980-83	2000-03	1980-83	2000-03	1980-83	2000-03	1980-83	2000-03
94	93	163	207	2097	3817	284	462

a. Labour force is the economically active population.

b. Labour productivity in agriculture, non-agriculture and economy-wise is the ratio between value added and the economically active population in respective sectors.

Source: Compiled from UNCTAD's LDC Report 2006, pp. 138.

grains production which was around 3 million tons in 1961-62 rose to 5.7 million tons in 1989-90 (the average annual growth rate was 2.1%). This growth was achieved mainly through the expansion in the area of cultivation despite the lack of irrigation facilities. Only 21 per cent of the total land under cultivation is irrigated. There has been decline in foodgrain production for the last 30 years. In financial year 2005-06 rice production declined by 2 per cent and wheat by 3.5 per cent. The agricultural growth fell down from 3 per cent in the financial year 2004-05 to 1.7 per cent in the financial year 2005-06. (Asian Development Bank, 2006). (See Table 9.1)

International Trade

Nepal's trade GDP ratio which was stagnant at 23 per cent of GDP in late 1980s increased to 41.6 per cent in 2000. During 1990-91–1999-2000, the average annual increase in export was about 30 per cent, whereas the average annual increase in import was 21 per cent during the same period.

With the adoption of Globalization in Nepal, trade sector has responded positively and pushed the GDP up. The ratio of export to GDP was 1.2$ in 1980s and increased to 20.7 per cent in 2001-02. But the share of import to GDP was greater than that of exports. In 1980s, ratio of export to GDP was 22 per cent which increased to 31.1 per cent in 2001-02. (Table 9.2)

Foreign Direct Investment (FDI)

There was distinct rise in FDI in Nepal with an average of $9.5 million per annum during 1991-2001 as compared to annual average flows of $0.3 million during 1980-90. (ILO, 2004b). The FDI inflow was at peak at $ 23.1 million in 1997. The increased flow of FDI was due to liberalization of trade and exchange rate, existence of bonded warehouse and duty drawback systems favouring export oriented industries.

FDI too played an important role in employment generation. Out of 2,93,000 persons engaged in manufacturing in 1999-2000, 52,969 persons were estimated to be engaged in FDI projects. Labour employment also increased in export-oriented industries. In garment industry, the increase in employment ranged from 44.4 per cent to 55 per cent which indicate the Labour intensive nature of garment industry. (ILO, 2004b) (Table 9.3)

Table 9.2: Foreign Trade of Nepal

Indicators	1985-86	1986-87	1987-88	1988-89	1989-90	1990-91	1991-92	1992-93	1993-94	1994-95	1995-96	1996-97	1997-98	1998-99	1999-2000
Total Exports % change	12.3	-2.8	37.5	2.0	22.9	45.3	85.5	26.0	11.7	-8.6	12.7	13.9	21.5	29.6	39.6
Total Imports % change	20.7	16.7	27.2	17.3	13.1	31.5	37.5	22.7	31.5	23.5	16.9	25.6	-4.9	-1.6	23.5
Exports / Imports % ratio	33.0	27.6	29.7	19.4	28.1	31.8	42.9	44.0	34.5	27.7	26.7	24.2	30.9	40.7	45.5
Outstanding Foreign loans/ Total exports %	335.6	503.8	506.1	696.4	713.7	805.5	517.4	506.3	528.5	640.6	644.0	583.5	585.3	474.8	382.6

Source: Babu Ram Bhattarai (2003), *The Political Economy of the People's War*, in Arjun Karki and David Seddon (edited) *The People's War in Nepal: Left Perspectives*, Adroit Publishers, New Delhi.

Table 9.3: Economic Indicators

(Average in %)

	1971-80	*1981-90*	*1991-2000*	*2001-02*
Per capita Income Growth	0.4	2.0	2.4	-1.5
GDP Growth	2.4	4.3	4.9	0.8
Share of Agriculture	62.7	52.8	41.8	38.8
Share of Industry	12.7	15.0	19.5	20.2
Share of Sources	24.2	32.2	33.8	41.0
Investment as % of GDP	13.1	19.4	23.5	24.1
Public Investment	3.9	7.9	7.0	6.1
Private Investment	9.2	11.5	16.5	18.0
Revenue to GDP	6.5	8.5	9.8	11.6
Expenditure to GDP	11.0	17.6	16.8	16.8
Deficit to GDP (after grants)	4.4	6.5	4.9	4.4
C/W Domestic financing	1.1	2.8	1.8	2.8
Export to GDP	12.1	12.0	22.8	20.7
Import to GDP	17.3	22.0	34.1	31.1
The Money and quasi money M2 to GDP	17.1	28.5	39.9	41.0
Domestic Credit to Govt. (Net)	2.7	12.3	10.8	11.9
Domestic Credit to Para Status (Net)	1.8	2.7	0.7	0.5
Domestic Credit to Private Sector (Net)	5.1	10.3	21.9	31.8
Inflation (CPI average)	7.8	10.2	8.3	2.8
Landing Interest Rates	13.5	15.6	11.6	7.7
Exchange Rates (NRS/US$)	11.4	19.6	58.6	76.5

Source: World Bank Staff Estimates from IM Fund and HMG Nepal Data (ILO, 2004b).

Inflation

Inflation in Nepal is a structural phenomenon rather than a monetary one. Nepal has a history of moderate inflation (see Table 9.4).

Table 9.4: Average Inflation Rate (in %)

	1981-85	*1986-90*	*1991-95*	*1996-2000*	*2000-06*
Overall inflation	9.7	11.6	11.3	7.9	2.4

During 1980s, inflation rate was about 10 per cent in average. This was due to budgetary provision despite, balance of payment deficit and devaluation (15%) during that period. During 1990-91–2000-01, the average inflation rate was 9.2 per cent whereas during 1980s it was 10 per cent. Since 1999 there has been a declining rate of inflation. The inflation was 3.5 per cent in 1999-2000 and 2.4 per cent in 2000-01. But in financial year 2004-05, it rose to 4.2 per cent. It again surged to 8 per cent in financial year 2006-07. Due to the exchange rate peg to Indian respect and an active trade between the two countries the inflation generally follows India's inflation rate.

The share of agriculture in GDP had declined from 51 per cent in 1990 to 39 per cent in 2001. The share of manufacturing in GDP increased from 5 per cent average in early 1980s to about 10 per cent in 1990s. The share of industry in GDP increased from 15 per cent in 1980s to 20.2 per cent in 2001-02. And the share of services in GDP increased from 32.2 per cent in 1980s to 41 per cent in 2001-02. (Table 9.1)

Employment

The annual population growth in Nepal is more than 2 per cent. About three hundred thousand people enter into labour market every year. Proportion of the employment in agriculture sector is declining while the proportion of wage earners is increasing. As trade grew during globalization period, employment too grew from 1,66,400 in 1991 to 2,73,931 during 2001. The growth was 64.4 per cent during 1991-2001. This indicates significant absorption of the labour force in trade sector.

As the structure and composition of export changed from being consisting mainly of primary goods to manufacturing goods, employment too increased.

Income Distribution

Income distribution is skewed in geographical, social and gender terms. Farm income is the major source of household income in Nepal, which was 64.4 per cent of total household income in 1984 and reduced to 61 per cent in 1996.

There has been a wide income disparity in urban areas as Ginni coefficient went up from 0.26 in 1985 to 0.43 in 1996. For the mountain region it went up from 0.11 to 0.21, 0.26 to 0.53 for the hill region and 0.26 to 0.66 for Terai. Income distribution disparity was most in central region and least in the mid-west. Ginni's coefficient was 0.66 for central whereas it was only 0.25 for the mid-west.

Poverty

Incidence of poverty in western and far western region are more pronounced than other developed regions. Proportion of poor in mountain region is twice higher than Terai. (*See* Table 9.5)

Table 9.5: Poverty Estimates of Nepal

Year	*International Poverty Line % of population below $1 (Measured in 1993 PPP per day consumption)*	*National Poverty Line % of Population below Poverty Line*
1995	39	–
1996	–	42

Source: UNCTAD, LDC Report 2006, p. 32.

Government gave priority to poverty reduction from Sixth Five Year Plan (1980-85). Eighth Five Year Plan (1992-97) and Ninth Five Year Plan (1997-02) gave top priority to poverty reduction. The Tenth Five Year Plan (2002-07) is caused as Poverty Reduction Strategy Paper (PRSP) and has focused more on reduction of poverty in Nepal.

About 42 per cent people (1996) of the total population of 17.9 million (1990) were living under poverty line, which according to Government estimates, have come down to 31 per cent (2004) of the total population of 25.3 million (2005).

Conclusion

Impact of Globalization in Nepal shows a mixed trend. Some of the positive impact of Globalization is that there has been slow growth in GDP which was 2.3 per cent in five year 2005-06 (ADB-2006). Contribution of agriculture to GDP has declined from 52.8 per cent in 1980s to 38.8 per cent in 2001-02. Though agricultural output has grown in past several years, it declined to 1.7 per cent in five years 2005-06 from 3 per cent in five years 2004-05.

Non agricultural sector has strengthened. The share of industry in GDP has increased from 15 per cent in 1980s to 20.2 per cent in 2001-02 and service sector has grown from 32.2 per cent in 1980s to 41 per cent in 2001-02. This indicates the structural change of the economy.

There has been growth of trade with more rise in exports. There has been diversification in direction and composition of exports. Mild inflation has been observed and there has been increase in employment opportunities in non-agricultural sector.

But there are negative aspects as well. Globalization has failed to reduce poverty to any significant extent. By the end of Ninth Five Year Plan, it was around 38 per cent and government estimate puts it at 31 per cent in 2005. The withdrawal of subsidy from agriculture sector changes in food distribution system, which had adverse consequences on poverty reduction strategy.

The impact of globalization on agriculture is less pronounced as majority of farmers are involved in cereal production. The slow growth of these crops and removal of agricultural subsidy adversely affected their income. It is clear that agriculture is not playing any significant role in poverty reduction.

Impact of globalization on employment and underemployment shows positive trend. Increased employment is provided by the growth of labour intensive garment industry. Labour productivity in non-agriculture sector has increased, but due to privatization several job opportunities are lost. Income distribution has not been equal.

Though policy reforms have been made but liberalization has not been effectively implemented. Also the political instability and Maoist insurgency has made internal macro environment unstable. Thus, as compared to other South Asian countries globalization has been less effective in Nepal. With the restoration of Seven Party-CPN (M) alliance Government globalization is expected to make a headway.

References

Asian Development Bank. 2003. *Moving the Poverty Reduction Agenda Forward.*

Asian Development Bank. 2006. *Country Operations Business Plan: Nepal 2007-09* www.adb.org/documents/adbplan.pdf Downloaded: 20th November, 2006.

Asian Development Bank (2006a) Nepal, *Asian Development Outlook 2006*, pp. 171-176 www.adb.org/documents/books/ado/2006/documents/nep.pdf-:csoft32 downloaded 14th December, 2006.

Asian Development Bank. 2006b. *Quarterly Economic Update: Nepal* III (2):1-12 www.adb.org/nrm. Downloaded 12-11-2006.

Boyle, Siobhan, Andy Brock. John, Mace and MO. Siblovns.2002. "Reaching the Poor. The Costs of Sending Children to School". *Synthesis Report, DFID Nepal.* www.dfid.gov.uk/DFID.rep.pdf Downloaded 25th November, 2006.

Cockburn, John. 2004. "Trade Liberalization and Poverty in Nepal: A Computable General Equilibrium Micro Simulation Analysis". *Cahiers de recherche 0513, CIRPEE.*

Datt, Ruddar and K.P.M. Sundram. 2006. "Globalization and its Impact on India". *Indian Economy (52nd ed.)*, edited by Ruddar Datt and K.P.M. Sundram: 265. New Delhi: S. Chand and Co. Ltd.

Department of International Development. 2005. *Annual Report 2005.* www.dfid.gov.uk/annualreport2005.pdf: downloaded 25th November, 2006.

DFID Nepal. 2004. "Monitoring in a Fragile State: country assistance plan. www.dfid.gov.uk/DFIDCAP.pdf Downloaded 25th November, 2006.

Encyclopedia Americana. Vol. 20: 97-100. 2006. Connecticut: Scholastic Library Publishing.

Ghose, R.N., Y.M. Melotte and M.A.B. Siddique, eds. 1996. *Economic Developments and Change: South Asia and the Third World.* New Delhi: New Age International Publishers (P) Ltd.

http://www.adb.org/documents/annualreport2003 Downloaded 25th November, 2006.

ILO. 2004a. "A Fair Globalization: Creating Opportunities for All, World Commission on the Social Dimensions of Globalization (WCSDG)". Geneva: ILO.

ILO. 2004b. "Consequences of Globalization in Nepal in terms of Employment, Income Distribution and Poverty". Geneva: ILO.

Karki, Arjun and David Seddon, eds. 2003. *The People's War in Nepal: Left Perspectives.* Delhi: Adroit Publishers.

Kiely, Ray. 1998. "Globalization (Post-) Modernity and the Third World". In *Globalization and the Third World*, edited by Ray Kiely and Phil Marflect: 1-22. London: Routledge.

Nepal Rashtra Bank. 2006. "Strategic Plan 2006-10", www.nrb.org/rashtrabank.pdf

Nepal, Ram Babu. "Auditing Economic. Reform: The Napalese Experience". http://www.asosai.org/asosai_old/journal1999/auditing_economic_reform.htm

Encyclopedia of nations. Nepal: Economic Development.

Ohmal, Kenechi. 2005. *The Next Global Stage: Challenges and Opportunities in Our Borderless World.* Singapore: Wharton School Pennsylvania and Pearson Education Pvt. Ltd.

Practical Action Nepal, Country Strategy 2004-08. www.practicalaction.nepal.com Downloaded 25th November, 2006.

Priorities and Outcomes, *Annual Report 2003*.

Rose, Leo E., T. Scholz. 1980. *Nepal: Profile of a Himalayan Kingdom"*. New Delhi: Select Book Service Syndicate.

Shukla, Vijay. 1993. *World Bank and Development of SAARC Nations"*. New Delhi: Deep and Deep Publication.

Situation Report. 2005. *Nepal: Political and Economic Update*. www.reliefweb.com

UNCTAD. 2006a. "*Least Developed Countries Report 2006*", www.unctad.org. Downloaded: 09-12-2006.

UNCTAD. 2006b. "*Trade and Development Report 2006*", www.unctad.org. Downloaded: 09-12-2006.

UNO. 2005. "Implementation of the Brussels of Action for the LDCs. For the Decade 2001-10 Progress Report: Nepal (2005), www.uno.org/brusselsperformamce.oraction.pdf Downloaded 30th November, 2006

WTO. 2005. Country Working paper–Nepal, TERI Report No.: 2004-GL22, www.wto.org/countrypapers-wto/cwp-nepal.doc18january2006. Downloaded: 14-12-2006.

www.ecn.ulaval.ca/CSAE/WPS/2002-11/tradelibandpoverty.pdf

10

Fiscal Federalism: The Indian Experience and Relevance for Nepal

Anil Kumar Jain and *Parul Gupta*

Introduction

In a federal set-up, along with political problem of division of functions, issues connected with fiscal arrangements have also to be sorted out in the backdrop of regional and local needs and aspirations. Fiscal balance need to be ensured through appropriate mechanism of resource transfer and financial adjustments between the two layers of Governments. The Indian Constitution has provided under its Article 280 for setting up a Finance Commission every 5 years to redress imbalances in revenue and expenditure of the Union and State Governments, arising out of a mismatch between the powers to raise resources and the financial responsibilities of the Governments, keeping in mind the objectives of equity and efficiency. The fiscal relations in India have evolved over time through political, institutional and functional changes within the provisions of the Constitution. In many ways, India's fiscal federal system has served the country well and has brought stability over an extended period of time, although it is also a fact that with growing fiscal stress and divergence in performance, the system has become the subject of increasing controversy, especially, in respect of vertical and horizontal imbalances.

We think that the rich and diversified experience of India in respect of fiscal federalism is of extreme relevance for Nepal so as to transform Nepal into a democratic, divergent and progressive nation state, for which federalism is necessary. Towards this scheme of restructuring Nepal into a 'nation state', it should recognize the equality of all cultures and languages: devolve powers to enable all groups to exercise powers to rule and promoting individual freedom. This task is full of challenges arising from diversities, presence of numerous ethnic groups, loyalty of certain groups to their community, different languages and dialects, etc. Therefore, the scheme of federalism must be agreed by all population and its characters need to be set forth by consensus.

Division of functions and resources between different layers of government is *sine qua non* of fiscal federalism. With the passage of time, more and more countries are moving towards federalism. Generally, there are two ways of moving towards federalism. In some countries, States surrender some powers to the federal government but each state has freedom of action and sovereignty in respect of all other matters (aggregation). In such a situation, federation is a creation of State as in the case of U.S., Australia and Switzerland. The other way in which federation may come into being is that government of the country establishes regional or State Governments and delegates some powers to them for reasons of efficiency and harmony (disaggregation) etc. such as Ethiopia, Austria, Spain, South Africa, etc. Federations are also suitable for those countries in which different ethnic and cultural groups occupy reasonably distinct areas. While Switzerland is a clear example of federation by aggregation, Canada and India are 'hybrid' examples, because some states were the result of aggregation while others were the product of disaggregation. Federalism is one of the popular devices to ensure the participation of different ethnic groups in the State. There is worldwide movement for federalism on account of collapse of one-party States, opening up of market economy and continuing importance of the politics of identity. Education and improved technology are further driving the discourse on federal idea.

The purpose of the present paper is to explain the meaning and essentials of federalism, the Indian scheme of division of function and resources between the Centre and the States, the Indian experience with federation, along with its historical perspective and draw lessons for Nepal which has already committed to become federal.

Meaning of Federalism

'Federation' is not a static or rigid concept and there is no standard model of federalism. It has evolved in different forms in different countries. According to Ron Watts, "Federalism provides a technique of constitutional organisation that permits action by a shared government for certain common purposes that relate to maintaining their distinctiveness, with each level directly responsible for its own electorate."[1] According to Encyclopaedia Britannica, "Federalism is a form of government in which the essential principle is that there is union of two or more states under the Central body for certain permanent objectives." In the words of professor R.N. Bhargava, "The term federal finance refers to the finance of the federal as well as of the State Governments and the relationship between the two."[2] Thus, in a federation, there is constitutional division of powers, functions and resources between the Central (federal) and State (unit) Governments. This becomes necessary because there are various duties and functions which can be more efficiently performed at the Central (federal) level, being in the nature of pure public goods and having good deal of externalities such as defence, services which cover more than one State, etc. On the other hand, in case of some public services, the exact need differ from area to area such as sanitation, medical aid, etc. Such services should be left in the hands of State and local government. In between these two extremes, there are functions, such as education, which can probably be handled efficiently by both layers of government. Such functions have to be kept in concurrent list where both the Central and State Governments may perform but care has to be taken to ensure that there is no duplication of efforts and no serious gap is left. Traditionally, federalism was used for reasons like geographical diversity and geographical distance, mutual defence etc. to being the government closer to the people and increase people's participation in public affairs. However, the emphasis in new federations has changed so as to reflect diversity of ethnicity and culture and the protection of minorities.

Financial Issues in a Federal Set-up

Government activities have financial counterparts–both in revenue and expenditure. Hence, in a federal set-up, along with political problem of division of functions between different layers of the government, issues connected with financial arrangements have also to be sorted out. This involves two issues of diversity and equivalence. As there are diversified regional and local needs and aspirations, they have to be satisfied to the largest extent possible and this results in variations in the level and composition of provision of public services in different regions. But simultaneously, there is also the need that no regions or locality is discriminated against. This implies that government should treat all regions on a parallel footing and variations in public services should reflect only their respective needs and aspirations. In other words, it means that public services may be categorised on the basis of their national, regional and local applicability and provided accordingly.

Similarly, between the Federal and State Governments, the taxing powers should be divided on the basis of identification of the tax bases. However, in practice, it is always not possible to avoid taxing the same base by two or more governments on account of tax competition. Some States may like to reduce or abolish certain taxes in order to attract trade and manufacture from other parts of the country which, many a times, may not be in national interest. It is very unlikely that needs and availability of resources will match on account of increasing upward trend in public expenditure, cyclical fluctuations, different nature of revenue sources, variations in the level and composition of income in different States, etc. Therefore, fiscal balance needs to be ensured between federal government and regional governments through appropriate mechanism of resources transfer and financial adjustments between them.

Principles of Federal Finance

While there can be no uniform principles which determine the allocation of functions and resources among component governments forming the federal structure, there are certain principles or norms which should be kept in mind while making such allocations:

1. Central and State Governments should be financially independent within their own spheres. This implies that scope of tax policy, expenditure policy and debt policy should be clearly demarcated between the Centre and the States.

2. There should be equitable and just allocation of benefit and sacrifices between different States. This implies that system of taxation and pattern of expenditure should, as far as possible, be uniform in all the States, unless circumstances and needs warrant otherwise.
3. There should be adequate means at the disposal of the federal, State and local governments so that they may meet their requirements, as determined by allocation of functions at any given time. However, here it is necessary, as observed by R.N. Bhargava, that "the scheme of resources must be set upon elastic system because no scheme, howsoever good, can be final for all times to come."
4. Resources should be so distributed among the federal components as to give each unit a fair share of revenue and equitable treatment to different taxable units.
5. In a federation, all States are not equal in terms of resources and level of development. Therefore, in the national interest and balanced development, it is essential that special attention is paid to the financial needs of relatively backward and poorer States.
6. It should also be ensured that division of resources should be flexible, Central and State Governments should collaborate in a manner so as to ensure maximum utilisation of national resources towards accelerated economic development and reduction in disparities between people and regions.

The Indian Federation

Indian federal structure is the result of gradual evolution from a centralized authority. British rulers unified Indian States for the purpose of 'facilitating the revenue collection' by creating a 'centralized governments system.' Until 1871, the provincial governments had no independent sources of revenue. It was only in 1904 that a system of divided heads was adopted on a quasi-permanent basis and was made permanent in 1912. "The trend of administrative evolution in India has been towards the transfer of a widening range of functions–in the field of social services and, more lately, also in the field of economic development–to the provinces or the States. There has, thus, been need for maintaining the financial viability of these units at expanding levels of expenditure."[3] One method of meeting these requirements was to divide revenue heads between Centre and units. This was tried under the Government of India Act, 1919 but The Government of India Act, 1935 (which came into force in 1937) laid a firmer foundation for financial federalism by prescribing Provincial Legislative List (94 entries), Federal Legislative List (59 entries) and Concurrent Legislative List (36 entries). In the same way, financial resources were also divided into three categories, namely, federal, Provincial and jointly federal and provincial. This structure, later on, formed the basis of financial federalism in India after Independence.

"It is now well accepted in theory of federal finance that inter-governmental fiscal relations should be constructed on the basis of the principle of adequacy, inter-state equity, autonomy, fiscal discipline and economic efficiency. All these principles are equally important but come into conflict to some extent in particular areas and hence a balance has to be struck among them so as to enable the two levels of government to fulfil their functions efficiently."[4] The Indian Constitution, which came into force on January 26, 1950, recognised such likely imbalances and mandated the setting up of a Finance Commission (Under Article 280) every five years. Article 268 (Duties levied by the Union but collected and appropriated by the States), Article 271 (Surcharge on Certain duties and taxes for the purpose of the Union), Article 272, as amended in 2006 (Taxes which are levied and collected by the Union and may be distributed between the Union and States), Article 275 (Grants from the Union to certain States), Article 279 (Calculation of net proceeds) have been incorporated in the Constitution which are relevant to the Finance Commission. The Seventh Schedule of the Constitution of India lays down the respective functions and financial resources for the Centre and the States. It contains three lists, namely, Union List (97 entries). State List (66 entries), Concurrent List (where both Union and States can legislate). Till 1992-93, the Indian Constitution did not have a compulsory place for local bodies. However, 73rd and 74th Amendments to the Constitution made it obligatory for the State to create local bodies. All these provisions have been incorporated in Constitution to avoid overlapping of the taxation powers of the Centre and the States.

The Finance Commission in India is a unique arrangement envisaged by the framers of the Constitution to redress the imbalances in the revenues and expenditure of the Union and State Governments arising out of a mismatch between the powers to raise revenues and the functional responsibilities of the governments. The Finance Commission is mandated to achieve this through approximate tax sharing between the Centre and the States and through grants-in-aid to the States which are in need of such assistance. The Finance Commission is also required to recommend the *inter se* allocation among States to their share in the Centre taxes. "The fiscal relations in this country have evolved over time through political, institutional and functional changes within ambit of the provisions of the Constitution. The Finance Commission has had an important role to play in this evolving structure because resource sharing based on constitutional division of functions and finances between the Centre and the States is a critical element in the federal system."[5] Since 1990s, a number of constitutional amendments have been effected in India to strengthen the finances of Municipalities and Panchayats. The State Finance Commissions (SFCs) are the instrument to achieve these objectives. A constitutional amendment was also necessitated when the vertical devolution process was sought to be simplified by making all taxes and duties in the Union List sharable with the States.

In India, Thirteen Finance Commissions have so far been appointed and they have submitted their reports. The primary task of the Finance Commission has been to decide about the distribution of net taxes of the Centre between Union and States, allocation between the States of the proceeds received from the Centre, principles governing grants-in-aid and to look into specific issues referred in the terms of reference from time to time. Such issues have changed with the passage of time. For example, the Twelfth Finance Commission was asked to suggest measures needed to augment the consolidated Funds of a State and the Thirteenth Finance Commission was asked to suggest a road map for fiscal consolidation.

It has been the endeavour of the Finance Commissions in India to recommend scheme of transfers that could serve the objectives both of equity and efficiency and result in fiscal transfers that are predictable and stable. The concept of "equalisation" which has been followed in Canada and Australia in different ways[6] is considered to be a guiding principle for fiscal transfers. However, conditions in India are different from those in Canada or Australia because the extent of differences in the resource bases is far large in India and there are larger inter-state differences in density and composition of population.[7] The problem is further aggravated by the disparity in the levels of development of various states that is partly caused by difference in the endowment of resources given by the nature and partly by manmade efforts in the process of development.[8] Such transfers in the form of tax devolution and grants are meant to correct both vertical and horizontal imbalances. Vertical imbalance refers to transfer from the Central Government to the State Government taken together, while horizontal imbalance refers to allocation of resources amongst states. The vertical imbalance arise because more revenue sources have been assigned to the Central Government and states have been entrusted with larger responsibilities. The horizontal imbalances have their roots in differential capacities and needs of the states as also differences in the costs of providing services.[9]

In India, resources are transferred from the centre to the states through many forms and roots. Statutory transfers consist of sharing of central tax revenues which have element of built-in flexibility (the percentage share of which stands of 30.5 per cent after the recommendation of the Twelfth Finance Commission and at 32 per cent after the recommendation of Thirteenth Finance Commission w.e.f.

Table 10.1: Transfer of Resources from the Centre to the States

(*Rs. in Crore*)

Year	*Share of states in Central taxes*	*Grants from Centre*	*Loans (Gross)*	*Gross Transfers to states*
1970-71	755	612	1028	2395
1975-76	1599	1289	1296	4184
1980-81	3792	2796	3146	9734
1985-86	7491	7067	8472	23031
1990-91	14535	13293	14522	42350
1995-96	29285	21577	19627	70489
2000-01	51945	37684	20490	110119
2001-02	53528	42489	24528	120545
2002-03	56841	43167	28231	128239
2003-04	67366	48430	25449	141245
2004-05	80159	53873	24806	158838
2005-06	95887	73677	5654	175218
2006-07	122330	93185	4970	217485
2007-08	153600	108377	6701	268683
2008-09 (RE)	161979	124362	8118	294459
2009-10 (BE)	166862	143957	6714	317533

Source: Ministry of Finance, (Govt. of India), Indian Public Finance Statistics, 2009-10, July, 2010, p. 102.

2010-11) and grants which can be unconditional and general purpose or conditional and purpose specific and can be targeted towards achieving a degree of equalisation. These statutory transfers under the recommendation of the Finance Commission are supplemented by grants from the Planning Commission and discretionary grants from the Central Ministries. The total gross transfers from Centre to the States in India in the form of share in central taxes, grants and loans have increased from Rs. 2,395 crore in 1970-71 to Rs. 42,350 crore in 1990-91, to Rs. 1,10,119 crore in 2000-01 and further to Rs. 3,17,533 crore in 2009-10 BE)[10] (Table 10.1). Transfers under the recommendation of the Finance Commission account for about 65 per cent of the total transfers.

With the growing fiscal stress in the form of increasing gross fiscal deficit, revenue deficit and primary deficits, especially in recent past, both in absolute terms and as a percentage of GDP for the Centre as well as States (Table 10.2), problem of horizontal and vertical imbalances have become subject of controversy. Some idea of prevailing horizontal imbalances may be obtained by comparing the per capita GSDP of the states. Inter-states disparities among general category states are not only high but have shown an increasing trend. In 1980-81, the per capita SDP in the richest state, Punjab was about three times that of the poorest, Bihar. In 2008-09, this difference increased to more than five times, with per capita SDP of Haryana, the richest state, at Rs. 68,914 against Bihar—still the poorest, as Rs. 13,663. An idea of vertical inequity can be derived from the fact that states raise about 34 per cent of the consolidated tax revenues but incur about 58 per cent of the total expenditure. Another adverse development that has taken place in India's fiscal federal relations is that over the years, the role of the Finance Commission has been weakened by three developments: expansion of the terms of reference, restrictions on its scope and emergence of multiple and overlapping agencies in making transfers.[11]

Nevertheless, despite large differences in fiscal capacities, a high degree of equalisation has been achieved in India. The fiscal relations in India have evolved over time through political, institutional and functional changes within the provision of the Constitution. In many ways, India's fiscal federal system has served the country well and has brought stability over an extended period of time.[12]

Relevance for Nepal

We think that the rich and diversified experience of India in respect

Table 10.2: Combined Deficits of Central and State Governments in India

(Rs. Crore)

Years	Gross fiscal Deficit[1]	Revenue Deficit[2]	Primary Deficit[3]
1990-91	53,580(9.4)	23,871 (4.2)	28,585 (5.0)
1991-92	45,850 (7.0)	21,912 (3.4)	14,858 (2.3)
1992-93	52,404 (7.0)	23,688 (3.2)	15,936 (2.1)
1993-94	70,952 (8.3)	36,529 (4.3)	27,938 (3.3)
1994-95	71,639 (7.1)	37,185 (3.7)	19,313 (1.9)
1995-96	77,671 (6.5)	37,932 (3.2)	18,598 (1.6)
1996-97	87,244 (6.4)	48,768 (3.6)	17,156 (1.3)
1997-98	110,743(7.3)	62,782 (4.1)	32,466 (2.1)
1998-99	157,053 (9.0)	110,618 (6.4)	63,957 (3.7)
1999-2000	184,826 (9.5)	121,393 (6.3)	74,375 (3.8)
2000-01	199,852 (9.6)	138,803 (6.6)	75,035 (3.6)
2001-02	226,425 (9.9)	159,350 (7.0)	84,039 (3.7)
2002-03	234,987 (9.5)	162,990 (6.6)	76,363 (3.1)
2003-04	234,501 (8.5)	159,408 (5.8)	56,928 (2.1)
2004-05	234,721 (7.5)	114,761 (3.6)	42,408 (1.3)
2005-06	239,560 (6.7)	99,312 (2.8)	35,583 (1.0)
2006-07	230,432 (5.6)	55,366 (1.3)	-399 (0.0)
2007-08	203,922 (4.1)	9,626 (0.2)	-51058 (-1.0)
2008-09	472,466 (8.5)	241,814 (4.3)	192,372 (3.5)
2009-10 (RE)	623,045 (9.5)	375,923 (5.7)	261,262 (4.2)
2010-11 (BE)	576,140 (7.3)	302,699 (3.8)	N.A.

Notes: Negative Sign (–) denotes surplus figure in parenthesis are percentages to GDP.

1. Gross fiscal deficit is the excess of total expenditure including loans, net of recoveries over revenue receipts (including external grants) and non-debt capital receipts.
2. Revenue deficit is the excess of revenue expenditure over revenue receipts.
3. Gross primary deficit is the difference between gross fiscal deficit and interest payments.

Sources:

(i) Reserve Bank of India: Handbook of Statistics on the Indian Economy (different years).

(ii) Reserve Bank of India: Annual Report 2008-09.

(iii) Ministry of Finance, (Govt. of India), Indian Public Finance Statistics, 2009-10, July, 2010.

(iv) Govt. of India, Economic Survey, 2010-11, p. 66.

of fiscal federalism is extremely relevant for Nepal so as to transform Nepal into a democratic divergent and progressive nation state. During the latter phase of Independence Movement in India, financial integration of erstwhile princely states was also in progress. They were either being merged into bigger units and called part B States or they were being merged into their neighbouring part A States (erstwhile British provinces). It was decided to bring the tax and expenditure structures of these erstwhile princely states in conformity with rest of India.

On similar lines, Nepal is a multi-ethnic, multilingual, multi-religious and multi-cultural society. The 2001 census of Nepal has recorded 103 caste/ethnic groups, 93 languages and dialects and 9 religious groups. Diversity is on the rise. The 1991 census collected data on 62 castes or ethnic groups whereas 2001 census found more than one hundred groups. Political parties in Nepal are moving through ethnic interests, people are turning more loyal to their community and there is the problem of equitable allocation of resources among federating units. It is a happy augury that restructuring of the state became the major objective of people's movements in Nepal and the Interim Constitution gives great importance to restructuring of the state for democracy, inclusiveness and social justice. An amendment in 2007 specifies that Constituent Assembly would make the final decision on the "federal system of state" putting federalism formally on agenda.[14]

Towards the scheme of restructuring Nepal into a 'nation state', it should recognise the equality of all culture and languages, devolve powers to enable all groups to exercise powers to rule and promote individual freedom. This task is·full of challenges arising from diversities, presence of numerous ethnic groups, etc. Therefore, the scheme of federalism must be agreed by all population and its characters need to be set forth by consensus.

Notes

1. Watts, Ron. 1994. *Comparative Fiscal Systems*, 2nd Edition. Montreal: McGill-Queen University Press.
2. Bhargava, R.N. 1971. *The Theory and Working of Union Finance in India*. Allahabad: Chaitanya Publishing House.
3. Twelfth Finance Commission. 2003. *Fifty Years of Fiscal Federalism*. April: 48.

4. Chelliah, Raja J. *Fiscal Federalism in India*: 98.
5. Rangarajan, C., *Perspectives of Indian Economy*: 22.
6. Rangarajan, C. and D.K. Srivastava. 2004. "Fiscal Transfers in Canada: Drawing Comparison and Lesson". *Economic and Political Weekly* 39(19). May 2004. "Fiscal Transfers in Australia: Review and Relevance to India". *Economic and Political Weekly* 39(33). August.
7. Rangarajan, C. and D.K. Srivastava. 2008. "Reforming India's Fiscal Transfer System: Resolving Vertical and Horizontal Imbalances". *Economic and Political Weekly* XLIII (23). June.
8. Bhargava, P.K. 2003. "Centre-State Resource Transfers in India: Need for a Pragmatic Approach". In *Fiscal Federation in India*, edited by P.K. Chaubey: 113-126. New Delhi: Deep & Deep Publication Pvt. Ltd.
9. Government of India. 2004. *Report of the Twelfth Finance Commission.* November: 9.
10. Ministry of Finance, Government of India. 2010. *Indian Public Finance Statistics*, 2009-10. July:102.
11. Rao, M. Govinda. 2009. *A Review of Indian Fiscal Federalism.* New Delhi: National Institute of Public Finance and Policies.
12. World Bank Report. 2005. *State Fiscal Reforms in India.* New Delhi: Macmillan: 58.
13. UNDP. 2008. *Federalism and State Restructuring in Nepal*, Kathmandu: UNDP. April: 2.
14. *Ibid.*, 3.

11

Bridging the Indo-Nepal Relations through Telemedicine Initiative

Preeti Singh

Introduction

Telemedicine is not a new technology today, but it is an innovative methodology for many developing countries, and in fact, it may have more profound influence on these countries than developed nations due to unmet demands for health and unprecedented health related challenges. In the health context of Nepal, telemedicine is rising and currently being implemented. Information Technology (IT) is poised to revolutionize healthcare trade through new thresholds in human connectivity. SAARC Telemedicine centre established in Nepal with the assistance of Rs. 4.88 crores from the Government of India is an initiative in this respect. Overall economic status of Nepal is far below India, there are vast areas of economic cooperation that must be identified particularly in the field of investment in joint ventures and transfer of technology ensuring benefits to both countries what is known as "Win-Win" effect. India's cooperation to Nepal is essential in a greater scale in future not only to sustain its development activities but also for poverty alleviation.

Prime Minister Nehru once stated in the Indian Parliament on 1950...... "We have had from immemorial times, a magnificent frontier that it is so say, the Himalayas. The principal barrier to India lies on the other side of Nepal and we are not going to tolerate any person coming over that barrier. Nehru had reiterated in 1954 "foreign policy of the Nepalese Government should be coordinated with the foreign policy of India. And today SAARC Telemedicine centre established in Nepal with the assistance of Rs. 4.88 crores from the Government of India is an initiative in this respect. Telemedicine will be an important alternative for treating people, in a country like Nepal which has large population and where majority of the population lives in remote and underdeveloped places with limited access due to poor road and insufficient infrastructure. Also, there is acute shortage of doctors in Nepal. The total number of allopathic doctors are 4000 and majority of them are staying in capital and other major cities. The public and doctors ratio is approximately 6000:1. Health workers in rural health care, who serve most of the population, are isolated from specialist support and up to date information. The advent of ICTs has unbridled new opportunities to the delivery of health services. Telemedicine may in fact have a more deep impact on developing countries like India and Nepal than on developed countries. In Nepal, top ten OPD diseases are related to communicable and infectious diseases which can be diagnosed and managed with the help of images and no physical examination of patient is needed. Further, simple change in health habits can help to reduce the burden of these diseases, which can be provided through tele-education.

Nepal and India have age-old historical, cultural and geographical bonding. So is economic relation that dates back to Nepal's entrepot trade with India before the Nineteenth century. After the induction of democracy in Nepal in 1951, India was a premier donor country that played an important role in mobilizing aid to Nepal under Colombo Plan. India's cooperation to Nepal especially in the field of bilateral trade, investment and transfer of technology has been instrumental in speeding up the pace of economic development in Nepal in recent years. However, Nepal's increasing economy is heavily reliant on India and deprived of the opportunity of maximizing benefits from the economy of big neighbourhood like India, an emerging economic muscle in the world. Although overall economic status of Nepal is far below India, there are vast areas of economic cooperation that must be identified particularly in the field of investment in joint ventures and transfer of technology ensuring benefits to both countries what is known as "Win-Win" effect. India's cooperation to Nepal is essential in a greater scale in future not only to sustain its development activities but also for poverty alleviation.

Potential for cross-border expansion between India and Nepal

Telemedicine is a new way of delivering healthcare allowing a change from a centralized service to one which is patient-centred, resource efficient and where decisions are made at a local level close to the patient, which is brought about by use of ICT applications to medicine (NST, 2009). Telemedicine, in particular, can be useful technology to deliver health care to remote and rural areas when backed-up by ICT infrastructure. It will allow integration of technology and information sharing, enhances accessibility to health service to people and to health providers, increases efficiency of treatment, lowers health related costs, and improves patient care (WHO, 2009). Caring patient at a distant, to needy people in the sense, is utmost important to level the unbalanced health system. Telemedicine could prove vital in delivering care even in urban centres and to nearby vicinities, especially in emergencies. This is possible only if technology reinforces with the existing health systems, and this is why telemedicine becomes more important. Since telemedicine uses information and communication technologies to deliver health care, it cannot be overseen without the development of ICT infrastructure. Both the information and communication technologies share in common-information sharing, and they can be used as installed bases to develop ICT infrastructure such as telemedicine. As such, the growth and development of telemedicine is possible only when ICT infrastructure is well developed. The population, Gross National Income (GNI) and GNI per capita is given below for selected SAARC countries (*See* Table 11.1).

As shown in Table 11.1, the GNI per capita is estimated to be US$ 250 and the size of GDP would level to US$ 6 billion, which is lowest in the SAARC region. Nepalese economy suffers from serious structural constraints accompanied by unprecedented political

Table 11.1: Population, GNI and GNI Per Capita of selected SAARC Countries

Country	*Population (Million)*	*GNI (Billion $)*	*GNI (Billion $)*
Nepal	2.4	5.9	250
Bangladesh	133.4	49.9	370
Pakistan	141.5	59.6	420
India	1.033	474.3	460
Sri Lanka	19.6	16.3	830

Source: World Development Report, 2003.

turbulence. Economy is choked by landlocked position, rough topography with limited cropland, poor resource base, a high extent of poverty, and uncontrolled corruption.

Despite the increasing role and importance of ICT in health, developing such infrastructures in Nepal is challenging. Some of the major problems that Nepal faces as hindrance to technological development are remote and inaccessible geographic terrain of the country, non-uniformity (and inequality) in the construction of infrastructure overall the regions of the country, lack of skilled human resources capable of using and applying newer technology, lack of timely supply of required human resources to particularly underserved areas, lack of motivation in the available human resources (lack of training, etc.), and, disturbances and damages in developmental works due to the political conflicts (Pradhan, 2002). There is huge gap between city and the remote areas in terms of health, education, and other basic needs. In addition, Nepal lacks effective monitoring and evaluation system, policy reformation, plan formulation and their implementation.

Telemedicine Concept

Telemedicine did not arise as a separate and well-defined discipline with specialized instrumentation standard and protocols (Norris, 2002) rather it developed as continuous efforts of people (Clinicians) trying to use technologies into medical practice and as information and communication technologies advanced to new heights. Telemedicine has pioneered the use of communication technologies within health care, and has been principally available for decades. (EHTEL, 2008). Often termed as 'distant medicine' Telemedicine initially developed to provide health service to remote and rural or underserved communities in primary and secondary care, and in emergency conditions and locations such as military services and natural disasters. (Norris, 2002). It has a long way from telegraphy and telephony to radio and television to digital technologies and is still in continuous process of development. It involves use of telecommunication such as a simple telephone line or a mobile telephone line or mobile phones and PDAs (Personal Digital Assistants), fax, internet, e-mail, web or a combination of these and dedicated computerized devices, hardware and software applications for instances, video-conferencing, Electronics Patient

Records (EPRs), robotics etc. Given below is the linkage of villages through telemedicine (Fig. 11.1).

Bridging the Relations through SAARC Telemedicine Network

SGPGI, Lucknow got connected to Central Hospital located in Thimpu, Bhutan under the SAARC Telemedicine Network Project funded by the External Affairs Ministry, Government of India implemented by Telecommunication Consultant India (Ltd.). The implementation of telemedicine is one of the cutting edge technologies that have surged to the forefront as a viable solution for solving cost, location, and many other issues. Since Nepal is one of the least developed and poorest countries of the world. With the annual growth rate of 2.25 per cent, the population of Nepal (2008) was estimated about 27 million. The urban population is about 13.9 per cent, i.e. more than 85 per cent of the population lives in rural areas. Internet connection is slow in Nepal, expensive and limited, therefore, access to information is also limited. According to 2008 figures, Nepal ranks the lowest 15th in the world and fourth lowest in Asia in terms of telephone subscriber rates, both mobile and fixed, which is about 6.4 per cent (ITU, 2010).

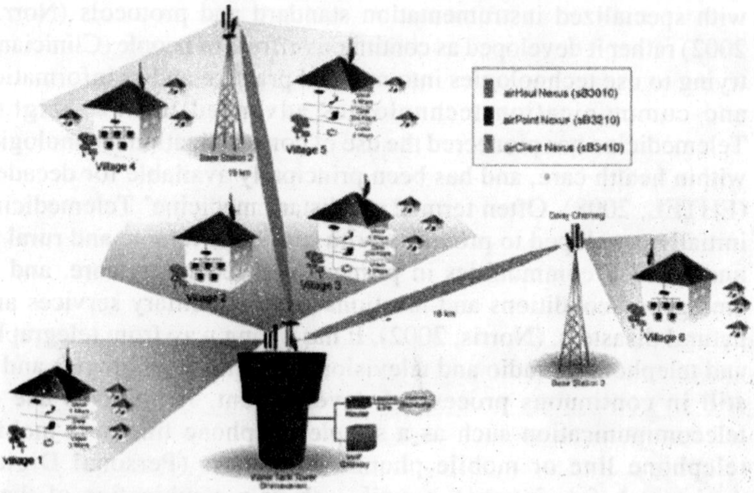

Fig. 11.1: Telemedicine Infrastructure.
Source: e-health, Vol. 2, Issue 5, May 2007.

The main purpose of establishing telemedicine centre was to provide patients with specialist care when needed. The telemedicine linkage would reduce the need to transfer patients to a site of medical expertise and decrease in the relocation of medical specialists to the patient. Indeed, it would make health care facilities better organized and less costly, ensuring quality service to the patients. It also ensures more efficient and effective use of medical and technological resources, which would result in enhanced diagnostic and therapeutic quality of care while opening up new possibilities for continuing education or training for isolated or rural health practitioners, and creating new opportunities for technical expertise, and to learn and practice new technology for IT personnel and doctors/consultants (*See* Fig. 11.2).

Figure 11.2 highlights the various villages connected through telemedicine in Nepal. Presently, more than twenty-five villages are benefited. Effective implementation of telemedicine includes many benefits from cost savings, to improved patient care, to more efficient distribution of doctors' expertise. Using telemedicine creates a virtual network that has no geographic barriers (*See* Fig. 11.3).

Video consultation usually lasts for 30-45 minutes, and involves usually three personnel in addition to the patient and/or accompanying patient member–IT staff, Doctor and the Consultant.

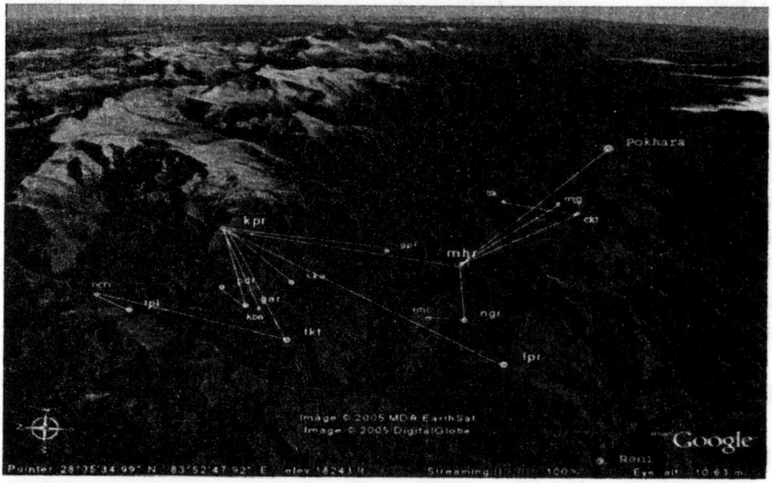

Fig. 11.2: IT Enabled Connectivity in Nepal.
Source: www.google.com

Fig. 11.3: Demo of Telemedicine Consultation.
Source: www.google.com

Discussion

Nepal is geographically difficult to access, and most health providers and doctors being centralized to cities, allows telemedicine to stand-in. Technology matters but not without users, and since it is about distance, doctors are not able to reach the patient as per the political situation of the country, and thus doctors do agree that technology would be helpful to widen their expertise and skills. The doctors are satisfied with the use of telemedicine service; however, they need formal training in IT skills, at least basics of IT, and knowledge in ICT. India is a neighbouring country and has open border with Nepal. Relatively, buying from India is cheaper than from other parts of the world and at the same time it is efficient. It is efficient in the sense that it is easy to replace damaged or malfunction equipments or to order their parts or order a new one. Telemedicine provides a common ground for doctors and patients, and is equally shareable in terms of use. For example, patients and doctors in Nepal can get expert advice and treatment plans, while Indian specialists can offer cross-border services to Nepal, using the same set of telemedical solutions. In other words, telemedicine provides a similar platform for different users with different motives. Thus, openness is an inherent property of infrastructures.

Conclusion

Technology has changed our lives. It has influence how we shape this world. Development of information infrastructures, computing technology and telecommunications, and so on, has envisioned us with a new way to see and perceive things. Advanced technology has paved a way for new health dimensions; more specific, more result oriented and unique. Advancement in computing technology, telecommunications, internet, web-based technology, etc. have given rise to new fields like telemedicine and concept of e-health, and literatures have shown that these have been largely proved valuable in managing patients with their illnesses. State-of-art equipments and processes dedicated at patient care have revolutionized the health care system.

Infrastructure development may be a difficult task in Nepal. There are many challenges to developing ICT infrastructure, and hence telemedicine implementation in the country. However, there are also possibilities. Infrastructure development, implementation and maintenance are very crucial for any country, and even more for developing countries. ICT infrastructure might be a boon for Nepal since it has many opportunities for development; however, a lot of hard work is required. Thus, it requires efforts from people and organizations at all the sectors of the economy—government and private—including donor agencies as well. In addition, it requires good strategies, far-vision and effective planning to achieve success. The collaboration of India and Nepal through telemedicine will be a "Win-Win" effect in shaping the future of both the countries by strengthening bilateral cooperation for the mutual benefit of the peoples of the two countries.

References

Bhasin, A.S. 1979. *Documents on Nepal's Relations with India and China, 1949-66*. Academic Books.

Brown, N. 2005. *Telemedicine Coming of Age*. Telemedicine Information Exchange. http://tie.telemed.org/articles/article.asp?path=telemed101&article=tmcoming_nb_tie96.xml

Cetingaya, B. 2009. Telemedicine: A Paradigm Shift in Healthcare. *Why Telemedicine might be the Answer:* http://burag.com/2009/12/19/why-telemedicine-might-be-the-answer/Coiera, E.

Edworthy, S.M. 2001. "Telemedicine in Developing Countries." *BMJ* 323: 524-525.

EHTEL. 2008. "Sustainable Telemedicine: Paradigms for Future-Proof Healthcare." A Briefing paper, Prepared for the Sustainable Telemedicine Task Force, European Health Telematics Association. [Cited 2010 March 3]. Available from: http://www.ehtel.org/forum/

tasks-sources/task-force-sustainable-telemedicine-and-chronic-disease-management/ehtel-briefing-paper-sustainable-telemedicine-paradigms-for-future-proof-healthcare-1

Hailey, D. 2002. "Systematic Review of Evidence for the Benefits of Telemedicine". *Journal of Telemedicine and Telecare* 8(S): 1-7.

ITU. 2010. *ICT Statistics*. International Communication Union. [Cited 2010 February 9]. Available from: http://www.itu.int/ITU-D/icteye/Indicators/Indicators.aspx

Dahal, Madan and Shankar Aryal. 2003. "Improving Nepal-India Economic Relations: A Study of the Impact of Foreign Direct Investment (FDI) and Transfer of Technology in Nepal."

Norris, A.C. 2002. *Essentials of Telemedicine and Telecare*. England: John Wiley & Sons Ltd., 6-10.

Pradhan, J. 2002. "Information Technology in Nepal: What Role for the Government?" *The Electronic Journal on Information Systems in Developing Countries* (*EJISDC*) 8 (3): 1-11.

Prakash. A. Raj. 1975. *Indo-Nepal Relations,* Future Prospects Press. http://www.ifa.org.np/pdf/prc/prakasharaj.pdf

Rudeep, Piya. 2010. "Scope and challenges of telemedicine in Nepal: a look towards future." http://www.ub.uit.no/munin/bitstream/handle/10037/2577/thesis.pdf?sequence=2

Shaha, Rishikesh. 1978. *Nepali Politics: Retrospect and Prospect.* Delhi: Oxford University.

Yellowlees, P. 2003. "Trends in e-health: Technological Advances that will Impact on Diagnosis and Treatment, Business Briefing". *Global Healthcare*: 1-4.

12
India's Economic Miracle and Its Impact on Nepal

Hari Bansh Jha

Introduction

For a long time, it was a common practice to identify the rate of economic growth in India as 'Hindu rate of economic growth'—a derogatory term used to denote lower annual growth rate of the economy. This was the state of affairs under the License Raj in India until 1980s, which was based on strict enforcement of licenses, regulations and red tape owing to protectionist and interventionist policies of the Government. As such, India's annual rate of economic growth from 1950s to 1980s could not grow more than 3.5 per cent.

Because of the defective economic policy, India ultimately experienced a major crisis in its balance of payments in early 1990s. This, however, proved a blessing in disguise. In order to resolve the crisis, the Indian government introduced significant reforms in trade, industry and investment sector in the process of liberalizing the economy. A new era began in which the long policy of isolation with the global markets, financial regime and technology flow was abandoned.

Emerging as World's Fast Growing Economy

Economic indicators show that the Indian economy soon attained the take-off stage under the new liberalized economic regime. The FDI which amounted to mere US $ 6.1 billion in 2001-02 shot up spectacularly to US $ 34.3 billion in 2007-08.[1] By 2020, India aspires to increase the FDI quite impressively from its present share of 0.1 per cent of the GDP to 3.5 per cent, particularly in areas like infrastructure, high technology-oriented units and sectors that could generate massive employment opportunities.[2]

In addition, the service sector exports grew from 7.2 per cent of GDP in 1990 to 20 per cent in the recent years. India's industrial growth is fundamentally software-led. In 1996-97, the software exports accounted for merely $ 1 billion, which increased to $ 23.4 billion in 2005-6.[3] Remarkably, the exports of computer software and business services shot up by 40 per cent per year during 2004-08. Similarly, the exports of merchandise grew by 20 to 30 per cent per annum.

Moreover, the exports trade in India doubled from $ 52.7 billion to $102.7 billion between 2002-03 and 2005-06 within the period of just three years. As a result, the share of India in world export trade became 1 per cent in 2005-06 from 0.5 per cent in 1990-91.[4]

India's savings rate shot up unprecedentedly from mere 23 per cent in 1990s to 35 per cent during the recent years. Indian economic growth rate registered 7.8 per cent in 2008-09. In 2010, the economic growth rate in India was 8.8 per cent. The higher rate of economic growth in India has made the country the second fastest growing economy in the world after China. In fact, it is the fastest growing free market economy in the world.

In 2009, the GDP in India in terms of Purchasing Power Parity (PPP) recorded US $ 3.5 trillion. It is expected that it would double every eight years or so at the present rate of economic growth of 8.8 per cent. On this basis, expectations are that India would emerge as the third largest economy in the world by 2040 when its GDP in PPP terms could reach over US $ 28 trillion, i.e. nearly 8 times of the current GDP. By then, the per capita income in India could reach US $ 20,000 in PPP terms.

With additional modest capital flows from abroad, India is in a position to make investment with its savings to the extent of 40 per cent of GDP per year. This 40 per cent investment in the economy is likely to help economy achieve 10 per cent economic growth assuming the capital-output ratio of four to one.[5]

Now Indian Prime Minister, Manmohan Singh is confident to achieve 10 per cent rate of economic growth based on the performance of Indian economy over the past years. No country other than China is in a position to maintain the steady economic growth rate of 10 per cent over the years, which now India is confident to achieve. Therefore, Goldman Sachs predicted that India's rate of economic growth would be not less than four times in 2020 as compared to the situation in 2007.

One of the factors that led to higher growth of Indian economy is the growth in the middle class population. As it is well known, India's middle class account for nearly 300 million, which is 30 per cent of the country's total population. In 1984-85, the middle class population formed as low as 10 per cent of the total population, but now half of India's population is likely to enter into middle class group between 2020 and 2040. Much of West and South India will turn into middle class by 2020 itself.

Recently, the Asian Development Bank has estimated that over the next two decades, the middle class population in India would reach 1 billion. In this context, the McKinsey Global Institute (MGI) estimated that India would emerge as the world's fifth largest consumer economy by 2025, up from 12th position at the moment. Now, that there has been massive growth of Indian middle class population, India has emerged as Asia's largest buying economy. The Indian middle class population is likely to assume the traditional role of the American and European middle classes.

The rise of the middle class population in India is important from different points of view. For the corporations, the middle class population provides significant business opportunities. They are the ones who buy bulk of consumer goods, including automobiles, mobile phones, televisions, computers and other electronic items. Besides, they are the ones who need financial services and also services in educational, health and different other sectors.

Unlike China, Japan and other Asian Tigers which have followed export-led growth strategy, India's growth is driven primarily by domestic consumption. Significantly, the domestic economy provides India greater cushion from external shocks than any of these countries. In India, the private domestic consumption accounts for 57 per cent of GDP, whereas it is only 35 per cent in China. The economy of India did not suffer due to the confidence in consumers. Because of India's less dependence on other countries, the growth in this country is much more sustainable. This is the reason why the Indian economy, particularly the banking sector largely escaped the adverse impact of global financial crisis when many of the world economies, including the USA, Europe and Japan were hardest hit. The banking sector remained largely unaffected partly due to its limited operations outside India and partly due to the fact that they had little exposure to sub-prime lending by foreign investment banks. The banking sector in India recorded 43 per cent in profitability in 2008 when the big financial institutions around the world lived in nightmare.

Economic Integration with World Economy

In a brief span of time, India has transformed itself from a country of 'snake charmers' to the 'country of charmers.' It is getting integrated with the world economy. In this process, the number of multinationals in India increased perceptibly. Be it the countries of European Union, including Britain, France, Netherlands, Italy, Germany, Belgium and Finland or Asian countries like Korea and Japan, they all have multinational companies in India. There is perhaps no sector left where foreign multinational companies have not made their presence in India. Finnish Nokia, Fiat, Piaggio, Ford Motors, Samsung, LG Electronics, Hyundai, Vodafone and McDonald are among some of the world's noted multinational companies in India. Even recently, a number of world's multinationals including Arcelor Mittal and Posco steelmakers expressed their commitment to make further investment in steel and power sector in this country.

Basically, the multinationals are interested in India because of macro-economic stability, labour competitiveness and attractive environment for FDI. With the increasing prospect for the development of civilian nuclear programme, more and more multinationals are expected to make their inroads into India. The multinationals are interested mostly in India's huge market. With over 1.21 billion population, India has created most conducive environment for investment. The average annual rate of economic growth of 8 to 9 per cent has enhanced people's purchasing power dramatically. Therefore, India has emerged as world's fastest growing telecom market. Each month over 1 million new mobile phone subscribers are added. Over 10,000 motor cycles are sold in the country each day. Of the total order for aircraft, private Indian airline companies alone account for 43 per cent of total order for aircraft—be it Air Bus or the Boeing. Each second a new baby is born in India and together with it there is corresponding increase in the demand for the bulk of the population.

It is not that only the foreign multinationals are making their inroads in India, Indian multinationals are equally becoming competitive to expand their network and base in other countries of the world. Thanks to the strong technical base in India that the Indian multinationals find themselves competitive to work abroad. In India, only 2 per cent of the applicants compete in Information Technology (IT) sector; whereas 10 per cent of the applicants succeed in world renowned institution like Harvard University. This clearly shows the quality of the manpower that India produces each year.

More than half of the world computer graduates are in India alone. It is, therefore, expected that India will be world's major centre for the production of ideas. This is one of the reasons why the Indians have penetrated every field be it in the field of journalism, Silicon Valley, Wall Street or fashion world. Indian companies including automakers, such as Tata Motors and Mahindra & Mahindra as well as Tata Tea have entered into international markets. It is expected that the Indian firms will produce more of multinationals in future as the Chinese, Russians, Koreans and other South-east Asian countries are doing.

In regard to the strength of the Indian multinational companies, it needs to be mentioned that the Indian companies like Infosys and Wipro recently expressed their plan to invest billions of dollars in Karnataka alone. Infosys, for example, announced its plan to set-up a new facility in Bangalore, which could provide employment opportunities to nearly 20,000 engineers.

Estimates are that India will have more multinationals than China because China is not opening up so much to foreign companies. More than 2,200 Indian companies are expected to open operations overseas over the next 15 years overtaking China.

India has emerged as world's number one country in terms of export of manpower. Also, it has become world's largest food producing country. The real problem in the country is not the lack of foodgrains. It is rather the distribution of foodgrains that is the problem. Therefore, when India's population crossed 1 billion marks in 2000, the warehouses were bulging with grain. Because of some of these activities, the magnitude of poverty has reduced in India.

During his recent visit to India, the American President Barak Obama mentioned that the sheer size and pace of India's progress in just two decades was one of the most stunning achievements in human history. The way Indian economy has fared well at the global level is a matter of pride for many of the developing countries in the world that aspire to take off.

India's Support to Nepal

As it is well-known, Nepal and India are closely linked together by history, geography, culture, religious, commercial and economic ties. Mutual trust and friendship and also the desire for peace and stability are the cornerstone in the relations between the two countries. Ever since the formation of the two states, there is open border with free movement of people from one country to the other. Such special relations at the people to people level have encouraged marriage relations, and also relations in health, cultural, educational, religious and economic affairs.

Ever since India achieved independence, it started extending extensive economic assistance to Nepal. Special privileges in trade and commerce have been granted to Nepal. The transit facilities as enjoyed by Nepal are something unprecedented as no other land-locked country enjoys so much transit facility.

Indian assistance programme is launched in almost all the seventy-five districts of Nepal. More than 400 projects are under implementation with total outlay of NRs. 60 billion. Indian support to Nepal in capacity building is significant. Under this programme, 9,000 Nepalese have been pursuing higher education. The concessional line of credit as made available by India to Nepal worth US $ 350 million could be used for the development of infrastructural facilities in Nepal.

Significantly, India's share in total direct investment in Nepal accounts for 45 per cent. Some of the major joint ventures with India in Nepal include Surya Nepal—a joint venture with ITC India, Dabur Nepal, Nepal Lever and United Telecom Nepal, Everest Bank, SBI Bank, LIC Nepal, Asian Paints, GMR India, IL&FS and Manipal.

Considering the growing demand for power both in Nepal and in India, Satluj Hydro Electric Project of India has made investment for the construction of 402 MW in Arun-III. On the other hand, GMR, an Indian infrastructure developer has made investment for the construction of 300 MW Upper Karnali at Tunibagar in Dailekh district. Also, Himtal Hydropower Company Pvt. Ltd. (in which GMR has 80 per cent share and the Nepalese have 20 per cent share) has made investment for the construction of 600 MW Upper Marshyangdi-II hydropower. IL&FS has 15 per cent share in 750 MW West Seti project. Besides, the Indian Government has also offered to construct 240 MW Naumure project under its grant assistance.

Indian investment has given Nepal access to new technologies and management skills. It also generated substantial revenues to the national exchequer. Besides, it promoted import substitution and exports of Nepalese goods to the Indian market. More significantly, about 30,000 Nepalese have been provided direct employment and twice this number have got indirect employment in various industries run through Indian investment.

Bilateral trade between Nepal and India doubled to US $ 4 billion during last five years. Credit for the surge in trade between the two countries largely goes to the treaty of trade signed between Nepal and India in 1996.[6] There is provision of preferential treatment for the Nepalese products in India at par with the Indian producers.

Impact on the Nepalese Economy

Despite India's support to Nepal in its drive for economic growth and modernization, Nepal ranks in the bottom 10 per cent of the countries in the world. The per capita income in the country is as low as $ 470. About 55 per cent of the people fall below the international poverty measures of $ 1.25 per day. There is a huge capital flight from the country. Liquidity crunch among the banking and financial institutions have shattered the investment climate both in the short and long-term perspective. The annual rate of economic growth of the country is as low as 3.5 per cent when India is having the growth rate of nearly 9 per cent. Virtually, Nepal is island of poverty in South Asia.

In such moments of economic breakdown, there has been a growing Indian concern not only about the health of the Indian investment in Nepal but also about the investment climate in the country. Today, the Indian investors in general feel quite insecure to make an investment in Nepal as the business environment in the country has been badly shattered mostly due to the frequent *bandhs*, prevailing culture of strikes, labour disputes, forced donations, poor law and order situation and above all the continuing political instability in the country.

There have been reports of diversion of third country goods from Nepal to India during the transit. Perhaps, affixation of an additional one time lock by Indian customs could resolve this problem, but it is not getting materialized. Besides, there is growing practice of copying the popular Indian brands and trademarks by certain unscrupulous Nepalese manufacturers. Such activity has eroded the reputation of the Indian brand. Besides, this created doubts in the minds of the Indian investors about the nature of fragile legal framework of Nepal in regard to the protection of intellectual property. This prevented the Nepalese consumers from getting quality goods from India. Some of the Indian business community also grudge that there is erosion in the margin of preference by the Nepalese Government on import of goods from India.

There are reports that many of the Indian investors have already started deserting the country as they feel that they have had to face certain tariff and non-tariff barriers and that they were being discriminated in the country in different ways. Some Indian companies who have made investment in Nepal feel that they were trapped as the concerned Nepalese wings hardly fulfilled their obligations made during the time of agreement. Meanwhile, certain forces have mixed up politics with economics and obstructed the implementation of different development projects, including the hydro-power projects undertaken by India in Nepal.

Because of the negative perception of Indian companies, no new Indian investment has made their entry into Nepal since 2003 when Indian companies at the global level have made a commitment to make investment to the tune of US $ 70 billion. All this led to the decline in investment, production and exports of goods resulting into deficit in balance of trade with India and affecting the economic growth of the country as a whole.

A Way Forward

It is amply demonstrated that India is largely integrated with the rest of the world. The country has maintained sustainable economic growth and it is gradually being transformed into modern, vibrant and merit based society. It continues to eliminate poverty and give its people a better level of living. Because of some of these factors, India, in fact, has become a model of economic growth for many countries of the world. By all likelihood, the 21st century is going to be India's century for which the government, planners, policy makers, farmers, industrialists, business persons, academics, civil society leaders and the elite groups have been trying their best to achieve. By all accounts, India has proved that diversity, democracy and development can go together.

Unfortunately, however, Nepal could not benefit that much from India's fast economic growth with market of 1.21 billion populations, despite the significant level of privileges made available by India to Nepal. Therefore, more and more engagement is required at business to business level to dig out potential opportunities, promote information dissemination, and organize trade fairs, exhibitions and different other business activities. Nepal could, of course, concentrate on investment in areas in which it has comparative advantage over India.

However, for all this an enabling environment will have to be created in the country to restore the confidence of Indian investors. In this regard, it will be worthwhile for Nepal to enter into investment promotion agreement with India. It is essential to make resolution of outstanding investment issues by sticking to obligations made during the time of agreement of the projects. The Government of Nepal also needs to discourage those Nepalese manufacturing firms who indulge in copying of popular Indian brands and trademarks at the cost of Nepalese consumers. And most importantly, it is essential to develop linkages with India in infrastructure sector such as in roads, air, irrigation, education, health, and flood and drought control.

The Nepalese Government should come forward with incentive schemes for promoting exports to India through Export Processing Zones (EPZs) with a view to targeting the large market of bordering states of India with 361 million customers.[7] Tariff and non-tariff barriers, if any, in trade between the two countries need to be removed to facilitate the process of economic integration possibly through the mechanism of Free Trade Arrangement (FTA) with provision of common external tariff with India.

Notes

1. Kumar, Rajiv and Pankaj Vashisth. 2009. "The Global Economic Crisis: Impact on India and Policy Responses". *ADBI Working Paper Series*, 164: 5. November.
2. Holslag, Jonathan. 2010. *China and India: Prospects for Peace.* New York: Columbia University Press: 66.

3. Bhagwati, Jagdish, N. and Charles W. Calomiris, ed. 2008. "Introduction" in *Sustaining India's Growth Miracle*. New Delhi: Stanza: 4.
4. Panagariya, Arvind. 2008. "Transforming India" in *Sustaining India's Growth Miracle*, edited by Jagdish N. Bhagwati and Charles W. Calomiris: 14. New Delhi: Stanza.
5. Swaminathan, S. and Anklesaria Aiyar, "India's Growth Fantasy" http://www.cato.org/pub_display.php?pub_id=11954.
6. Jha, Hari Bansh. 2009. "Trade treaty: A Paradigm shift". *My Republica*. November 25.
7. Jha, Hari Bansh. 2009. "Better opportunities lie with India than China". *My Republica*. December 13.

13

Developing Women Entrepreneurship in Nepal through Small Scale Industries

Usha Kiran Rai and *Monica Srivastava*

Introduction

Entrepreneurship, first and foremost is a mindset. An Entrepreneur is one who creates a new business in the face of risk and uncertainty for the purpose of achieving profit and growth by identifying significant opportunities and assembling the necessary resources to capitalize on them (Zimmerer and Scarborough, 2005). Literature on entrepreneurship is diverse and interdisciplinary, with roots in sociology (Weber,1904), economics (Schumpeter, 1934) history (Cole, 1959) and other disciplines (Venkatachalam and Waqif, 2005). However, all these entrepreneurial research reveal that entrepreneur is intimately associated with three elements. They are risk-bearing, organizing and innovating. Thus, an entrepreneur can be defined as a person who tries to create something new, organizes production and undertakes risks and handles economic uncertainty involved in enterprise (Khanka, 2007).

Women entrepreneurship, in a formalized sense, is a relatively new phenomenon in Nepal. Although certain ethnic communities in the country, especially the Newars and Tibeto-Burman Highland Groups such as the Sherpas, Gurungs, Thakalis are known to have a long tradition of women being involved in small business enterprises (CEDA, 1981), it is only within the last ten years that the concept of women entrepreneurship has progressively gained some acceptance in the overall dominant majority within the Nepalese society. With the growing recognition that women have unique talents which could be harnessed for development and for creating employment opportunities for others who are not suited to an entrepreneurial career, developing women as entrepreneurs has become an important part of national development planning and strategies.

Gender equality and economic development go hand in hand. Since the early 1980s, the policy-makers and planners have become acutely aware of the economic significance of women's productive activities and the nature of their contribution to income generation. It has been firmly established that women in Nepal are vital and productive contributors to the national economy but their access to knowledge, skills, resources, opportunities and power still remain rather low (Stri Shakti, 1995).

Although women constitute a little over one half of Nepal's population, they rank lower than men in almost every social indicator in the country. Within the increasing tides of poverty in Nepal, women are the poorest of the poor, a relatively more deprived segment even from among the poor (World Bank, 1991).

Forty-five per cent of women aged 10 and above are listed as economically active, while the corresponding figure for men is 68 per cent (Census, 1991). The growth rate in the female labour force exceeded that of males between 1981-1991, but they are still confined to a few activities indicating their disadvantaged position in reaping the benefits of diversification in many areas of employment.

Over the past fifteen years women's participation in economic activities has also moved beyond agriculture into the local market economy. In search for wage employment, women are moving into small business and self-employment ventures thereby creating many formal and informal opportunities for work. Women are increasingly migrating to urban areas for employment in a range of cottage industries, such as carpet weaving, textiles and handicrafts.

Some 82 per cent of working women are self-employed and 12 per cent are wage-employed, as compared to 69 per cent and 27 per cent in the case of men. More than 4 per cent of women are unpaid family workers, the only category where women have outnumbered men. Less than 1 per cent of the working women hold the status of "employer". Women's participation in the informal sectors has increased significantly in both urban and rural areas. Vending, petty trade, liquor making, and vegetable selling are some of the more common employment ventures undertaken by women (Census, 1991).

Full-scale unemployment in Nepal is relatively low, but the extent of underemployment is markedly high. The proportion of household underemployed by net workdays is estimated at 46.4 per cent for urban and 33.3 per cent for rural areas. Underemployment rates for males and females are estimated at 41.8 per cent and 51.1 per cent respectively. For urban Nepal, this is estimated at 23.8 per cent for males and 46.6 per cent for females. An estimate of 0.2 million persons are entering the labour market every year. By 2010, 3 million additional jobs will have to be created to achieve full employment.

The vicious circle of backwardness and poverty can be eliminated by transforming the agrarian economy into a dynamic one through industrialization. The contribution of industry to national income in Nepal is about 6 per cent of GDP; besides organized industries in the country, there is a large number of micro enterprises operating on a small cottage basis which contribute about 4 per cent of GDP.

The major industrial strategies employed in Nepal are both import substitution and export promotion. In these circumstances, one major way to achieve the goal of industrial development could be through establishment of small-scale enterprises. For this to happen, it is recognized that entrepreneurship development can be the key to raising the prospects for increasing the share of small-scale and cottage industries in the national income (Aryal, 1992).

It is against this backdrop of industrial development and women's role and participation in the national economy that one must critically view the emerging needs of and scope for women entrepreneurial development. The history of entrepreneurship development programmes in Nepal is quite recent. While Nepal has been interested in the development of small-scale and micro enterprises since the late 1970s, issues and questions relating to the promotion of women entrepreneurs have only been raised more recently (UNIDO, 1988). The number of women who come under the category of entrepreneurs in a formal sense is still negligible. The representation is somewhat better in the informal sector with a higher percentage of women applying for loans for cottage industry enterprises. However, this does not necessarily mean that these women intend to enter the economy as entrepreneurs. They may simply remain self-employed and limit the scale of their enterprise to meet the requirements of household consumption.

Therefore, some of the fundamental questions that need to be explored in connection with women and entrepreneurship are:

- What kinds of factors restrain or obstruct women from entering the entrepreneurial field in a full-fledged manner?
- Are women less entrepreneurial than men?
- Is their entrepreneurial talent different from that of men?
- Should they adopt the same skills that men have?
- Why are there not more capable women operating small enterprises?
- Should entrepreneurship development be promoted for women, and if so how?
- Would this require a women-specific approach and methodology, or is women entrepreneurship development a gradual dynamic growth that will come, following on from the increased empowerment of women?

There is not an extensive body of work in the entrepreneurial research arena in Nepal and the topic of women entrepreneurs virtually remains untouched, with the exception of a few studies carried out within the last five years which have merely scratched the surface. The need for more substantial research, especially an exploration into the gender perspectives of this issue cannot be overemphasized, especially in view of the fact that a fair degree of awareness has already been raised, particularly among the urban elite, about entrepreneurial ventures, challenges and scope in small and cottage industries in Nepal.

Objectives of the Study

The overall objective of the study, therefore, is to examine the gender issues involved in entrepreneurship development for women, and to examine the gender differences that inhibit restrain and obstruct women from advancing in the field of entrepreneurship or availing of the opportunities which promote it.

The factors affecting women entrepreneurship development are to be studied within three broad categories, as demarcated by the specific objectives below:

(i) To examine and assess the socio-cultural/educational and legal barriers to women's entry into enterprise, as well as performance and growth in entrepreneurship;

(ii) To identify and examine personality traits *vis-à-vis* entrepreneurial functions;

(iii) To examine and assess women's access to economic opportunities and formal inputs which promote entrepreneurship development; and

(iv) To provide recommendations on how to promote and strengthen the potential for enhancing women entrepreneurship in Nepal.

Literature Review

Entrepreneurship for women is often seen as a journey out of poverty and a march towards equality. Studies have proven that entrepreneurship, in the form of small and medium sized enterprises, can indeed empower women and through time, fundamentally transform power relations within a society, making it a place where women can lead. However, in the past, women's entrepreneurship in much of the developing world has gone little beyond informal business ventures which ensure daily survival for women and their families. In Nepal, embedded structural and socio-cultural constraints challenge women entrepreneurs and make it hard for them to realize their potential as leaders in business. This article suggests policy measures, business and management training, and the promotion of entrepreneurial networking systems, as potential ways to empower women entrepreneurs and create leadership opportunities, in the hope of bringing women into the mainstream business sector in Nepal.

During the last few decades, recognition has been given to the importance of women's entrepreneurship as a prerequisite for household-level poverty alleviation, national economic development, and the empowerment of women (Mayoux, 2001a). The term 'entrepreneur' has been defined as anyone who 'undertakes the organization and management of an enterprise involving innovativeness, independence and risk, as well as the opportunity for profit' (Timmons and Spinelli, 2006, 10). Innovation enables an entrepreneur to venture into new technology, products, and markets, while independence and risk-taking is required in every stage of the business from start-up to expansion (Ming-Yen, 2007).

A focus on women's entrepreneurship has been particularly strong in low-income countries since the Micro-Credit Summit in Washington in 1997. The summit goals focused on the development of credit measures for '100 million of the world's poorest families by 2005, especially focusing on women household members for self-employment and other financial and business services'. More recently, the Global Micro-credit Summit held in Halifax, Canada in 2006 set new goals to 'lift more than 500 million people out of extreme poverty by 2015, and to ensure 175 million families have access to credit, particularly targeting women'. This has resulted in a shift in development projects and government policies in many developing countries. Women's entrepreneurship has been underlined as a key strategy for both poverty reduction and empowerment. According to some, women's entrepreneurship is recognized as a crucial way to fight against poverty and gender inequity in society, and acts as a vehicle in the promotion of empowerment and leadership for women (UNIFEM, 2000). However, critics have pointed out that the conflation of the goals of women's empowerment and entrepreneurship has resulted in a 'magic-bullet' approach to development which, far from empowering women, subjects them to the disciplinary power of the market (Lairap-Fonderson, 2002). Neo-liberal ideas of market-led growth promote the development of women's entrepreneurship, mainly because they are seen as harder workers and better at meeting credit repayments than men (Rogaly, 1996). Various micro-financing schemes aligning with this concept work on the assumption that group activities will 'empower' women; and that women can be lifted out of poverty through development projects. However, women's entrepreneurship may have an insignificant effect on generating meaningful and sustainable employment opportunities for women, and an even lesser effect on the country's economic advancement and its entrenched gender relations (Mayoux, 2001b). While it may enhance personal well-being and family security on a temporary basis, embedded traditions and structural constraints make for only marginal increases in women's independence and abilities to lead in business.

What does the theory say about gendered barriers to entrepreneurship?

Research into the general issues facing women entrepreneurs sheds light on a number of gender-specific factors and challenges. A study by Das (2000) puts forward the idea that women entrepreneurs can be categorized into *three* types:

- 'Chance' entrepreneurs, who start their business without clear goals, their business may have evolved from hobbies or been passed to them by a family member.
- 'Forced' entrepreneurs, who have been compelled to start their business because of financial circumstances.
- 'Created', or 'pulled' entrepreneurs, who were motivated through entrepreneurship programmes, or who were looking for a challenge and wanted to build their own identity, develop leadership skills, and contribute to society through their venture.

The following key points gathered from studies indicate both the social and personal characteristics that are considered impediments for aspiring women entrepreneurs:

- Traditional stereotyping of sex roles relegates women to being 'home oriented' (Parasuraman, 2001).
- Women may experience low social integration due to the few ties they have to the core social system (Shapero, 1982).
- Women require flexible financial support mechanisms. In the absence of co-coordinated effort among government and other lending institutions, women entrepreneurs cannot be successful (Mayoux, 2003).
- As there are relatively few veteran women entrepreneurs, there tends to be little solidarity within their group-networking is not established to the same degree as with male entrepreneurs. A high degree of group solidarity or cohesion within such a marginal group is seen as necessary to counteract whatever opposition may be forthcoming from mainstream groups within the larger social system (O'Donnell, *et al.*, 2001).
- Women are generally low risk-takers, due to their primary responsibility for dependents (Goffee and Scase, 1985).
- Women's perception of risk involves loss, danger, ruin, and hurt. Though the risk tolerance ability of women in day to day life is high compared with that of men, in business it is found to be the opposite (Greene, 1999).

Women's Entrepreneurship in Nepal

Comparatively little information has been gathered about the problems women face in Nepal when starting businesses, whether in light of gender disparities or the kinds of interventions needed to support women in developing ventures. The aim of this article is to give a snapshot of the current situation faced by women entrepreneurs in Nepal. To understand the difficulties women face, it is first helpful to get a general sense of Nepal's development level, through the composite indices contained in the 2007-08 Human Development Reports (Human Development Report 2007; Human Development Report 2008). These highlight the low level of development for the country as a whole. The Human Development Index (HDI) of 0.534 ranks Nepal 142nd out of 177 countries, while the Human Poverty Index (HPI) value of 38.1 ranks Nepal 84th among 108 developing countries for which the index has been calculated. The Gender Development Index (GDI) further reveals the positioning of women in society. Nepal ranks 134 out of 156 countries in the GDI, and is ranked 86 out of 93 countries in the Gender Empowerment Measure (GEM).

Women Entrepreneurs in Nepal

While struggling to improve their lives in an environment of high unemployment and political unrest over the past ten years, more and more Nepalese women have entered into private enterprise. In line with the 1995 Beijing Declaration, the government adopted the rhetoric of women's participation, and introduced various gender-based initiatives, increased microfinance support systems, and created an opening for the introduction of gender policies and programmes in many government bodies and NGOs. Measures to address gender-specific barriers to women's entrepreneurship include gender-equity measures, such as equal access for both men and women to education and skill-training in business management, which were legislated under the Tenth Five Year Plan (Nepal National Planning Commission, 2002). But due to the violent insurgency by the Communist Party of Nepal and overall political instability, the means to enact the legislation were unavailable; even men made few gains under the legislation. It is currently estimated that, in Asia, nearly one-third of new small enterprises are being set-up by women, and in many cases these businesses are creating employment faster than the countries' domestic averages (Thapa, 2004). It is estimated that over 7,000 women entrepreneurs are now registered and more than 5,00,000 are involved in business activities countrywide. However, although their combined contribution to the national economy is estimated at 40 per cent of the GDP, they remain the largest underrepresented group in terms of visibility as owners of enterprises (De Gobbi, 2005).

It is very difficult to accurately estimate the current number of women entrepreneurs in Nepal, due to the absence of up to date statistics and gender disaggregated data. In addition, the statistics do not reveal who actually controls and runs women's businesses: even though women may be officially registered as owners of a business, in frequent cases it is the husband or father who is operating the business. This 'surrogate entrepreneurship', a phrase coined by Ganesan (2003) makes the task of accurately capturing the number of actual women entrepreneurs very difficult. However, reports from the Nepal Labour Survey in 2000 indicate that out of the 9.5 million people working in Nepal, only 1.5 million (16%) were paid. Of that number, only about 4,00,000 were women, with 82 per cent of these paid women being self-employed, while 12 per cent were wage-employed. The figures for men were 69 per cent and 27 per cent, respectively (Central Bureau of Statistics, 2003).

Although women entrepreneurs have always been common in some ethnic groups, especially in Newar, Sherpa, and Gurung communities, the idea of women in business has only recently become more common across the country (Tuladhar, 1996). On average, female-headed enterprises earn about two-thirds of what male-headed enterprises earn annually, and working hours tend to be at least three to four hours longer each day for women compared with men, due to the additional responsibilities women have in the home. These factors severely limit women's abilities to lead flourishing and profitable businesses.

From the above, it can be noted that although statistics are lacking, the number of women entrepreneurs either in absolute or relative terms has not reached the critical mass necessary to make an impact on the economic system, or to raise awareness in the country of the role women can take in the workplace and society. The subtle manifestation of the gender phenomenon is often reflected in the size of the business, product line, growth, composition, and management, which can be seen from the profiles of women entrepreneurs in this article. 'A typical woman entrepreneur's enterprise is very small, in traditional manufacturing, small shop or informal vending with low turnovers, a low number of employees and no professional assistance' (Acharya, 2000: 21).

How to Promote Entrepreneurship among Women Entrepreneurs of Nepal

- Assist women in identifying projects, programmes, and schemes for upliftment. Encourage women entrepreneurs to market their products and compete in the market successfully.
- Organise exhibitions, seminars and vendor development programmes. Assist women to learn and acquire entrepreneurial qualities through several programmes. Provide infrastructure facilities to the members with an objective to encourage industrial growth.
- Conduct exhibitions and send its delegations around Nepal and internationally to get market information, thus helping in market promotion.
- Act as a liasion between Government and Entrepreneurs by providing necessary information and help women entrepreneurs by providing necessary consultancy.
- Help entrepreneurs overcome gender-related barriers.

Conclusion

The paper can be concluded best by citing the Nepal Human Development Report of 2004 which clearly state the condition of the women in Nepal.

Nepal Human Development Report 2004

- Literacy rate 35 per cent compared to 63 per cent for men.
- Maternal mortality of Nepali women rank among highest in the world; one out of every185 women dies because of pregnancy and childbirth related complications.
- Property rights–Absence of property rights hinders the economic development and empowerment of women.
- More than 70 per cent are *trapped in low-wage, low-skilled sectors.*

- Violence is accepted and perceived as normal behaviour due to stereotyped roles and economic dependence.
- Ongoing conflict: Many female migrants find work in the informal economy in unregulated sectors such as domestic work, entertainment and the sex industry.
- Women's political participation and access to positions of power are restricted.
- A local women's group report in 2000 found *118 laws which discriminated against women* including abortion law--women are still serving sentence for having an abortion.
- Gender Mainstreaming: While Nepal struggles to find a political consensus on the path ahead it is encouraging to note that women have not been totally left behind.
- Proposed laws: Citizenship Rights, Property Law and at least one-third representation of women in Nepal's governmental infrastructure amongst others.
- Women's empowerment is not only strongly linked to economic empowerment, but is its very basis.

References

Acharya, M. 2000. *Labour Market Development and Poverty: With Focus on Opportunities for Women in Nepal.* Kathmandu: Friedrich Ebert Stiftung 21.

Aldrich, H. and C. Zimmer. 1985. "Entrepreneurship through Social Networks". In *The Art and Science of Entrepreneurship,* edited by D.L. Sexton and R. Smilor: 3-23. Cambridge, MA: Ballinger.

Central Bureau of Statistics. 2000. "Report on the Nepal Labour Force Survey".

Central Bureau of Statistics. 2003. "Women in Nepal: Statistical Facts".

Government, National Planning Commission Secretariat Report.

Das, D.J. 2000. "Problems Faced by Women Entrepreneurs". In *Women Entrepreneurship,* edited by K. Sasikumar. New Delhi: Vikas Publishing House.

De Gobbi, M. 2005. "Nepal and Pakistan, Microfinance and Microenterprise Development: Their Contribution to the Economic Empowerment of Women". *SEED Working Paper No. 69, Geneva, International Labour Office.*

Ganesan, S. 2003. *Status of Women Entrepreneurs in India.* New Delhi: Kanishka Publishers.

Goffee, R. and R. Scase. 1985. *Women in Change: The Experiences of Female Entrepreneurs*. London: Allen & Unwin,

Human Development Report. 2007. United Nations Development Programme.

Human Development Report. 2008. United Nations Development Programme.

Factors affecting Women Entrepreneurship in Small and Cottage Industries in *Nepal: Opportunities and Constraint* (http://www.ilo.org/public/english/region/asro/bangkok/paper/fac_npl.htm)

14

Millennium Development Goals and the Status of Nepalese Women

Anjoo Sharan Upadhyaya and *Afreen Khan*

Introduction

The status of women is one of the major hinges around which the Millennium Development Goals revolve. Of the world's 1.3 billion poor people, it is estimated that nearly 70 per cent are women. Between 75 and 80 per cent of the world's 27 million refugees are women. There are many countries where women are still treated as second-class citizens, though equal rights are proclaimed in the Constitution. The status of women in Nepal assumes a critical position as the state has suffered violence for long. The patriarchal society of Nepal has in the past constantly denied women their rightful place, resulting in their very adverse socio-economic indices. However, of late this situation is gradually undergoing a change. This is evident from the fact there is greater presence of women in the social, political and economic sectors of the country. Their overwhelming participation in Political bodies holds a promise of favourable changes in future. In this paper we will explore the changing status of women in Nepal with the purpose of examining the achievements of the Millennium Development Goals as stipulated by the United Nations Organizations.

The United Nations has defined the status of women in the context of their access to knowledge, economic resources, and political power, as well as their personal autonomy in the process of decision making.

In Nepal still very few women have the power of decision making though their access to education, employment and gender equality is enhancing. Nepal hold 115th rank out of 134 countries in Global Gender Gap (GGG) Report, 2010; in 2009 it had 110th rank out of 134 countries and 120th rank out of 130 countries in 2008 while in 2007 its rank was 125th out of 128 countries. In the sub-index of GGG report 2010, namely Economic Participation and Opportunity it was placed on 112th rank, in Educational Attainment it has 126th rank, in Health and Survival Index it has 110th rank and in the sub-index of Political Empowerment it has 44th rank.[1] The data shows that Nepal has moved forward in gaining gender equality.

Socio-economic and political developments in Asia have brought with them profound changes in the status of women. Worldwide women's condition has improved with economic development and socio-political changes that favours equality and individual rights. At the same time, cultural traditions, especially those related to family life, continue to have a strong influence on the status of women in the region. Until recently in most Asian countries, few women attended secondary school or university, and few worked outside the home. Over the past 50 years, larger and larger proportions of women have completed primary and secondary school. The proportion of women attending university, although much smaller, is also growing. More recently, women have started taking up paid employment in greater numbers, particularly in the manufacturing, clerical, and service sectors.

The past three decades have witnessed a progressively escalating consciousness of the need to empower women through measures to increase socio-economic and political equity, and broader access to fundamental human rights, improvements in nutrition, basic health and education. Along with awareness of the subordinate status of women has come the concept of gender as an overarching socio-cultural variable, seen in relation to other factors, such as race, class, age and ethnicity.

The last decade has been an age of tumultuous changes in Nepalese society because the political structure of the country has been in the process of tumultuous change. However, many people believe that the age old patterns in the society have not changed and things have changed only on the surface. A closer look reveals that situation in Nepal is constantly in the process of change for the better.

Social Status of Women

Nepal is a country of great geographic diversity and the regions differ significantly in terms of population, land, access to food and foodgrain production. Consequently, the extent of malnourishment and undernourishment of populations also varies. Half of the population is illiterate and the country ranks the second lowest in South Central Asia in the human development index (138 of 169).[2] Nepalese per capita income is the lowest in South Asia. Most of the inhabitants live on agriculture on the hills and in the *Terai* region.[3] The access to remote areas is highly limited due to the underdeveloped infrastructure and topographical variation. Consequently, hunger remains prevalent in endemic forms as food is not evenly distributed.[4] The rapid decline of forests, which often is an independent source of subsistence against shortages for women and children, the environmental aspects like heavy monsoon rains and the civil war have taken their toll on the livelihoods of the poor.

According to the Census Report of 2001, women constitute half of the population (50.04%). This factor may mislead us to believe that the position of women is superior to the rest of the South Asian countries as their ratio in other South Asian states is much inferior. However, this is not so. The position of women in Nepal though varies from one ethnic group to another and from one region to another, by and large their status in society remains largely underprivileged. Though there also exists great geographical and cultural diversity between Sherpa women living on the foothills of high mountains and Maithali Brahmins and Tharus living in the *Terai* which is not very high from the sea level their position remains vulnerable as the unequal socio-cultural norms are highly tilted in favour of men. Similarly, there is diversity amongst caste and ethnic groups such as *Brahmins, Chhetris, Newars, Tamangs, Magars, Rajbanshis, Sattars, Buddhists, Kirantis, Gurungs, Thakalis, Chepangs, Tharus, Danuwars*, and Muslims etc. and the consequent impact that this situation has on the status and position of women.[5] Brahmins or Bahun are at apex and Dalits at the bottom.[6] Women of these high castes (*Brahmins, Chhetris, Newars*) have better opportunity to get empowerment but Dalit[7] and other backward class women remain least empowered. Population groups, castes and languages are numerous, which results in great variability in gender equality.[8]

The different ethnic groups have their specific beliefs, institutions and languages. Yet, some characteristics are quite similar countrywide. The caste system is unofficial, but strongly controls the society, which sets unique distinctiveness into women's life, e.g. within some groups widows are considered impure. Women carry heavy general workloads, high risks of pregnancy and child-birth, worse general health, poor nutrition and education, all of which remains a cause of higher female mortality rate.[9] Traditionally husbands and older family members hold the authority over decisions in financial, social and family planning issues. Even if a woman develops a substantial intra-family status, the community factors still limits her autonomy.

Nepalese society entertains strong traditional values in favour of males. Consequently, gender disparity is found to be widely prevalent. A recent study[10] on an assessment of the major changes in women's lives in Nepal over the past decade has shown that despite higher attainment of literacy, social mobility and awareness, women still remain confined to their traditionally prescribed and socially acceptable roles, lower status and subordination to men within the patriarchal socio-cultural, economic, political and legal frameworks. Male centred process of socialization makes different expectations and preparations for their adulthood. Nepalese society creates a distinct role for men and women since its formation. Men are the "breadwinner", "protector", "provider" and hold a superior position within the "domestic mode of production" and control the distribution of resources and goods in the family. It is widely believed in a traditional family that the birth of a son paves their way to heaven (*chhora paye swarga jaane*). Parents prefer to wait till they have given birth to a son (*dhilo paye, chhora paye*) as sons are the only source of maintaining the family line.[11] The Nepali society continues to remain largely influenced by patriarchal norms and values. These patriarchal norms and values have extensively limited Nepali women's mobility and their participation in the economic life outside the homes.

According to the Nepal Marriage Registration Act, 1972 marriages may be registered, registration is not compulsory. The minimum legal age for marriage in Nepal is 21 for men and 18 for women. But as per the census report of 2001, almost 68 per cent of the married women are married off between the age group of 15 to 19 years (*see* Table 14.1).[12] The number of married girls aged 10–14 is the highest in *Terai* areas at 19,555. The Mountain regions have

Table 14.1: Marital Status of Women, Nepal (1981-2001)

Indicator	*1981*	*1991*	*2001*
Per cent ever married in the age group			
10–14	14.3	7.4	1.8
15–19	50.8	46.3	33.5
20–24	86.9	86.1	78.5
All	70.8	73.6	70.3
Women in polygamous marriage			559.250
Urban	—	—	65,592
Rural	—	—	493.656
Women in polyandrous marriage			2.147
Per cent divorced/separated	0.4	0.7	0.1
Per cent widows	5.5	7.2	3.7
Per cent remarried			2.7
Urban			2.9
Rural			1.1

Source: Acharya Meena, 2003, "Changing Gender Status: Achievements and Challenges" In *Population Monograph of Nepal,* CBS, Kathmandu, Nepal.

the lowest number (1,192), because of the lower total population. In terms of percentage, this area lags behind the Hill region, where 5,397 girls in this age bracket were already married. Marriage age laws are often ignored as these sacred events are performed in religious ceremonies and are seldom officially registered. The kin pressures ensure that the first child is born by the age of 15 to 16. Families start controlling their fertility only after giving birth to a boy.[13] Besides continuing the family name, sons can perform funeral rituals and are expected to provide support in the old age. If the first wife does not deliver a son, the husband may take another wife for religious purposes. The status of a mother of sons is therefore considered superior to that of a daughter only and thus for a woman, a male progeny is nearly always her most manipulative link.

Traditionally, boys are conditioned for 'productive' work and 'decision-making', while girls are brought up to be housewives, mothers and service providers. Girls have a lack of access to information, knowledge and resources, as they spend their life at home. Normally, the female youth has no access to health or sex education or health services to deal with their problems, which as well contributes to infant mortality, being one of the highest in the Asian region.[14] Currently over half of the under five year-olds are stunting.[15] Malnutrition is more common on the mountains than on the *Terai* plains. Some demographic facts show light on the present status of women in Nepal. According to the census, total population of Nepal in 1991 was 18,46,907 out of them women were 51.3 per cent while male population was 48.7 per cent.[16] Thus, female population was 2.6 higher than that of male. But in 2001, female population was 50.5 per cent while male population was 49.95 per cent. Though the female population in 2011 was 0.55 higher than that of male, there was a marked decline in this ratio from 1991.[17] The average growth rate of population between 1991-2001 was 2.24 per cent.

Concerning the status of women in Nepal, some positive changes have certainly taken place but still a friendly atmosphere has not yet been formed to that extent in which both men and women can equally participate in development activities of the country.

Women and Education

Education is one of the important tools for the empowerment of the women. Data on education reveals that there is rapid advance in the field of education. However, a very high percentage of girls are not even enrolled in primary schools in spite of state's commitment towards "Education for All by 2015". However, reason for low enrolment and low retention in primary schools has been both poverty of the people and rigidity of the formal system of education. In recent years, it is being felt that enrolment numbers can go up through non-formal approaches of imparting education that can be made available for a large majority of children, especially girls. Statistical data of literacy point out that literacy rate is low among females. Female literates are more concentrated in urban areas. The Female Literacy Rate and Educational Attainment among Various Caste/Ethnicity are different (*See* Table 14.2). The absolute difference in number of male and female literates is still quite enormous. Women are still lagging behind. The progress in literacy levels of the younger group is quite significant. During the 1991-2001 period the difference in male/female literacy levels has declined by half in the 15-19 age group. However, in the younger age group the progress has been much slower. This difference has declined by only 2.4 percentage points (*See* Table 14.3).

According to the census of 2001, national literacy rate is 54.1 per cent. Male literacy rate is 65.5 per cent while female literacy rate is 42.8 per cent. District-wise the lowest female literacy rate is 9.3 per cent in Mugu and the highest is 66.6 per cent in Kathmandu.[18] Lower

Table 14.2: Female Literacy Rate and Educational Attainment among Various Caste/Ethnicity in 2001 (in %) (Population Includes 6 Years of Age and Above)

Social Categories	*Literacy (Female)* %	*Graduate & Above (Female)* %
Madheshi	27	0.3
Hill Social Groups (Hill Janjati/Dalit)	40	0.2
Newar	63	2.5
Chhetri/Thakuri	48	0.6
Bahuns	66	1.8

Source: Yadav, Ram Pakash, 2007, Poverty, Deprivation and Social Justice: A Report, Kathmandu: Poverty Alleviation Fund.

Table 14.3: Gender Differences in Literacy Rates (%)

Age Group	*1981*	*1991*	*2001*
Overall	22.0	29.0	22.7
15-19	30.7	32.9	16.2
10-14	29.6	12..8	10.4

Source: Population Census, 2001.

literacy rates in females are due to various reasons such as historical, economic and social. Some main reasons are: poverty, social prejudices against female education, low social status granted to females, the system of early marriage and low participation of females in formal education. But the situation is changing rapidly and females have greater access to primary as well as upper levels education. Progress in female education will improve the social, eeonomic and political condition of women in Nepal. In recent years, expansion of educational facilities, implementation of free education up to secondary level and awareness of people have helped to enhance educational attainment. Nepal is spending its huge share of national budget on education. In 2003-04, about 16 per cent of national budget was allocated for educational sector.[19]

Women in Economy

Although women play a great role in Nepal's economic life, their domestic work, as well as the agricultural work they do is still not considered in the national income estimation. A large part of women's work is not considered as economic activity. As a result, in the Census of 2001 only 51.7 per cent women as compared to 67.60 per cent men are classified as economically active (*See* Table 14.4). The occupational structure reveals that 92.5 per cent population was involved in agriculture sector in 2001. Women's input in agriculture is ignored because most women participate in subsistence farming.[20] 73 per cent women are involved in agriculture and 43 per cent women in labour force while 27 per cent women are working in non-agricultural fields. Women are mostly engaged in unpaid, low wages and low skill sectors. 4 per cent of economically active women work in the formal sector in comparison to 12 per cent men. 63 per cent of women were engaged in unpaid jobs compared to 24 per cent men.[21]

The majority of women in the formal sector worked as semi-skilled and unskilled workers. In virtually all food, drink, tobacco and match industries female workers were mainly concentrated in packing the finished product and in related processes.[22] Overall, the participation rate is higher for males than females, the percentage of female workers in rural and agricultural occupations is higher than the consequent percentage for male workers, the percentage of female workers employed in the organized sector is much lower than the consequent percentage of male workers and underemployment affects female workers more than male workers. Thus, not only the female

Table 14.4: Representation of Women (Various Castes and Ethnic Groups) as Minister, State Minister and Assistant Minister during the Periods from 1951 to April 2006

Castes/Ethnic Groups	*(1951-2006)*		*Percentage of Population in 2001*	*Proportional Share Index (PSI)*
	Total No	*%*		
Bahuns	20	46.5	12.7	3.66
Chhetri/Thakuri	15	34.1	17.3	1.97
Newar	3	6.8	5.5	1.24
Sub-Total	**38**	**87.4**	**35.5**	**2.43**
Madheshi	1	2.3	33.0	0.07
HSG	5	11.3	29.0	0.39
Others	0	0.0	2.5	0.00
Sub-Total	**6**	**13.6**	**64.5**	**0.21**
Grand Total	**44**	**100.0**	**100.0**	

Source: Yadav, Ram Prakash, 2007, Poverty, Deprivation and Social Justice: A Report, Kathmandu: Poverty Alleviation Fund.

workers are confined to less productive and less remunerative jobs, they also have fewer employment opportunities than males. It is possible to argue that the labour market disadvantages female workers, partly because they are less skilled and less educated than male workers, but also because there continues to be discrimination against women in education and skill development programme. In other words, gender based discrimination in the labour market in part reflects the generally low social status of women. Available data indicates that women face higher levels of unemployment and underemployment in both rural and urban areas.

Since 1990, microfinance programme is focusing women as target because it is not only tool for poverty alleviation but also the strong tool for women empowerment. By access to income and control over it, women are able to make economic, social and political decision. Besides, efforts for increasing women's access to banking, many smaller training-cum-income generating projects have been started for women by the government, semi-government and various private foreign agencies. At present there are Women Training Centres in all five regional headquarters. These centres conduct skill-based training programmes. Because of these programmes, women have become more self-reliant in generating income of their own. In urban areas women are believed to be engaged in large numbers in tourism (hotels, airlines and travel agencies) and other tourist related services such as restaurant, carpets and handicrafts manufacturing. The sectors that employ women in substantial numbers are: agriculture, commerce, manufacturing, personnel and community services.

Legal Rights of Women

1990 Constitution of Nepal states that there will be no discrimination of any kind on ground of sex, caste, religion and race. Yet there were certain national codes which privilege men. The rights to inheritance to property, marriage and divorce, tenancy and transaction rights favoured men. The social and human aspects also do not seem congenial for women, as there still remain certain clauses in public law (*Mulki Ain*) that put women in a vulnerable position. For example, before the promulgation of Interim Constitution of 2007 property laws allow a daughter to inherit the deceased parent's property only when there is no surviving male (son or son's son) of either parent. The law did not recognize any transaction carried out by a wife without the consent of her husband. A family with only one son is prohibited from giving him up for adoption. In the case of a single daughter, her adoption would be legal. There are no legal safeguards against sexual harassment of domestic violence targeted at women.[23] Similarly, The Army Act, 2016 V.S. (1959) bans the recruitment of women into the Royal Nepal Army. But parallel to women guerrillas in the 'people's war', Nepali women have been joining the police and the army. Women were recruited in the Nepal Army for the first time in 2003, in non-ranking post and they were engaged in the sectors like policing, exchange, transportation and administration etc. The fact one should not forget here is that women activists had been demanding for long to enrol women in the national army by amending the military law. By whatever reasons women have been joining the Nepal Army in all kinds of job. It is estimated that the proportion of women is 5 per cent in Nepal Army.[24]

Earlier women had no property rights but this too is undergoing a change now. With the 11th Amendment Bill 2002[25] regarding property and inheritance rights daughters are accepted as heir of the family from birth. The new law establishes a wife's equal right to her husband's property immediately after marriage, rather than after she reaches 35 years of age or has been married for 15 years as before. A wife's share is provided to her before the decree of divorce and widow also gets full right to inheritance of property.

However, women have to return parental property when they get married, that is a severe weakness of this Act. But now women have better property rights because the Interim Constitution, Article 20 clause (4) mentions that—"Son and daughter shall have equal rights to their ancestral property."[26]

The Bill gives women the right to seek divorce from her husband if he harasses her physically or psychologically; if he establishes sexual relationships with other women; if he is incapable of producing children; or if he is affected by STD, including HIV/AIDS. Previously, the law allowed a wife to claim only food stuff from her husband for the five years following their divorce. Today, a woman can also claim property.[27]

Polygamy is still rampant in Nepal, though it was declared illegal in 1975. Previously, those who violate the law in this regard face a punishment of 1 to 3 months in prison or a fine of 1000 to 2000 Rupees, or both. The new amendment increases these punishments; a man can now face 1 to 3 years in prison or a fine of 5,000-25,000 Rupees, or both.[28]

Previously, abortion was illegal unless a doctor advised that continuation of pregnancy was a threat to the mother's life. Charged with this crime, dozens of women are imprisoned across Nepal. The new law legalizes abortion on some conditions. In normal case, a woman can make her own decision to go through with an abortion, though only within the first 12 weeks of pregnancy. However, if the child's delivery endangers the mother's life, or if a women becomes pregnant through rape or incestuous sexual relations then abortions can take place within 18 weeks of pregnancy. Nepal is the first South Asian country to legalize abortion in this way.[29]

Rape is one of the major issues that have been raised by the women's movement in Nepal. In this regard, the amendments to the civil code make the law stronger and increase the punishment for rapists. According to the new provisions, a rapist can be imprisoned for 10-15 years, if their victim is below 10 years of age; 7-10 years of imprisonment, if their victim is between 10 and 16 years of age; and 5-7 years of imprisonment, if the victim's age is above 16 years. In each category, an additional five years of prison can be given if the victim is a pregnant or disabled woman.[30]

It is a big achievement that women have been granted more legal rights with this amendment. But, there are issues to be addressed. The struggle to achieve rights based on gender is ongoing. If gender equality has not been achieved even when important goals are met then the struggle should continue. The Interim Constitution has recognized women's rights as fundamental right. Besides, there are many positive provisions in the Constitution in this regard. After this, various discriminatory laws have been reformed and some policies have been formulated. It will not be wrong to say that the women rights movement is taking place with expected achievements now. However, there is need of proper implementation of these policies to eliminate the discrimination and obtain equity and equality between men and women in the real sense. There is a bigger challenge ahead of the women's movement. Until and unless women and men in wider society are aware of these new legal instruments, they cannot bring any remarkable change to the real lives of Nepalese women. In this regard, it is the role and responsibility of the women's movement to make women and men aware of their legal rights. At the same time, social and bureaucratic structures including those in civil society and government must institutionalize these changes. Only in this way will feudal and traditional attitudes towards women's rights have the hope of change. To ensure the impact of these legal rights, authority should be delegated in a practical way and the implementing apparatus should be correctly managed. The women's movement can lead the campaign to make people aware and to check that the law is implemented properly. We can prove that legal instruments are important tools and play a crucial role in creating gender equality in society.

Women and Politics

Women's participation in the various political processes in Nepal has been relatively significant. Their presence in the Constituent Assembly has been sizeable and so has their status in various committees of the CA. However, this situation has not been that promising in the past. Though women constitute about 50 per cent of the total population of Nepal but yet their participation at the various levels of decision-making is negligible. The major reason for their inefficacy has been rampant violence, corruption and manipulations, which are widespread in the society. Many women who have excellent leadership qualities are unwilling to participate in politics because of these Four M factors (Man, Money, Muscles and Mafia).[31]

The role of Nepalese women in politics is increasing. As late as early 1990s women's participation in politics was a meagre 5 per cent. However, after the political change in 1990, some women got opportunities to organize themselves. It was a good sign that more and more women's organizations were coming to support women to express their problems and experiences but after a few years they disappeared. Though the urban women's participation in politics has become reasonably significant but in rural areas their participation in politics is very peripheral. Women's recruitment in the Peoples Liberation Army has brought about a change of their outlook on public spaces and has ironically led them to perceive politics in a more positive stance, but the jostling and manipulations in public spaces has limited their role to being far from significant. This applies to both urban politics and rural politics. Many women avoid politics, as there is no adequate representation and participation of women in the national politics.[32]

From the general elections of 2000, a total of 12 out of 205 (5.9%) women were elected as Members of the Parliament. There were 57 women in the Interim Parliament formed on 15th January, 2007 with a total of 330 Members (17.3%). The Interim Parliament had 36.1 per cent women Members from the CPN (Maoist), 14.4 per cent from CPN (UML), 7.5 per cent from NC and 13.1 per cent from all other parties. From the elections held in 2008, 32.8 per cent women have been elected in the Constituent Assembly which also oversees the responsibility of the Parliament. Figure 14.1 presents the comparative description of women's participation in the Parliament and the Government from the date before second popular movement to till date.

In the Interim Constitution women obtained a quota of 33 per cent seats. However, their demand grew for a quota of 50 per cent seats, a demand that was acceded to on 15th June, 2007 by an Act/ resolution of the Parliament.[33] In the Constituent Assembly women constitute a large number and won 196 seats out of 601 seats and there is about 33 per cent representation of women in the historical Constituent Assembly formed in 2008. That is an immense achievement. From among 30 women Members elected under FPTP system, 24 are from CPN (Maoist), 2 each from the NC and MJFN and one each from CPN (UML) and TMDP. Under the proportionate system, 18 political parties out of 25 have made women's representation to the CA. CPN (Maoist) has 50 women Members, the largest number under this category. Under the Nomination category, there are 3 women Members from CPN (Maoist), largest under the category as well. Figure 14.2 presents the number of women

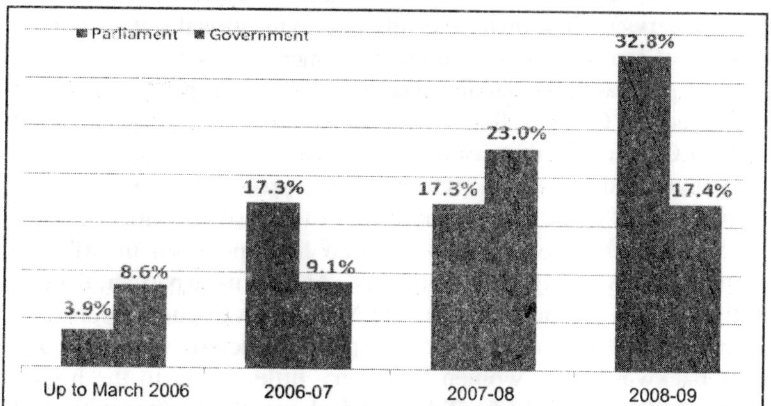

Fig. 14.1: Comparative Status of Women's Participation in the Parliament and the Government before and after the Second Popular Movement.

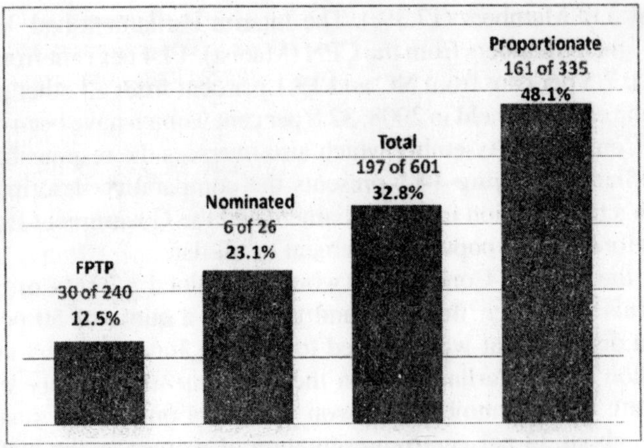

Fig. 14.2: Number of Women in the Constituent Assembly.

CA Members elected under FPTP, Proportionate and Nomination categories.

Women's political participation and access to positions of power are restricted for several reasons. Women's mobility is limited; they have fewer opportunities to mix with those in power; they have the sole responsibility for household maintenance and child care activities, they feel it as an extra burden on themselves; and they face political nepotism that favours men. Women's access to positions of power is further restricted by the inflexible entrance and promotion rules of the civil service, their own relatively poor educational status, and the primacy of family responsibilities in women's lives.

The general understanding that women have of politics was best expressed by Chhaya Jha, an active member of an NGO called HURDEC, who said that politics is the game of power and money so women are hesitant to join.[34] Gender based problem is very high and women cannot come forward because of these social barriers.

Most of the women who reached high position mostly are 'martyrs' wives and dynastic daughters'. As their male partner, women of high classes (Bahun, Chhetri, and Newar) have better opportunity to get empowerment and positions in power structures but Dalits and other backward class women have very little access to the higher positions (*See* Table 14.5). Table 14.5 shows the representation of women in various castes and ethnic groups as Ministers, State Minister and Assistant Ministers during the periods from 1951 to 2006. Data

Table 14.5: Access to Positions of Power: Percentage of Women in various Positions of Power

Detail	*1991-92*	*2000*
Per cent in Parliament	3.8	6.4
Number of women in the Cabinet	2	2
Per cent executives of the major political parties	7.8[1]	8.3[2]
VDCs	0.45	7.7
Municipal executives	0.38	19.5
DDCs	0.65	6.7
Government administration	na	7.8
Officers	4.39	6.2
High government positions - first and special class	2.46	2.4
Professionals and technicians	15.1	19.0
Administration and management	9.3	13.8

Source: Acharya Meena, 1994, *The Statistical Profile of Nepalese Women: An Update in the Policy Context*, Kathmandu: IIDS.

Acharya Meena, 2003, "Changing Gender Status—Achievements and Challenges." In *Population Monograph of Nepal,* Kathmandu: Central Bureau of Statistics.

1. Five nationally recognized parties (NC, UML, RPP, SJN, and NSP).
2. Seven Parties in the Parliament (NC, UML, RPP, SJN, NSP and NPWP).

shows clearly that 46.5 per cent Bahun and 34.1 per cent Chhetri/Thakuri women grab the position but Madheshi and other hilly social groups have very little opportunity. Even though common women took active part in *Jana Andolan I & II* and in Madheshi Andolan, and though women did rise to significant popularity but was not given any berth in the Ministry. Instead one who was defeated in the election was appointed not only a Minister but also as Prime Minister of the country. This obviously has a very dampening effect on women who have political ambitions.

Nonetheless some prominent women leaders who are making good strides are Yogmaya Devi, Kamaksha Devi, Shailja Acharya, Durga Acharya Ghimire, Durga Pokhrel, Sahana Pradhan, Sadhna Adhikari, Sushila Sherestha, Pampha Bushal, Ambika Basnet, Hisila Yami, Sujata Koirala, Sita Khadka, Shashi Shrestha, Shanta Manavi, Uma Adhikari, Radha Gyawali, Khuma Subedi, Jayapuri Gharti Magar etc. After Maoist movement women from the grass roots level are also becoming aware and taking active interest in the making of *Naya Nepal*. Now many of them are nominated in Interim Government and work hard as Parliamentarians. For the first time in Nepali constitutional history, the Interim Constitution has recognized social security as a right for women and others in need of security (though a law to address the issue still needs to be legislated). Such provisions can be critical for helping women who are victims of violence.

There are many NGOs, working for women empowerment and provide them opportunity and training to enhance their capability. Some of them are, ABC/Nepal: Anti-Trafficking, Basic Human Rights and Cooperatives, EWN (Empowering the Women of Nepal), FEDO (Feminist Dalit Organization), Jagaran Nepal, Manushi, Nagarik Aawaz, WACN (Women Awareness Centre Nepal), SAATHI, FWLD (Forum for Women, Law and Development), Didi Bahini, Sancharika Samuha (SAS), and ECWD (Education Centre for Women in Democracy).

With the democratic changes of the early 1990s, women have been mobilized extensively into groups by various NGOs/INGOs and government programmes. They were also mobilized by the political parties for participation, especially after the mandatory provision in Local Self Governance Act, 1999. Gender consciousness among the women's wings and sister organizations of the political parties have increased rapidly, as has women's political consciousness due to their socio-political mobilization by various institutions. A survey conducted by an organization named GEFONT in 2003 among female and male workers reported that 27 per cent of the interviewed women had joined a woman's organization, but many of these women could not continue such membership due to familial and social non-acceptability and household responsibilities. Another study conducted by Bennett/ Gajurel, in 2005, based on information for about 2,000 men and women from 60 villages of different parts of the country also found that women were more empowered today than in 1978 regarding their mobility and voice within household decision-making.[35] Nevertheless, compared to men, women had less confidence in utilizing government/NGO services, police, and courts, although a larger percentage of women were group members than men. Women from Brahmin/Chhetri castes were much more empowered in terms of their access to services and confidence in dealing with law enforcement agencies or service providers than women and even men from other ethnicities and castes. Dalits were most disadvantaged in this respect.

The facts presented above show the low socio-economic status of Nepalese women. But now they are trying to confront multitude of problems and challenges simultaneously. It is the presence of both opportunity and challenges that spurs Nepalese women into action. They have already succeeded a great deal in sensitizing a large section of society towards the gender sensitive issues like women's property right, legislation need for increased reservation for women in different levels of polity to enhance their political participation.

Some segments of women in the middle class have gained by having access to education, urbanization and changing norms. The processes of modernization and development have been retrogressive to women in general. Herein lies the greatest challenge for all women leaders, politicians, activists, researchers and building up a broad countervailing unity and solidarity, cutting across all the conventional barriers, in order to attain their cherished goal of full equal position because women's development is very much related with politics. Today we can say that in Nepal there are very strong women politicians, leaders and activists who raise their voice over the issues related to women development. Now the hitherto unheard voices of Nepalese women find spaces and women are making their presence felt in New Nepal. If this trend continues in a healthy mode there are chances of Nepal approximating the MDG. Among these are areas of critical importance to women, where progress which has been achieved so far, still falls short of minimally desirable standards; for example literacy, health and nutrition.

Given the very sluggish political development of the country as a whole it becomes amply clear that the road ahead for Nepal is not a smooth one.

Notes

1. Hasumann, Ricardo, Laura D. Tyson and Saadia Zahidi. 2010. *Global Gender Gap Report*. Geneva: World Economic Forum.
2. UNDP. 2010. *Human Development Report,* available at http://hdr.undp.org/en/reports/global/hdr2010/chapters/
3. Chhetry, D. 2001. *Understanding Rural Poverty in Nepal.* Asian Development Bank, Asia and Pacific Forum on Poverty.
4. Pyakuryal, B., Y. B. Thapa and D. Roy. 2005. *Trade Liberalisation and Food Security in Nepal.* International Food Policy Research Institute (IFPRI), Markets, Trade, and Institutions Division (MTID) *Discussion Paper* 88.
5. Majupuriya, Indra. 2007. *Nepalese Women: Gender Approach to Development.* Kathmandu: Rohit Kumar.

6. *Census Report.* 2001. Kathmandu: Central Bureau of Statistics.
7. Dalit groups as identified by Dalit Ayog (2002) are as follows: Hill Dalits–Kami, Sarki, Lohar, Sunar, Gaine, Badi, Parki, Chunara, Kuche and Kadara. Newar Dalit–Kusule, Chyame, Pode, Dhaier (Dyhala) and Terai Dalits–Tatma, Paswan, Dushad, Batar, Mushahar, Khatway, Chamar, Dom, Halkhor, Badimar, Gothi and Jhangar.
8. Niraula, Bhanu and Samira Luitel. 2004. *Economic Reform and the Status of Women in Nepal.* Canada: IDRC. Available at www.idrc.ca/en/ev-58036-201-1-DO_TOPIC.html
9. Majupuriya, Indra. 2007. *Nepalese Women: Gender Approach to Development.* Kathmandu: Rohit Kumar.
10. Acharya, Meena. 2007. *Gender Equality and Empowerment of Women.* Kathamndu: UNPFA.
11. Malla, Sapana Pradhan. 2000. "Property Rights of Nepalese Women". *FES Nepal.* March. http://www.nepaldemocracy.org/gender/property_rights.htm Accessed on 20th June, 2011.
12. *Census Report.* 2001. Kathmandu: Central Bureau of Statistics.
13. Leone, T., Z. Matthews, and G. Dalla Zuanna, 2003. "Impact and Determinants of Sex Preference in Nepal." *International Family Planning Perspectives* 29(2) June.
14. UNICEF. 2006. "Situation of Women and Children in Nepal 2006". Chapter 7: 9. http://www.un.org.np/reports/UNICEF/2006/situation-analysis (1.4.2007)
15. UNICEF. 2007. "The State of the World's Children 2007". http://www.unicef.org/sowc07/profiles/inequality_household.php. (1.4.2007)
16. *Census Report.* 1991. Kathmandu: Central Bureau of Statistics.
17. *Census Report.* 2001. Kathmandu: Central Bureau of Statistics.
18. Majupuriya, Indra. 2007. *Nepalese Women: Gender Approach to Development.* Kathmandu: Rohit Kumar.
19. Manandhar, T.B. & K.P. Shrestha. 2003. "Population Growth and Educational Development". *Population Monograph of Nepal* I. Kathmandu: Central Bureau of Statistics.
20. National Planning Commission. HMG-N. *The Ninth Plan (1997-2002) and The Tenth Plan (2002-07).* Kathmandu.
21. *Nepal Human Development Report.* 2008. Kathmandu: Nepal South Asia Centre.
22. Acharya, Meena. 2001. "Women and the Economy: The Key Issues". In *Gender and Democracy,* edited by L.K. Manandhar and K.B. Bhattachan. Kathmandu: Centre Department of Home Science—Women Studies Programme.
23. Niraula, Bhanu and Samira Luitel. 2004. *Economic Reform and the Status of Women in Nepal.* Canada: IDRC; Available online at www.idrc.ca/en/ev-58036-201-1-DO TOPIC.html

24. *Nepal Samacharpatra*, August 17, 2006:4.
25. The battle for equal rights to parental property has been one of the main gender issues fought for last decade. A Bill to amend the National Code 1963 was tabled on January 13, 1997 in the 11th session of Parliament by Government. It was in accordance with the Supreme Court directive in 1993.
26. *Interim Constitution of Nepal*. 2006. Kathmandu.
27. Pandey, Binda. 2002. *Workers News* 32. March.
28. *National Report*. 2002. Vol. II. Kathmandu: Central Bureau of Statistics.
29. Pandey, Binda. 2001. *Women's Property Right Movement and Achievement of the 11th Amendment of Civil Code*. Kathmandu.: Friedric-Ebert-Stiftung. Available online at http://www.nepaldemocracy.org/gender/property_rights_movement.htm
30. Majupuriya, Indra. 2007. *Nepalese Women: Gender Approach to Development*. Kathmandu: Rohit Kumar.
31. Based on an Interview with Urmila Aryal in June 2007. She is a Centre Committee Member of CPN-UML and a former Minister of State for Women, Children and Social Welfare. Her constituency is Parsa in Terai region.
32. Sarup, Kamala. 2007. "Nepalese Women Seek Greater Political Role". *American Chronicle*.
33. *Kathmandu Post*. 2007. Kathmandu. 15 June.
34. Based on an Interview with Ms. Chhaya Jha, in June 2007, she is an active member of the NGO called HURDEC and a teacher in Padma Kanya Campus, Kathmandu.
35. Acharya, Meena. 2007. *Gender Equality and Empowerment of Women*. Kathmandu: UNFPA (United Nations Population Fund).

ANNEXURE

Chronology of Events

1768	King Prithvi Narayan Shah unifies small principalities through military conquest that now constitute modern Nepal.
1846	Jung Bahadur establishes an hereditary Rana military oligarchy alongside the hereditary monarchy. The Prime Minister holds the dual role of head of government and commander of the army while the king is confined to his palace.
1854	Jung Bahadur introduces the Civil Code that essentially codifies law for the first time in Nepal's history. In 1856, the Lal Mohar (royal order) assigned all political power to the Jung Bahadur and fixing the line of succession. It was fixed that Mukhtiyari, or executive head of the government, or Prime Minister (including Supreme Commander of the Army) would pass from Jung Bahadur to his brothers and then to his son.
1948	Padma Shumshere Rana (Prime Minister) introduces the first written constitution, Government of Nepal Act or the Rana Constitution that is opposed by conservative forces.
1951	A popular revolt overthrows Rana military oligarchy and revives the Hindu monarchy under a democratic interregnum.

1951	Interim Government of Nepal Act, 2007 promulgated with the approval of the monarch. The king promises elections for a Constituent Assembly but abandoned this promise later.
1959	The Parliamentary Constitution of 1959 based on the Westminster multiparty model of democracy announced abrogating the Interim Government of Nepal Act which came into force with Nepal's first multiparty Parliamentary elections held on 18th February, 1959 (with NC sweeping the polls headed by B.P. Koirala), the formation of Nepal's first elected government on 27th May, 1959, and on 24th July, 1959 when king inaugurated the joint session of Parliament—Nepal's historic experiment in representative government.
1960	In December, King Mahendra overthrows the first elected government of B.P. Koirala and revives the absolute monarchy.
1962	The King promulgates the Panchayat Constitution to institutionalize an absolute monarchy. During the Panchayat years, political pluralism was outlawed.
1980	King Birendra, who succeeded to the throne in 1972, in the face of student unrest, orders a national referendum offering the choice between 'panchayat with timely reforms' and 'multiparty democracy.' The first option wins by a slim majority.
1981	King Birendra introduces limited democrátic reforms by introducing adult franchise, direct election to the National Legislature, appointment of Prime Minister on the recommendation of legislature, and the Prime Minister to be accountable to the legislature.
1990	Restoration of multiparty democracy as a result of *The Jana Andolan I* (spring uprising) forces King Birendra to introduce multiparty Parliamentary Democracy under a constitutional monarchy. Politically, it signifies the beginning of a new stage in Nepali politics.
1991	Nepal's second multiparty Parliamentary election returns NC with a majority. The CPN-UML, the second largest party, leads the opposition.

1992	First local election gives NC majority with CPN-UML in second position.
1994	Prime Minister, G.P. Koirala, at the height of unpopularity, calls for fresh polls. CPN-UML emerges as the largest party to form a minority government.
1996	In February, CPN-M launches a 'people's war' to topple Parliamentary Democracy and monarchy.
1997	Second local elections held with NC and CPN-UML in control of most seats.
1999	Third Parliamentary elections held with NC capturing the majority of seats in the House of Representatives.
2001	In June, King Birendra and his entire immediate family assassinated in the royal palace. His younger brother Gyanendra, the seniormost surviving member in the line of descent is named king.
2002	October 4, Prime Minister Sher Bahadur Deuba recommended the postponement of Parliamentary elections for more than a year. Gyanendra fired Deuba, describing him as "incompetent", and assumed all executive powers on an interim basis but indefinitely postpones elections scheduled for November 13. This laid the basis for a period of royal absolutism which marked uncertainty and new tensions in Nepalese political life.
2003	January 29, The constitutional parties formerly in government and CPN-M agree to ceasefire.
	April 27, First round of talks held between governing parties and CPN-M.
	May 9, Second round of talks makes slow progress.
	August 17, Talks resume, government presents its reform agenda.
	August 27, Talks collapse after CPN-M breaks ceasefire.
2004	May 30, King sought nominations of persons with a "clean image" for the position of Prime Minister. The major political parties such as NC and CPN-UML rejected the offer.

	June 2,	King reappointed Deuba as Prime Minister, less than two years after he had dismissed him as "incompetent".
2005	February 1,	King dismissed Deuba for the second time, indefinitely postponed Parliamentary elections, and imposed direct rule, proposing to introduce 'meaningful democracy.'
	Nov 22,	Political parties and CPN-M sign a 12-point "understanding" to end "absolute monarchy".
2006	March 19,	Political parties and CPN-M sign an "understanding" to establish democracy.
	April 6,	Movement for the restoration of democracy (*Jana Andolan II*), supported by CPN-M, launched.
	April 21,	The King requested political parties to name a Prime Minister. The offer was dismissed as a concession that came too late and offered too little.
	April 24,	People in large numbers continued to defy curfew and shoot-at-sight orders. The King was forced to restore the House of Representatives by issuing a late night proclamation. Political parties suspend the *Jana Andolan II* but CPN-M said the movement should have been allowed to continue to reach its 'logical conclusion.'
	May 18,	House of Representatives issued a proclamation to drastically cut the King's power, turn His Majesty's Government into the Nepal Government and Royal Nepal Army into Nepal Army. Nepal was declared to be secular, multiethnic, multireligious, multiracial country.
	June 16,	SPA and CPN-M sign an 8-point agreement to implement the 12-point understanding.

	August 9,	Nepal Government and CPN-M send separate but identical letters to UN asking it to monitor the arms and armies of Nepal Army and CPN-M and holding of elections for the CA.
	November 7,	Both Nepal Government and CPN-M agree to put their arms and armies under UN monitor and supervision.
	November 21,	Nepal Government and CPN-M signed a Comprehensive Peace Agreement to end insurgency that claimed 15,000 lives and left millions displaced.
	November 28,	Tripartite arms management agreement signed between UN, Nepal Government and CPN-M.
2007	January, 15	House of Representatives promulgates Interim Constitution. House replaced with 330-members Legislature-Parliament which combined the members of the House as well as CPN-M nominees and some civil society members. The Legislature-Parliament in the very first session endorsed the Interim Constitution and agreed to hold elections by June 2007.
	April 1,	CPN-M members inducted into the Interim Government.
	April 13,	Election Commission announced that CA elections were not possible on June 20, as scheduled because of the security situation and the absence of the necessary legislation to conduct the elections.
	August 23,	Cabinet decides to nationalize seven royal palaces.
	September 17,	CPN-M Ministers resign *en masse* and announce protest programmes to sabotage elections.
	September 25,	NC and NC-Democratic formally unify.
	October 6,	Elections to the CA postponed indefinitely.

	December 10,	Four lawmakers from Terai region resign to launch a regional party.
	December 28,	Third Amendment to the Interim Constitution declaring Nepal a 'Federal Democratic Republic' subject to endorsement by the CA.
2008	January 11,	Cabinet decided to hold CA elections on April 10, 2008.
	April 10,	Elections held for the CA described by independent monitors as generally fair and free.
	28 May,	Abolition of 240-years old monarchy formally by the CA.

Index